CUSTODIAN OF THE
TWO HOLY MOSQUES
KING FAHD BIN ABDUL AZIZ

# Custodian of the Two Holy Mosques King Fahd bin Abdul Aziz

## Fouad Al-Farsy

KNIGHT COMMUNICATIONS

Published by Knight Communications Ltd, Dixcart House,
Sir William Place, St Peter Port, Guernsey, Channel Islands

First published in 2001

A CIP catalogue record for this book is available from the
British Library.

ISBN 1 874132 17 8

Project Management by Paul Georgiou and Gladis Bethlehem

Design by Tim McPhee
Maps by Pete Welford
Typeset by Cambridge Photosetting Services, Cambridge
Design and production in association with
Book Production Consultants plc, Cambridge

Colour reprographics by East Central One Media Limited, London.
Printed in Scotland by Bath Press Colour Books

# CONTENTS

# INTRODUCTION

*There have been monuments built to mark the passing on earth of great men. Across the Red Sea, the pyramids still stand as giant tombs to long-dead pharaohs. King Fahd has a finer monument – a nation and a country that he has left far better than he found it.*

## GEOGRAPHICAL FACTORS

THE ARABIAN PENINSULA is a land mass which constitutes a distinct geographical entity, stretching from the Red Sea in the west to the Arabian Gulf in the east and bounded in the south by the Indian Ocean.

In earlier times, the Arabian Peninsula was almost certainly joined to north-east Africa (with what is today Egypt, Sudan and Ethiopia), forming part of a single, vast continental mass – but movements in the lower mantle of the earth opened a fissure in the igneous rock, creating a rift valley (the Red Sea and the Gulf of Aden) which separated the Arabian Peninsula from Africa.

The Arabian platform is tilted and, with its highest part in the extreme west along the Red Sea, it slopes gradually down from the west to the east. Thus the Red Sea coast is often rugged and mountainous, whereas the Arabian Gulf coast is flat, low lying and fringed with extensive coral reefs which make it difficult to approach the shore in many places.

Saudi Arabia itself is a vast country of some 865,000 square miles [2,240,000 sq km] occupying more than four fifths of the Arabian Peninsula. The Kingdom is bounded on the north by Jordan, Iraq and Kuwait; on the east by the Gulf, Bahrain, Qatar and the United Arab Emirates; on the south by Yemen and the Sultanate of Oman; and on the west by the Red Sea.

Much of the land is desert. In the southeast of the Kingdom is the vast expanse of desert, the Rub al-Khali or Empty Quarter, and much of the rest of the interior is desert but, bounding the desert, are mountain ranges and coastal plains.

The climate of the Kingdom is generally distinguished by heat and a lack of

> The average temperature in July in the capital, Riyadh, is 108 degrees Fahrenheit [42 degrees C]. Riyadh, being in the heart of the Arabian Peninsula, has low humidity.
>
> In Jeddah, on the Red Sea coast, the average temperature in July is 87 degrees Fahrenheit [30.6 degrees C]. In Jeddah, being on the coast, has high humidity.

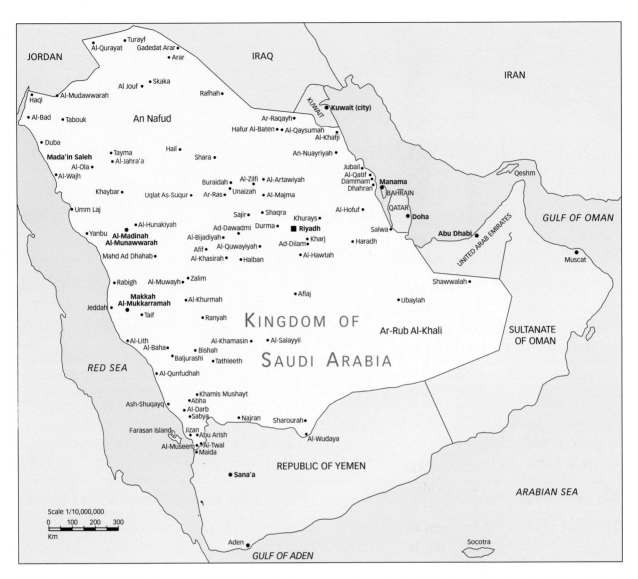

The stereotype of the Kingdom as a dry, barren desert devoid of almost all flora and fauna is far from correct. Of course, both plants and animals have had to adapt to the rigors of the climate but, for those who look, there is a wealth of wildlife to be discovered, even in the desert regions – and there are parts of the Kingdom, notably the southern region, which enjoy ample rainfall and support a wide variety of crops as well as plants and animals.

rainfall. Along the long coastline of the Kingdom, the level of humidity is high. Inland, the heat is dry. Average rainfall in the Kingdom is 4 inches [100 mm], but the rainfall is not evenly distributed throughout the vast territory that makes up Saudi Arabia and, while some regions enjoy much higher levels of rainfall, many areas, for years on end, receive much less rainfall than the average figure might suggest – and some, none at all.

Although the level of rainfall in much of Saudi Arabia is low, the desert to the north and west of the Rub al-Khali is well endowed with fertile oases which, as the nomadic population has settled, have become villages and towns.

Another distinguishing feature of the Saudi Arabian climate is the Shamal, a wind that can sweep across the country in spring or early summer, whipping up sandstorms that reduce visibility and cause general inconvenience.

The importance of Saudi Arabia's geographical position is quickly apparent:

*A green land in the desert*

it is strategically located between Africa and mainland Asia and has frontiers on both the Red Sea and the Arabian Gulf. As a result, from ancient times it was a land that traders came to know well. By the sixth century, the Hijaz was well established as a major trade route for commerce between Egypt, the Byzantine Empire and the East. In recent times, its geographical importance has been further enhanced by its proximity to the Suez Canal.

From about 600 BC for almost a thousand years, western Arabia enjoyed considerable prosperity as highly prized spices and other luxury goods were carried north along the trade routes from southern Arabia to the affluent in the fertile crescent, the lands that border the eastern Mediterranean.

## RELIGIOUS SIGNIFICANCE

The religious importance of Saudi Arabia, as the birthplace of Islam, is unique. The Holy Places of Makkah and Madinah are revered by one billion Muslims around the world. To understand the history of the Kingdom, its political, economic and social development and, most relevant here, the thinking that has underpinned King Fahd's life, both public and private, it is necessary to realize that Islam, which permeates every aspect of a Muslim's life, also permeates every aspect of the Saudi Arabian State.

Because this is so, it is worthwhile summarizing the five Pillars of Islam which constitute the basic religious duties which every Muslim, high or low, must perform.

### Al-Shahadah (or Testimony)

The first of the five tenets of Islam is the testimony and the pronouncing of the words that "There is no God but Allah and Muhammad is His Prophet." This Shahadah, or testimony, when recited by a person of sincerity, sound capacity and without any mental reservations, constitutes the first major requirement for being a Muslim. Of parallel importance and in accordance with the Shahadah is the solemn belief in a general resurrection, in the final day of judgment, in all the prophets of God and in the Scriptures of God and the total submission to the will of the Creator and acceptance of fate – be it good or bad.

### Al-Salah (Prayer)

Prayers are of such great significance that some leading scholars of the religion describe them as the backbone of Islam. Each Muslim is required to pray five times daily, in a prescribed manner. The first prayer is at dawn; the next is at high noon; then in the afternoon; after sunset; and finally at night. The formalized prayer consists of a sequence of obeisances made first from a standing position and then from a kneeling one. Muslims may pray in any place, alone or in the company of others. When praying, the Muslim faces in the direction of the Holy City of Makkah.

Inseparable from prayers in Islam is the Tahara, that is, the complete cleanliness of clothes, body and place. Without the Tahara, a Muslim's prayers will be rendered null. It is the Muslim's obligation, therefore, to be clean at the time of each prayer before facing his Creator.

### Al-Siyam (Fasting)

The imposition of fasting, which means complete abstention from food, drink and sexual intercourse from sunrise until sunset during the month of Ramadan, is the third basic tenet of the Islamic religion. Ramadan is the ninth month of the Hijira calendar. Fasting in Ramadan, besides being a religious duty, is no doubt of great benefit as it trains one to be patient, wise, well disciplined and to share the feelings of others.

Ramadan, traditionally held to be the month in which the Prophet Muhammad, peace be upon him, received his first revelation and the month in which the Holy Quran was revealed to the Prophet, is considered particularly holy by Muslims.

### Al-Zakat (Almsgiving)

In various parts of the Holy Quran great stress is laid on the Zakat, that is, almsgiving to those who deserve it. Each able Muslim should give a certain percentage of his annual income, either in money or in kind, to the poor and the indigent. In Saudi Arabia, the religious obligation of Al-Zakat has been officially recognized by the establishment of the Department of Zakat under the auspices of the Ministry of Finance. Al-Zakat on the individual's annual income from any legal source amounts to almost 2½%.

### Al Hajj (The Pilgrimage)

The fifth and last Pillar of Islam is the Hajj. It is explicitly stated in the Holy Quran that every physically and financially able Muslim should make the Hajj to the Holy City of Makkah once in his or her lifetime. The Hajj is considered the culmination of each Muslim's religious duties and aspiration.

For those readers who live in a largely secular, materialistic society, it may be difficult to grasp the extent to which Islam infuses the Saudi State and its people. The constitution of the Kingdom is the Shariah, Islamic law. The entire indigenous population is Muslim. The Five Pillars of Islam impose obligations on all Muslims, obligations which impinge on every aspect of life throughout every day of life. When we recount any of King Fahd's numerous personal acts of generosity, we should not see a king performing a gratuitous act of charity but a man fulfilling one of the basic obligations of his religion.

*It is a tribute to King Fahd's vision and tenacity of purpose that, whatever the economic circumstances, he has never been deflected from maintaining those policies, based on Islam, which have infused his thinking.*

## THE LIFE OF KING FAHD BIN ABDUL AZIZ AL SAUD

This unique land, birthplace of one of the great monotheistic religions, this vast territory almost the size of western Europe, is then the backcloth for the life recounted in this book.

King Fahd's life spans an extraordinary period in the history of the Arabian Peninsula and an extraordinarily difficult and challenging period in the history of the Middle East. It has been a time when many Arab States have been adjusting to the post-colonial era; a time when the goal of Arab unity has proved elusive; a time when the repercussions of the formation of the State of Israel have kept the region in a permanent state of tension. It has also been a time when Saudi Arabia has had to decide how to use its oil power and how to spend its oil revenues.

This book looks at the work King Fahd has performed in the Kingdom which he was eventually to rule as King and Prime Minister; in the Arab world where he was prepared to lend his support to any worthy Arab cause; in the Islamic world of which every corner has seen the benefits of the Kingdom's benevolence; and in the wider world of international affairs where King Fahd has always been ready to involve himself in the most intractable of problems.

It is common practice now, in giving an account of any individual's life, to seek out details that demean the subject. It is as though we need to diminish the great to the level of the ordinary, for fear that otherwise, by comparison, we ourselves might feel belittled. Ironically, such a process demeans us all. We should perhaps learn once again to accept that some men and women contribute to the common good more wholeheartedly and more effectively than others. We should willingly concede that, while the majority may see no way forward, some are capable of identifying, maintaining and fulfilling a bold vision of a better future. We should acknowledge that, while the public's attention is often focused on false heroes who strut upon the world's stage, seeking their own aggrandizement above all else, there are others who, through the decades, work for the common good, as far as possible from the glare of publicity. We should perhaps learn to celebrate once again the greatness in such individuals for, as fellow members of the human race, their contribution elevates us all, just as it benefits most profoundly those directly affected by their achievements.

As with any such account of a public life, there have been failures as well as successes. Political initiatives have not always succeeded. Economic factors, especially fluctuating revenues ensuing from an unstable oil price, have presented financial and social challenges. The process of development itself, implemented at an unprecedented pace, has sometimes meant that the meeting of modernity and tradition has not always been entirely harmonious. But, taken in the round, the achievements of King Fahd, set out in this book, deserve to be acknowledged within and beyond the unique country he has served for so long.

*King Fahd's legacy at home is not the buildings, the roads, the ports and airports; it is the people who, through education and social services, have been transformed from simple, generally illiterate tribesmen or traders into literate individuals, capable of holding their own and competing in the modern world.*

# BRIEF ACCOUNT OF THE HISTORY OF AL SAUD

IN CONSIDERING THE life of King Fahd bin Abdul Aziz, it is important to know something of the history of the Al Saud. That history is rich in events and in changing fortunes. Periods of great leadership and success have been interspersed with periods when fortune has been less kind. No doubt much of the character of a man is born in him but how that character develops and expresses itself is powerfully affected by experience and by a knowledge of the past.

The history of the House of Saud, the Royal Family of the Kingdom of Saudi Arabia, goes back over two centuries and falls into three distinct phases: the first phase begins with Muhammad bin Saud, the first ruler of the Saudi Dynasty, and spans the period from 1744 through 1818; the second phase comprises the continued succession of the Saudi house from 1824 through 1891; the third phase focuses on the ascendancy of the Royal Family initiated by Abdul Aziz in 1902, and continuing through the current era.

The name "Al-Saud" which means "Family of Saud" or "House of Saud", comes from Saud bin Muhammad bin Mugrin, who lived in the early eighteenth century.

The first ruler of the First House of Saud was Muhammad bin Saud. He started as ruler of Ad-Dir'iyah where he was to join forces with Sheikh Muhammad bin Abdul Wahhab, the eminent religious leader, in what could be called the first alliance.

Imam Muhammad bin Abdul Wahhab was born in the town of Uyaina in Najd of a highly respected and religious family. Showing a keen interest in religion and dismayed by contemporary deviations from Islamic teachings, the Sheikh invited his followers to return to Islam in its pure form, stripped of the heresies and abuses which had grown up around it. For that he was persecuted and forced to leave his town. He took refuge at Ad-Dir'iyah, the home of Al Saud, under the protection of Amir Muhammad bin Saud.

*Antiquities in Ad-Dir'iyah historical city*

Perceiving the value of Imam Muhammad bin Abdul Wahhab, Muhammad bin Saud concluded an agreement with him that together they would bring the Arabs of the peninsula back to the true faith of the Islamic religion. They confirmed this agreement with an oath in 1744. They were successful.

Muhammad bin Saud's son, Abdul Aziz bin Muhammad bin Saud, ruled from 1765 through 1803, retaining the association with Imam Muhammad bin Abdul Wahhab in the same capacity as his father and continuing to reform Islam in the peninsula. Abdul Aziz successfully captured the city of Riyadh in 1773. The combination of a deeply held theological conviction and military

success proved irresistible to many. As a result, the Saudi State began to spread rapidly and within fifteen years had extended its authority all over Najd.

After the death of Abdul Aziz, his son, Saud, ruled from 1803 through 1814. In 1803, Saud, provoked by the Sharif of Makkah, marched on the Holy City and took it. There he and his men performed Hajj. The Saudi Kingdom now stretched from Najd to Hasa in the west and south towards Najran.

Such an increase in authority was not to pass unchallenged. The Turkish Empire concluded that action must be taken and invited Muhammad Ali, the Viceroy of Egypt, which at that time came within the Ottoman sphere of influence, to dismantle the work of Muhammad bin Saud, his son and grandson, and to put an end to the emerging nation. Before Saud died in 1814, Muhammad Ali retook the Hijaz.

Saud's successor, his son Abdullah (who ruled until 1818), was unable to halt the Egyptian advance. Ad-Dir'iyah was taken and Abdullah removed to Istanbul where his captors executed him. Riyadh was captured in 1818. From 1818 to 1824, the Ottoman Empire maintained a few garrisons in Najd, as a gesture of their dominance. Thus, the first temporary decline in the House of Saud occurred.

Within a few years, however, the fortunes of the House of Saud were to revive. In 1824, Turki, a cousin of Saud bin Abdul Aziz, assumed the Amirship of Najd. In the course of his rule (1824 to 1834), Turki retook Riyadh. While continuing the Saudi drive for consolidation of the area, he recognized the symbolic suzerainty of the Viceroy of Egypt, Muhammad Ali.

In 1834, Turki was assassinated. Turki's eldest son, Faisal, defeated the assassin and became Imam. Faisal bin Turki refused to acknowledge the Viceroy of Egypt. The Viceroy, Muhammad Ali, was not prepared to see his earlier victories so quickly reversed.

In 1838, Egyptian forces defeated Faisal bin Turki, retaking the Najd. Faisal was taken captive and sent to Cairo. Later, when Muhammad Ali declared

Egypt's independence from the Ottoman Empire and was forced to withdraw his troops stationed in Najd in order to support his own position in Egypt, Faisal bin Turki escaped from Cairo (after five years of captivity), returning home and resuming his reign which lasted until 1865. By then, the House of Saud once more controlled most of Najd and Hasa.

On Faisal's death, however, Saudi fortunes declined once more. Disagreements between the sons of Faisal weakened the House of Saud. At the same time, a tribal leader of the Shammar, Muhammad bin Rashid, based in Hail, created a strong political force which rapidly covered the greater part of Najd, and by 1871, after concluding a pact with Turkey, captured Al-Hasa. In 1889, the third son of Faisal, Abdul Rahman bin Faisal, managed to confirm the rule of the Saudi dynasty by assuming the leadership of the family. At that time, the authority of the Saudi family centered on Riyadh but, in 1891, the House of Saud faced a further setback. Muhammad bin Rashid completed his control of Najd by capturing Riyadh, the citadel of the House of Saud. Adbul Rahman was forced to leave the city. He settled for months with the Murra tribes at the Great Waste, in the outskirts of the Rub al-Khali, the Empty Quarter, accompanied by his son, Abdul Aziz, the future King of Arabia. Eventually he left for Bahrain, to gather his family, and then went to Kuwait to live there in exile.

The son of Abdul Rahman, Abdul Aziz (better known in the West as Ibn Saud), was deeply concerned with thoughts of his home territory, Najd, the land of his ancestors. He anticipated that he would some day go back again and regain control of that part of Arabia.

When he was twenty-one, he decided to move on Riyadh with forty of his devoted friends. Having departed from Kuwait in December 1901, Abdul Aziz reached Riyadh in January 1902. The difficulties of taking Riyadh with so small a force were obvious. Abdul Aziz asked for volunteers to accompany him in the execution of a plan which seemed to have only its boldness to recommend it.

Under the darkness of night, together with his cousin Abdullah bin Jelawi and several other volunteers, Abdul Aziz stealthily made his way to a part of the city wall which he knew they could easily scale unobserved. The wall he chose was adjacent to the house of a man who had served Abdul Rahman, Abdul Aziz's father, some years before when the Al Saud had still ruled in Riyadh. When the wife of this man realized that the son of Abdul Rahman had come to reclaim his birthright, she vouchsafed some useful information about Ajlan, the Amir of Riyadh, the man Abdul Aziz would have to oust.

Once within the walls of Riyadh, the small group quietly made its way to an empty house close to Ajlan's residence. They entered the house, climbed to the roof and, by leaping from one roof to the next, reached the Amir's residence. There they waited.

At dawn, after prayers, Ajlan emerged from the Mosque into the street. As

*Al Masmak Fort in Riyadh*

soon as he saw Ajlan, Abdul Aziz gave vent to a loud battle cry and sallied forth from Ajlan's residence to attack. Ajlan fled back towards the Mosque, with Abdul Aziz and his companions in hot pursuit. Quickly cornered, the Amir defended himself briefly until the sword of Abdullah bin Jelawi cut him down.

The garrison of Riyadh was utterly demoralized by the unexpected attack and by the death of their leader. Assuming that such an assault could have been mounted only by a large and well-equipped force, they surrendered without further resistance.

So it was that, in 1902, Abdul Aziz had reasserted the authority of his family on the city of Riyadh and reestablished Al Saud rule over that area.

Naturally, this was not the end of the journey for Abdul Aziz; it was merely the beginning. His father, Abdul Rahman, who was the legal and rightful ruler of Najd, was recalled from Kuwait, and in a council formed of the Ulema (religious leaders) and other eminent citizens, he abdicated his rights and declared Abdul Aziz his successor. From 1902 to 1904, through a sequence of military campaigns, Abdul Aziz extended his authority over the whole of the Najd. He was now, however, faced with a much greater task – unifying the various tribes in Arabia.

Through a unique combination of the strength of his personality, judicious marriage alliances and force of arms, Abdul Aziz's drive for consolidation was so successful that by the end of 1904, he had managed to break the stranglehold of the Rashid and push them into the area at Jabal Shammar in northern Najd. The Rashid, desperately, appealed to the Turks who sent them reinforcements. Nevertheless, Abdul Aziz's desert fighters kept control of the situation in Najd. Through diplomatic negotiations at one time, and guerrilla warfare at another, Abdul Aziz forced the Ottoman Empire to recall its troops from Najd. Thus on the death of the leader of Al Rashid in 1906, Abdul Aziz had won complete control over Najd.

Having accomplished this objective, Abdul Aziz turned his attention to Al-Hasa and the area of the Arabian Gulf which was still under Turkish rule. Calculating on the Ottoman Empire's preoccupation with uprisings in Europe, and on his belief that Britain, considering the situation a domestic affair, would remain neutral, he launched a successful assault, and by 1913 his sovereignty was extended to both Najd and Al-Hasa.

Having reached this goal, Abdul Aziz once more confronted the perennial problem of the Bedouins and their practice of raiding and moving from place to place at will. This way of life was a recipe for insecurity and instability. He realized that, if he were to succeed in unifying the country, he must inspire a greater loyalty, one that transcended tribal allegiance. To this end, he implemented a brilliant two-stage plan. First, he sent preachers to various tribes, teaching them the essence of Islam and encouraging them to engage in agricultural labor. Secondly, he settled the Bedouins in agricultural settlements established according to the Wahhabi teachings, in Najd. The first of these projects was so successful that many others (sixty) followed. By 1916 the settled tribes constituted a formidable political-military force which enabled Abdul Aziz further to consolidate his rule over Najd and Al-Hasa. These settlers, known as the Ikhwan (meaning "brethren" in Arabic), became such a powerful force that Abdul Aziz assumed personal command of them.

In 1916, Abdul Aziz concluded a treaty with Britain, which recognized him as the sole ruler of Najd and Al-Hasa. This agreement gave Abdul Aziz the tacit right to eliminate any residual influence of the Rashid family. By 1918 his authority had reached the outskirts of Hail, the capital of the Rashid. During the next year clashes occurred between the forces of Sharif Hussein of Makkah and a force of the Ikhwan but Abdul Aziz withheld his troops from attacking the Hijaz. In 1920, he moved further south and consolidated Asir. The following year, he completed his campaign against the Rashid in Hail which fell under his control but still he refrained from moving into the Hijaz. Abdul Aziz was waiting for the right moment.

During the following three years, relations between the Sharif of Makkah and Britain began to deteriorate. The Sharif's maladministration of the Holy Cities further isolated him from other Arab countries. When, in March 1924, the Sharif proclaimed himself King of Arabia and Caliph of Islam, Abdul Aziz's patience was exhausted. In September of that year an army of the Ikhwan captured the city of Taif. With little delay and only minor resistance, Makkah, Madinah and the whole area of Hijaz came under the sovereignty of

Abdul Aziz. This final consolidation of the Arabian Kingdom was accomplished by the end of 1925. In the following year, Abdul Aziz, responding to popular demand from the people of Makkah, became the King of Hijaz and the Sultan of Najd and its Dependencies.

In September 1932, the Kingdom of Saudi Arabia was officially founded and acquired its present name. The consolidation of the Arabian Peninsula by Abdul Aziz within a period of thirty years is an outstanding example of nation building through courage, charisma and leadership.

In 1933, a discovery to prove of the greatest political and economic significance was made. A survey of the new Kingdom's natural resources, commissioned by the King, confirmed the existence of oil in the eastern region. By 1938, the exploitation of these oil fields, which contain approximately 25% of the world's proven oil resources, had begun.

In the course of his long reign, King Abdul Aziz gave studious attention to the development of international relations. In 1945, on board the *USS Quincy*, the Saudi King met the US President Franklin D. Roosevelt. (It was at that famous meeting that the American President gave his undertaking to the Saudi King that Arab interests in Palestine would not be sacrificed to Jewish aspirations for nationhood.) The concern of the Al Saud for the Palestinians and for Jerusalem is a constant in Saudi Arabian foreign policy.

*King Abdul Aziz*

The economic and technical cooperation which exploitation of the Kingdom's oil demanded and a community of political interest in many areas ensured that the friendship between the Kingdom of Saudi Arabia and the United States of America, initiated by King Abdul Aziz, was to grow in succeeding decades. Despite political differences in some areas, notably on the issue of Palestinian rights, that special relationship still survives and flourishes today.

On his death in 1953, King Abdul Aziz was succeeded by his son, Saud who, after a reign of eleven years was succeeded by his brother Faisal. King Faisal had been carefully groomed for leadership from an early age and it was during his reign that the

| KINGS OF SAUDI ARABIA | REIGN |
|---|---|
| King Abdul Aziz | 1932–1953 |
| King Saud | 1953–1964 |
| King Faisal | 1964–1975 |
| King Khalid | 1975–1982 |
| King Fahd | 1982–the present |

*King Saud bin Abdul Aziz*

Kingdom's industrial development began in earnest. King Faisal brought stability to the economy and then utilized the Kingdom's vast oil wealth to finance the country's ambitious development program. The last five years of his rule saw the implementation of the first of the Kingdom's Development Plans.

In 1975, King Faisal was succeeded by his half brother, Khalid. King Khalid

*King Faisal bin Abdul Aziz*

*King Khalid bin Abdul Aziz*

oversaw the implementation of the second Five-Year Plan (1975–80) and the preparation of the third. During this period, great progress was made in the building of the Kingdom's infrastructure and the policy of industrialization was pursued with vigor under the leadership of the then Crown Prince Fahd, brother to the King.

| | PERIOD |
|---|---|
| First Five-Year Plan | 1970–1975 |
| Second Five-Year Plan | 1975–1980 |
| Third Five-Year Plan | 1980–1985 |
| Fourth Five-Year Plan | 1985–1990 |
| Fifth Five-Year Plan | 1990–1995 |
| Sixth Five-Year Plan | 1995–2000 |
| Seventh Five-Year Plan | 2000–2005 |

In 1982, on the death of King Khalid, Crown Prince Fahd, who had already served as Minister of Education and Minister of the Interior in previous administrations and as Crown Prince throughout Khalid's reign, became King.

King Fahd has presided over the implementation of the third, fourth, fifth, sixth and seventh Five-Year Plans. The distinguishing feature of all the plans has been an unqualified commitment to the educational, industrial and agricultural development of the Kingdom, with the aim of providing the greatest possible opportunities for all Saudi citizens to fulfill their potential within a stable political framework, firmly based on Islamic precepts.

*King Fahd bin Abdul Aziz*

# KING FAHD AND EDUCATION

KING ABDUL AZIZ was well aware that there were two essential requirements if the Kingdom were to develop as he wished. A first-class infrastructure would be needed to facilitate the movement of people and goods. Even more important, the people must be educated. In 1949, he established a Shariah College in the Holy City of Makkah. This was followed by a teacher training college, also in Makkah, with an extension in Taif.

The task of establishing a national educational system fell to Prince Fahd. It must have been an extraordinarily daunting task. Literacy rates were low, except amongst the religious scholars. There were very few elementary schools for the general population, let alone secondary schools or universities. Only 35,000 schoolchildren were attending any kind of school at the time. There was no mechanism for a broadly based, educational syllabus. In other words, Prince Fahd, who was appointed the first Minister of Education in 1953 at a relatively young age, began with a clean slate.

In undertaking this intimidating task, Prince Fahd had at least some advantages. He himself was totally committed to meeting the challenge. He combined vision of what could be achieved and the benefits that would accrue with a determination to succeed. Like his father, he could see that, if the young Kingdom were to cohere, develop and play its full role amongst the community of nations, the key lay in education. Prince Fahd also recognized that, at the end of the day, the true wealth of any nation is its people and the drive and initiative they are able to deploy (a recurring theme in King Fahd's thoughts and speeches throughout his life). He knew that the only way to unlock the potential of the people was through education. In this respect, the interests of the citizen and the State were entirely coincident.

Another advantage was that, as the Kingdom's revenues grew, the priority which the Saudi Government attached to education meant that there was no shortage of financial resources. Anyone who has had to take responsibility for a major project will know that merely having sufficient resources by no means guarantees success – but the absence of such resources is certainly a serious impediment. Resources were not a problem.

Despite these advantages the scale of the task was awesome. Prince Fahd had to contend with the natural resistance of a nomadic or agricultural people to the introduction of a formal, modern, structured educational system. In addition, the implementation of such an educational system had to be reconciled with the traditional religious education which the Ulema provided for Muslim scholars and students. Above all, the sheer size of the country, the absence of qualified teachers and the general lack of educational facilities posed a challenge that would give even the most dynamic and competent organizer pause for thought.

The early years were difficult but, under Prince Fahd's leadership, those employed by the Ministry of Education made strenuous efforts to lay the foundations for a comprehensive educational system. A virtuous circle was established as the people responded to the educational opportunities provided by the Government and the Government continued to invest ever larger sums and ever more resources into the educational system. Even with the determination of Prince Fahd and his successors at the Ministry of Education, and with the generous resources provided by the Government, it took time to fulfill the original ambitious goals but, as an indication of what was achieved between 1970 and 2000 we provide figures for the number of schools and the number of students in the Kingdom in that period.

| Year | Number of Schools | Number of Students (males and females) |
|------|-------------------|----------------------------------------|
| 1970 | 3,283 | 547,000 |
| 1975 | 5,634 | 984,000 |
| 1980 | 11,070 | 1,462,000 |
| 1985 | 15,079 | 2,149,000 |
| 1990 | 16,609 | 2,934,000 |
| 1995 | 21,284 | 3,934,000 |
| 2000 | 22,770 | 4,774,000 |

It is not simply the scale of development that should be understood; it is its nature.

From the start, Prince Fahd recognized the importance of providing educational opportunities to girls as well as boys. Promoting the concept of equal educational opportunities for the sexes posed another problem but one that was ameliorated by Islam's insistence on the importance of learning in general (Muslims are exhorted "to seek knowledge from the cradle to the grave") and the high status accorded to women within Islamic society in particular. Once again, the figures will show how educational opportunities for girls were developed between 1970 and 2000.

| YEAR | MALE STUDENTS | FEMALE STUDENTS | TOTAL |
|------|---------------|-----------------|-------|
| 1970 | 412,000 | 135,000 | 547,000 |
| 1975 | 673,000 | 311,000 | 984,000 |
| 1980 | 951,000 | 511,000 | 1,462,000 |
| 1985 | 1,273,000 | 876,000 | 2,149,000 |
| 1990 | 1,624,000 | 1,310,000 | 2,934,000 |
| 1995 | 2,022,000 | 1,912,000 | 3,934,000 |
| 2000 | 2,405,000 | 2,369,000 | 4,774,000 |

Today, the Kingdom has an educational system of which it can be justly proud.

*Children studying the globe*

There are four levels of education below higher education. First, there is the pre-school level, which is a small sector of educational activity, currently confined mainly to cities and towns. Secondly, there is the elementary level, which caters for the educational needs of children from the age of 6 to 12. Thirdly, there is the intermediate level, which caters for children from 12 to 15. And, fourthly, there is the secondary level, which caters for children from 15 to 18 and prepares for higher education those who are to take their education further.

Primary and secondary education is largely the responsibility of the Ministry of Education which caters for male pupils and the General Presidency for Girls' Education. (Although there is a private educational sector, the vast majority of children are educated through the State system.) The Government has as its goal the provision of a high standard of primary

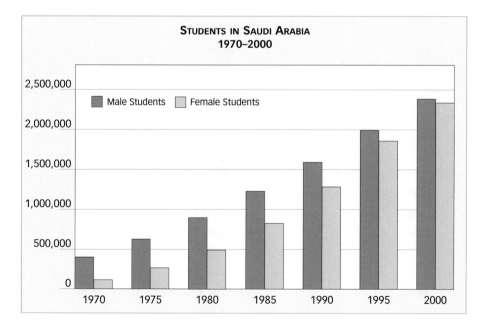

*King Fahd reviewing a model of Imam Muhammad bin Saud Islamic University*

and secondary education for all boys and girls, since it is an essential component of the Kingdom's policy to ensure that the entire population should be literate and numerate.

There is however a more ambitious goal, intended to benefit both the individual citizen and the State. The Government has, as one of its major objectives, the "Saudization" of jobs. Earlier and, in the initial phases of development, necessary reliance on expatriate workers has been reduced at all levels and Saudi citizens, now largely Saudi educated and trained, are taking over the work previously performed by foreigners. To ensure there are citizens qualified to assume the more demanding responsibilities, it is necessary for the Kingdom to produce a steady flow of graduates.

The Kingdom now boasts eight major universities:

- King Saud University in Riyadh, founded in 1957 as Riyadh University and renamed King Saud University in 1982
- Islamic University in the Holy City of Madinah, founded in 1961
- King Abdul Aziz University in Jeddah, founded in 1967
- Imam Muhammad bin Saud Islamic University in Riyadh, founded in 1953 and given university status in 1974
- King Faisal University in Dammam and Hofuf, founded in 1975
- King Fahd University of Petroleum and Minerals in Dhahran, founded in 1963 and given university status in 1975
- Umm Al-Qura University in the Holy City of Makkah, founded in 1979
- King Khalid bin Abdul Aziz University, founded in May 1998

For further details of the Kingdom's universities, see Appendix 1.

Of all the challenges facing the Kingdom in its social and economic development, there can be no doubt that the need to create a pool of highly educated Saudi Arabian citizens, capable of managing a complex modern economy, has been paramount.

It is in this context that the Kingdom's massive expenditure on education at all levels, but particularly at the higher level, must be seen. Clearly, the implementation of the development plans necessitated the assistance of tens of thousands of expatriate managers, scientists, engineers and teachers. But, while the development program was pursued with their help, the Government allocated resources to ensure that, as soon as reasonably possible, its own citizens should be able to assume full responsibility for their own future.

It is not only the more gifted who have benefited from King Fahd's uncompromising belief in the life-enhancing value of education. The Saudi Government has also made provision for those who are physically or mentally challenged by setting up educational establishments for the blind, the deaf and the mentally handicapped.

*King Fahd laying the foundation stone of Umm Al-Qura University in the Holy City of Makkah*

From the time when he was Minister of Education to the present, King Fahd has shown a continuous and unfaltering commitment to education. This commitment can be seen in the text of every Five-Year Development Plan and in the provisions of every annual budget. It has, of course, been in the Kingdom's interests to ensure that its population is properly educated. At the same time, it is clear from King Fahd's conduct and speeches that his belief in education is centered on the benefits it brings to the individual, not simply in improving employment opportunities but in understanding, appreciating and enjoying life.

# The Development of Infrastructure and Social Services

THIS CHAPTER ON the development of the Kingdom's infrastructure describes how, under King Fahd, the Kingdom's resources have been used to enable the Saudi economy to diversify, how the Saudi Government has created the economic and social conditions in which diversification could be achieved. It also indicates the emphasis that King Fahd, throughout his life, has placed on empowering Saudi citizens to play a full role within their society.

With the benefit of hindsight, it is clear that, although the Kingdom's development plans were ambitious, they were achievable. Nevertheless, it is worth emphasizing that, when each of the plans was announced, it was not unreasonable to question whether they could be fulfilled. Success should not detract from the enormity of the challenge, nor from the courage it took to take bold decisions in sometimes difficult political or economic circumstances.

## TRANSPORT

In devising a comprehensive and practical transport system, it is difficult to overestimate the challenge posed by the size of the Kingdom and the nature of its terrain. From the time of King Abdul Aziz it was obvious that it was crucially important to provide the best possible transport system for a vast country with three major focal points: Riyadh in the heart of the Arabian Peninsula, Jeddah and the Holy Cities on the west coast and Dammam, with its oil fields to the east. King Fahd has maintained the policy of facilitating travel and transportation in the Kingdom by every conceivable means, thus effectively bringing every part of the Kingdom closer together.

In this section, we look at all the features of transportation of people and goods in the Kingdom – roads, railways, air and sea. We include a brief section on overall transportation strategy.

*Makkah–Jeddah highway*

The statistics on each aspect of transportation give further evidence of the speed with which, in line with King Fahd's overall vision for the Kingdom's future, the infrastructure has been built to meet the demands of the Kingdom's development plans in the industrial and agricultural sectors of the economy.

### Roads

Linking all regions of the country, the extensive road network is a salient feature of the modernization of the Kingdom. The Kingdom of Saudi Arabia has, within three decades, built an advanced network of roads, bridges and tunnels. In addition to its obvious social and security benefits, the network of roads also serves the agricultural, industrial and commercial sectors.

With the massive increase in traffic that has ensued from the Kingdom's industrial and agricultural development, it has been necessary under King Fahd to upgrade many of the intercity roads to expressways, with anything up to eight lanes for traffic. Many overpasses and underpasses have been built within the cities to relieve congestion in city centers and a number of cities now enjoy the benefits of modern ringroads.

The length of the roads network, which satisfies high standards of safety, has expanded from 5,000 miles [8,000 km] in 1970 to 28,500 miles [45,500 km] in 1999. The following are some of the motorways in the Kingdom:

- Riyadh–Taif road, covering 467 miles [752 km]
- Makkah–Madinah road, covering 261 miles [421 km]
- Riyadh–Dammam road, covering 238 miles [383 km]
- Riyadh–Sudair–Al Qassim road, covering 197 miles [317 km]
- Jeddah–Makkah road, covering 37 miles [60 km]

*Roads in Saudi Arabia*

*Al Baha Descent*

While a major effort has been devoted to intercity and in-city road-building, agricultural communities have not been neglected. Even isolated villages are now connected by road to the main road network, so that the Kingdom can now boast a fully integrated, modern, nationwide network of roads. In 1999 the earth-surfaced road network totalled 66,050 miles [106,300 km] in distance.

The climate and the terrain of the Kingdom are inimical to road-building. Burning hot deserts and high mountain ranges, each pose different but equally challenging problems for contractors. Nowhere were these problems more intimidating than in the southwest of the Kingdom, where mountain ranges soar to 10,000 feet [3,000 m]. A series of viaducts has been built so that even the more inaccessible parts of the Kingdom in this region may now be reached by road.

Probably the most spectacular road construction project of all has been the building of the King Fahd Causeway, connecting the Kingdom with Bahrain.

*King Fahd Causeway*

On 11th November 1982, the cornerstone of the bridge was jointly placed by King Fahd and the then ruler of Bahrain, Sheikh Isa bin Salman Al-Khalifa. This is a four-lane highway. It is 82 feet [25 m] wide and about 16 miles [26 km] long. The cost of US$ 1.2 billion was paid by the Saudi Arabian Government in line with King Fahd's policy of increased cooperation with the Member States of the Gulf Cooperation Council. The causeway was completed in 1986 and was opened to traffic at the end of that year.

The Ministry of Communications is currently completing a number of dual carriageways linking various cities.

With the building of the road network, it became possible to expand the public transport services. In 1979, the Saudi Public Transport Company (SAPTCO) was established. From small beginnings, SAPTCO has grown into a national bus service, providing cheap public transport within and between major population centers. SAPTCO's services continue to expand as it increases the size of its fleet and upgrades the quality of its vehicles. Each year, SAPTCO faces and meets a particular challenge when pilgrims arrive from all over the Kingdom and from all over the world to perform the annual pilgrimage to the Holy Cities of Makkah and Madinah. SAPTCO assigns about 2,000 buses every season for services in the Holy Cities. It also operates regular international passenger services between the Kingdom and Egypt, Jordan, Syria, the United Arab Emirates, Qatar, Kuwait, Bahrain and Turkey.

**Railways**

Railways remain the least developed means of transportation in the Kingdom. With such vast distances to cover, in often adverse environmental conditions, it is inevitable that airline services seem to be a more practical mode of long-distance transportation.

The Kingdom's railways currently consist primarily of a single track, standard-gauge line, running for 350 miles [570 km] from Riyadh to Dammam in the eastern region. This line, which was opened in 1951, passes through Dhahran, Abqaiq, Hofuf, Harad and al-Kharj and has benefited from substantial renovation in recent years. An additional line joining Hofuf with Riyadh was opened in 1985.

The Kingdom's railways are managed by the Saudi Government Railways Organization, established in 1966, as an independent public utility, governed by a board of directors.

In 1999, there were 804,000 railway passengers.

**Air Transport**

Civil aviation occupies a special place in any account of the Kingdom's transportation systems.

In 1945, Franklin D. Roosevelt, President of the United States of America, presented a DC-3 Dakota to King Abdul Aziz. Quick to realize the contribution that air travel could make to the development of the Kingdom, the King promptly ordered two more planes.

These three planes formed the embryo of what has grown into Saudi Arabian Airlines, the Kingdom's flag carrier, and now one of the world's leading airlines – an airline which has in its fleet today more than 100 aircraft (including a number of Boeing 747s, Boeing 777s and Airbuses), which carried 10.6 million

| YEAR | BLOCK HOURS FLOWN (THOUSANDS) | PASSENGERS CARRIED (MILLIONS) |
|------|------|------|
| 1990 | 190.5 | 10.6 |
| 1991 | 165.0 | 9.8 |
| 1992 | 195.3 | 11.6 |
| 1993 | 203.3 | 12.4 |
| 1994 | 210.1 | 12.5 |
| 1995 | 206.0 | 12.0 |
| 1996 | 213.0 | 12.3 |
| 1997 | 211.1 | 12.2 |
| 1998 | 214.1 | 12.2 |
| 1999 | 231.0 | 12.7 |

passengers and 218,000 tons [198 million kg] of cargo in 1990. By early 1999, Saudi Arabian Airlines had 24 local and 52 international stations and was transporting 12.7 million passengers annually and 279,000 tons [253 million kg] of cargo.

The table to the left shows the number of hours flown and number of passengers carried by Saudi Arabian Airlines from 1990 to 1999.

The network of air transportation comprises 25 airports in the Kingdom, including 14 local, 8 regional and 3 international airports. In 1981, King Khalid opened the King Abdul Aziz International Airport in Jeddah. This airport, which has special facilities for handling the annual influx of pilgrims performing Hajj, has a land area of 40 square miles [105 sq km].

The King Khalid International Airport was opened in 1984. Located 22 miles [35 km] north of Riyadh, with a land area of 87 square miles [225 sq km],

*Internal view of King Khalid International Airport – Riyadh*

*General view of King Khalid*
*International Airport*

the King Khalid International Airport is a masterpiece of modern architecture, blending traditional Arab design with the requirements of efficiency, and incorporating into the whole the essential Islamic character of the Kingdom. It has four terminals and, from its inauguration, had the capacity to handle 7.5 million passengers a year. By 2000, its capacity had doubled.

The third international airport, the King Fahd International Airport, is at Dhahran. The King Fahd International Airport has an area of 300 square miles [780 sq km], making it the largest airport in the Kingdom. There are two parallel runways, each 13,120 feet [4,000 m]. The Airport has the capacity to handle seven million passengers annually. In addition to the construction of these three international airports, domestic airports are being systematically expanded.

Civil aviation has grown in parallel with the Kingdom's ambitious development plans. Its advantage over road and rail, in terms of speed for users, has made it the transportation mode of choice and its contribution to the Kingdom's successful progress cannot be overestimated.

## Shipping and Ports

As the coasts of the Kingdom of Saudi Arabia extend some 930 miles [1,500 km] along the Red Sea and Gulf coasts, great attention is given to continued expansion and modernization of seaports and maritime transport sectors. As a result, the Kingdom's trade activities have expanded and seaports and harbors account for 90 to 95% of total export and import trade. The Ports Authority was established in 1976 with a mandate to modernize and upgrade the operational efficiency of the Kingdom's seaports to meet the increasing volume of imports and industrial exports. The Ports Authority has successfully met these objectives through the use of modern techniques in operation and management. The number of berths at main seaports rose from 27 in 1975 to 183 in 1999.

The Kingdom has five major commercial ports and two major industrial ports. The commercial ports are at Jeddah, Dammam, Jizan, Jubail and Yanbu. The industrial ports are the King Fahd Industrial Port at Jubail and the King Fahd Industrial Port at Yanbu. There is also the oil port of Ras Tanura, as well as a number of minor ports.

### The Jeddah Islamic Port

The Jeddah Islamic Port is the oldest and busiest of all the Kingdom's ports. It is the principal commercial port and the main port of entry for pilgrims on their way to the Holy Cities of Makkah and Madinah. King Fahd has given special attention to this port to ensure pilgrims' comfort. The Jeddah Islamic Port has 54 quays and is wide enough for 135 ships to anchor simultaneously. All the Kingdom's major ports, including the Jeddah Islamic Port, are equipped with modern tugboats. They are able to anchor ships, extinguish fires, combat oil pollution and rescue ships in distress. In 1999 the volume of cargo handled at the Jeddah Islamic Port reached 17,903,000 tons.

### The King Abdul Aziz Port at Dammam

The King Abdul Aziz Port at Dammam ranks second to Jeddah as a commercial port. It is located on the Gulf and is the gateway for both the eastern and central regions. Like Jeddah it boasts a fully equipped repair yard. In 1984, King Fahd opened the King Fahd Ship Repair Complex, with an area of 161,460 square yards [135,000 sq m] and two docks for ship repair and maintenance. The Port also has an advanced center for training Saudi staff in repairing ships. It has a tower 310 feet [95 m] high as well as special stations for handling bulk cereals, containers and cold or frozen foods. In 1999, the King Abdul Aziz Port handled 10,163,000 tons of cargo.

### Commercial Port at Jizan

The Commercial Port at Jizan, which is the main port in the south of the country, serves the development projects in the region. It has twelve modern quays receiving giant commercial ships. Furnished with modern equipment for handling goods, the Port has storage areas for various types of goods. It also has a tower 200 feet [61 m] high, a quality control laboratory and a computer center. In 1999, it handled 675,000 tons of cargo.

*King Abdul Aziz Port at Dammam*

*Jubail Commercial Port*

The Jubail Commercial Port functions as a commercial and industrial port. Fifty miles [80 km] north of Dammam, the Commercial Port is famous for fishing and pearl harvesting. The Port has modern equipment for loading and unloading, 125 storage hangars and a control tower 170 feet [52 m] high. In 1999, the volume of cargo handled was 1,979,000 tons.

*King Fahd Industrial Port at Jubail*

The King Fahd Industrial Port at Jubail lies on a sea-lane to the north of the Jubail Commercial Port, extending 5,617 miles [9,039 km] into the Gulf. The Port is designed to handle export and import of solid and liquefied substances and bulk goods. It can also handle imports of iron ore and exports of bulk sulfur and fertilizers. It has 23 quays and a maritime station for tankers. It handled 28,113,000 tons of cargo in 1999.

*Commercial Port at Yanbu*

The Commercial Port at Yanbu is located 128 miles [206 km] northwest of Jeddah and has storage facilities for all types of goods, in addition to a modern pilgrims' hall. It handled 808,000 tons of cargo in 1999.

*King Fahd Industrial Port at Yanbu*

Situated near the Commercial Port, it contributed to the setting up of Yanbu Industrial Complex, exporting its products to various parts of the world. Extending 16 miles [25 km] along the coast, it is the biggest port on the Red Sea for loading oil. It has 22 quays and receives tankers ranging in capacity from 1,000 to 500,000 tons. Its control tower is equipped with radar, modern communication devices and data recorders. In 1999, it handled 28,402,000 tons of cargo.


## ELECTRICITY

In any program for industrial development, electricity plays an indispensable role and the need to extend electrification throughout the Kingdom was recognized early in the Kingdom's life. How the Kingdom has approached this task and, in particular, the way the strategy has evolved is worthy of note.

As the Kingdom's demand for electrical power in the industrial and agricultural sectors of the economy grew, the Government replaced the old fragmented system of electrical power generation (provided by numerous small companies) with SCECOs – Saudi Consolidated Electric Companies – each providing electricity for a whole region of the Kingdom.

The first SCECO (SCECO-East) was created in 1977, with a capital of SR 5 billion. This was followed in 1979 by SCECO-South, with a capital of

SR 4 billion, serving more than 1,447 cities and villages and SCECO-Central, with a capital of SR 8 billion, serving more than 600 cities and villages, including Riyadh. Electricity for the southwest of the Kingdom was provided by SCECO-West, established in 1982, with a capital of SR 8 billion.

The General Electricity Corporation (GEC) was given overall responsibility for the Kingdom's electricity system and a direct responsibility for the provision of electrical supplies to rural areas not covered by the consolidated companies. The GEC has represented the Government equity holdings in all the independent electricity-generating companies and has been a source of finance for those companies' capital requirements.

The Saline Water Conversion Corporation (SWCC) also began to produce electricity from its dual-purpose plants on the coasts of the Kingdom, selling electricity to the electricity facilities in these areas.

To improve and strengthen the power industry, in 1998, the Council of Ministers issued Resolution Number 169 for the restructuring of the electricity sector, aiming to reform its finances and increase the participation of the private sector in its ownership, management and energy conservation. The resolution stipulated the following:

- Establishment of a joint stock company for electricity to be called the Saudi Electric Company (SEC).
- Merging all the local electricity utility companies, as well as the electricity facilities owned by the General Electricity Corporation into the Saudi Electric Company.

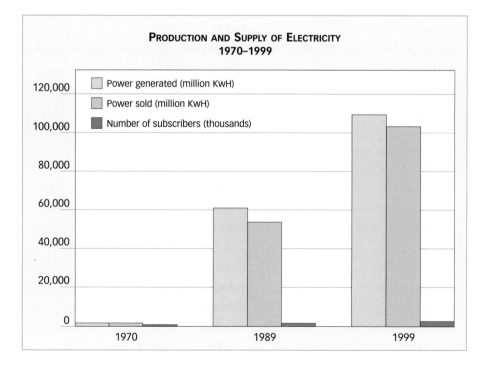

**PRODUCTION AND SUPPLY OF ELECTRICITY 1970–1999**

Power generated (million KwH)
Power sold (million KwH)
Number of subscribers (thousands)

- Creation of an independent agency during the first year of the company's establishment to review periodically the costs and tariffs of the electricity service according to defined principles.

|  | 1970 | 1989 | 1999 |
|---|---|---|---|
| Power generated (million KwH) | 1,825 | 61,568 | 114,624 |
| Power sold (million KwH) | 1,690 | 55,201 | 105,612 |
| Number of subscribers (thousands) | 216 | 2,259 | 3,372 |

- Liquidation of the General Electricity Corporation. A ministerial committee would undertake the development and execution of the liquidation plan, including the settlement of its liabilities, while preserving the full rights of its staff.

In 2000, the Minister of Commerce issued Resolution Number 2047, announcing the establishment of the Saudi Electric Company.

The table above shows the increase in electricity production from 1970 to 1999.

## POST AND TELECOMMUNICATIONS

Of all the indicators of social and economic progress in a modern society, probably the most obvious is the development of postal and telecommunication services. Certainly, efficient communications are a prerequisite of success.

### Telephone Service

King Abdul Aziz was well aware that an efficient telecommunications system was essential to his plans for consolidating and developing the Kingdom and it was during his reign (in 1930) that the first telephone exchange was installed in Al-Dira.

In 1953, the Ministry of Communications was formed and amongst its responsibilities were postal and telecommunication services. Within a year, the Saudi Arabian Radio Telecommunication Scheme RT-1 was installed, providing a multi-channel telephone and telegraph network, linking Riyadh, Dammam, Jeddah, the Holy Cities of Makkah and Madinah, and Taif.

In 1977, the Ministry of Post, Telegraphs and Telephones (which had taken over PTT responsibilities from the Ministry of Communications) embarked upon an ambitious plan to establish a modern telecommunications network, comprising telephone, telegraph and telex services, for the entire Kingdom. The Ministry's achievements have been remarkable by any yardstick.

In May 1998 Saudi Arabia's telecommunications service was privatised. The new company, known as the Saudi Telecommunications Company (STC), has a capital of over SR 10 billion during the first phase. STC will become one of the Kingdom's largest employers, providing jobs for more than 70,000 Saudis. There are plans to add 1.7 million new telephone lines across the country during the next three to four years.

To give some perspective to the magnitude of this achievement, we set out to the right a table showing the telephone exchange capacity and the number of telephones operating between 1985 and 1999.

| YEAR | EXCHANGE LINE CAPACITY (THOUSANDS) | NO. OF TELEPHONES OPERATING (THOUSANDS) |
|---|---|---|
| 1985 | 1,290.0 | 935.6 |
| 1986 | 1,301.0 | 966.3 |
| 1987 | 1,374.0 | 1,033.5 |
| 1988 | 1,413.0 | 1,094.9 |
| 1989 | 1,499.0 | 1,181.7 |
| 1990 | 1,569.0 | 1,278.4 |
| 1991 | 1,625.6 | 1,361.8 |
| 1992 | 1,670.3 | 1,451.1 |
| 1993 | 1,688.8 | 1,496.1 |
| 1994 | 1,766.4 | 1,530.3 |
| 1995 | 1,898.6 | 1,567.5 |
| 1996 | 2,094.8 | 1,737.1 |
| 1997 | 2,279.4 | 1,877.0 |
| 1998 | 2,694.4 | 2,157.2 |
| 1999 | 3,848.9 | 2,706.2 |

## Mobile Telephones

In January 1996, the Global System for Mobiles (GSM) was launched in the Kingdom with the aim of installing 500,000 GSM mobile telephones. By late September 1996, more than half were in operation. By the end of the project, 45 Saudi cities and towns and all the major highways will be covered.

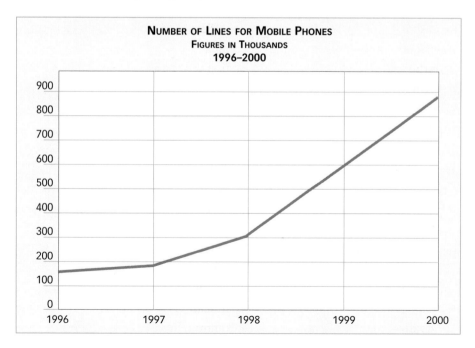

**NUMBER OF LINES FOR MOBILE PHONES**
**FIGURES IN THOUSANDS**
**1996–2000**

## Postal Services

The development of the Kingdom's economy has generated a massive increase in the volume of mail which the postal services have had to handle. In a continuing process of expansion, the Fourth Development Plan provided for five new central post offices (in the Holy City of Madinah, Abha, Buraidah, Jizan and Skaka) to complement the three main postal complexes in Riyadh, Jeddah and Dammam. Indeed, an efficient postal network now covers all the cities and villages of the Kingdom, with 488 main and 175 branch post offices. The total number of domestic correspondence has increased from 19.1 million postal items in 1970 to 345.6 million items in 1999.

## Telex

The development of telex services in the Kingdom has kept pace with every innovation in telex technology. From the early days of electro-mechanical devices, through the installation of electronic machines in 1978, to the introduction in the 1980s of the most sophisticated equipment, capable of handling Arabic and Latin text simultaneously, the Ministry of Post, Telegraphs and Telephones (PTT) has ensured that the Kingdom's ever-growing need for efficient telex communication services has been handsomely met. Telecommunications experts agree that the Kingdom of Saudi Arabia possesses one of the most advanced telex networks in the world. This network is actively able to support the business community and, with it, progress and prosperity in the Kingdom.

Having equipped the Kingdom with one of the most modern telex networks in the world, the Ministry of PTT has been able to proceed with the introduction of a high-speed data transmission service (Teletex), to which existing telex subscribers will have easy access.

## Satellite Communications

In 1985, with the launch of two communications satellites, ARABSAT (the Arab Satellite Communications Organization – formed by the Arab League in 1976) became operational. The ARABSAT satellites are positioned in geostationary orbit above the equator.

Communications satellites facilitate the almost instantaneous transmission of many forms of data, including alphanumeric text, voice, still pictures and moving pictures. Their use, in news dissemination, in business, in entertainment and in education is limited only by the imagination and resources of the user.

The Kingdom is playing an active role in the development and exploitation of this exciting medium of communication.

The King Fahd Satellite Communications City in Jeddah is the largest complex in the Middle East. It comprises four ground stations, two dealing with INTELSAT, one with ARABSAT and the other with ANMASAT for maritime communications to provide services to all ships, planes and vehicles. These stations provide telephone, telex, TV and cable services.

### The Internet

In 1999, the Internet service became available in the Kingdom, with all the connections routed through the State server, sited at the King Abdul Aziz City for Science and Technology. The Ministry of Post, Telegraphs and Telephones provides the external means to access the Internet and the service is available for research establishments, academics and public and private companies.

## HEALTH

The Kingdom's policy on health is simply expressed – the provision of free health services for the benefit of all the citizens of Saudi Arabia – and King Fahd has shown, throughout his reign, a very real understanding of the importance of adequate health provision for those who need it, both within and outside the Kingdom.

Healthcare is the responsibility of the Ministry of Health, which provides both general and specialized hospital services. Amongst the Kingdom's specialized hospitals are the King Faisal Specialist Hospital, the military hospitals and some Ministry of Health hospitals, which offer, amongst other advanced

*King Fahd inaugurating Al-Fanateer Hospital in Jubail*

medical techniques, open-heart surgery, kidney transplantation and cancer therapy.

The general health service is complemented by other agencies which provide health services for their staff (e.g. the military agencies) or segments of the general population (e.g. the Royal Commission for Jubail and Yanbu). There is an active Red Crescent Society in the Kingdom, which provides medical emergency services and plays a key role in providing medical assistance during the period of the annual pilgrimage, the Hajj. In his primary role as Custodian of the Two Holy Mosques, King Fahd takes a very direct interest in ensuring that healthcare provision during the Hajj meets the highest standards. The Kingdom's universities are also involved in healthcare, not only by providing primary and specialized healthcare for their own staff and students, but through research, training and the implementation of health education programs.

The Ministry of Health policy reflects the Government's national development strategy, which is committed to improving the quality of life of the Saudi people, and to helping them to participate fully in the development plan and to benefit from it.

To carry out this policy, the Ministry of Health provides a whole range of health services (preventive, curative, educational and rehabilitative) to the entire population. This is achieved through a network of hospitals and primary healthcare centers which are distributed throughout the country.

The health system used by the Ministry of Health stresses the importance of preventive healthcare as the basis for providing comprehensive health services to the citizens and residents, and uses a referral system for patients who need specialized diagnosis or hospital care. At the same time, the Ministry of Health gives much attention to upgrading and improving the quality of manpower in the medical field through expanding in-service training, particularly amongst Saudi personnel, as well as improving administrative effectiveness and health research.

The principal health policy of the Kingdom is to provide comprehensive healthcare to all citizens and residents throughout the country. To meet the increased demand for healthcare, the Government's annual expenditure on the health sector in 1999 was estimated at SR 12 billion. The Ministry of Health has finalised plans to establish eight new hospitals and renovate and expand 215 existing hospitals.

At the beginning of the First Five-Year Plan in 1970, there were only 74 hospitals in the Kingdom, with Riyadh Central Hospital as the only referral hospital. During the Second Plan (1975–80) five large referral hospitals were constructed and opened in various parts of the country. The five hospitals had 2,275 beds and cost a total of SR 3,500 million. During the Third Five-Year Plan (1980–5), 32 hospitals with 7,632 beds were built, costing approximately

SR 9,100 million. By mid-1984, the King Khalid Specialist Eye Hospital was opened in Riyadh with a capacity of 220 beds and the ability to provide high-quality ophthalmic care. In 1985, 24 new hospitals with 5,306 beds and costing about SR 5,700 million were in operation. By the end of the Fourth Development Plan (1985–90) most of the eighteen hospitals under construction (with 4,165 beds) at a cost of SR 5,100 million were in operation. Among these hospitals are King Fahd Medical City in Riyadh (1,400 beds) and Al-Khaleeg Hospital in Dammam in the eastern region (640 beds). In 1999, there were 314 hospitals in the Kingdom.

The great expansion in healthcare all over the Kingdom requires a large number of health personnel and therefore the health manpower in the Ministry has increased considerably. In 1970 the Ministry's total health manpower was 4,438; this number had risen to 73,314 in 1999. The number of physicians has increased from 789 to 14,786, nursing staff from 2,253 to 36,340 and allied health personnel from 1,396 to 22,188 in the same period.

In addition to the Government's healthcare facilities, the private sector also runs 128 general and specialized hospitals, has 16,716 physicians, 29,186 nursing staff and 19,575 allied health personnel.

To meet the increased demand for health manpower, the Ministry of Health planned and opened health institutes for males and females all over the country. The Ministry also plans to open intermediate health colleges in various parts of the country to improve the standard of the nursing staff and allied health personnel.

*King Khalid Specialist Eye Hospital – Riyadh*

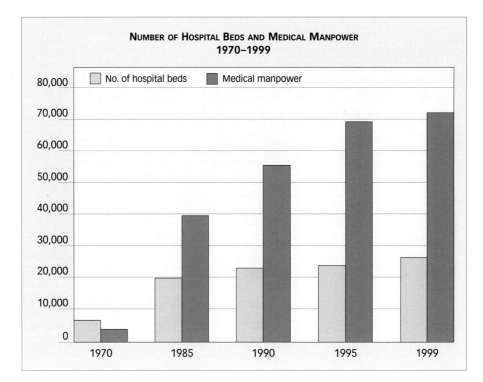

| YEAR | MINISTRY OF HEALTH | | | | OTHER AGENCIES | | | |
|---|---|---|---|---|---|---|---|---|
| | HOSPITALS | HOSPITAL BEDS | HEALTH CENTERS | MEDICAL MANPOWER | HOSPITALS | HOSPITAL BEDS | HEALTH CENTERS | MEDICAL MANPOWER |
| 1970 | 47 | 7,165 | 519 | 4,411 | 27 | 1,874 | 72 | 1,736 |
| 1985 | 105 | 20,796 | 1,306 | 40,050 | 71 | 10,163 | 522 | 30,036 |
| 1990 | 163 | 25,835 | 1,668 | 57,412 | 94 | 13,616 | 1,385 | 40,180 |
| 1995 | 175 | 26,737 | 1,725 | 70,668 | 110 | 15,179 | 1,575 | 53,421 |
| 1999 | 186 | 27,794 | 1,756 | 73,314 | 128 | 17,935 | 1,750 | 65,477 |

Although the responsibility for providing healthcare to the population of Saudi Arabia rests with the Ministry of Health, there are several Government agencies which also provide health services.

In addition to hospitals of the Ministry of Health, there are the university hospitals, military hospitals, the King Faisal Specialist Hospital and King Khalid Specialist Eye Hospital; most of these hospitals have highly advanced technology and operate as referral hospitals.

**The Red Crescent Society**
The Red Crescent of Saudi Arabia (the Muslim equivalent of the Red Cross) was founded in 1963. It provides emergency medical services in five administrative regions of the Kingdom of Saudi Arabia. By 1995, the Society had 146 First Aid Centers, staffed by 1,560 doctors, nurses and medics, with 471 ambulances.

The Red Crescent has a particular role to play during Hajj (the annual pilgrimage to the Holy City of Makkah), providing on-the-spot first aid and using its fleet of vehicles (760 in 1991) to take emergency cases to the nearest medical facility.

*Saudi Red Crescent Society vehicles in Mina*

## SOCIAL DEVELOPMENT

One of the underlying purposes of the building of the Kingdom's infrastructure, and the expansion of the industrial and agricultural base, has been to encourage social development in its widest sense. Over and over again, King Fahd has declared in his public pronouncements his Government's commitment to ensuring that all Saudi citizens participate in the Kingdom's development, both in terms of enjoying the benefits and contributing to its success.

The social services provisions of the Kingdom of Saudi Arabia are extensive by any standard. They are designed to redress existing imbalances, to improve living standards and the quality of life of the population, to stimulate citizen participation in community development activities, and to provide remedial care and assistance for the disabled and the deprived.

The Ministry of Labor and Social Affairs, on behalf of the Government, is in charge of carrying out programs and projects designed to improve living conditions for the population and to smooth the processes related to the rapid transformation of the socio-economic system. There are a number of social rehabilitation, care and remedial services, designed to assist the physically or mentally disadvantaged, to protect vulnerable members of society, and to deal with problems such as juvenile delinquency. Special attention is given to raising the living standards of the poorest sections of the community, particularly in the villages and the less developed districts of the towns and cities.

These services are provided through a network of facilities which, in 1999, comprised 16 orphanages, 22 social guidance and probation institutions, 5 residential nurseries for handicapped children, 2 centers for paralysed children, 28 centers for rehabilitation of the disabled, 11 offices for vagrancy control and 10 homes for the elderly.

In addition, there are 173 benevolent societies, of which 20 are for women. These receive technical assistance and financial grants from the Government. In 1999, the subsidies provided to them amounted to SR 54.8 million. These societies provide help and care for the disabled and families in need and seek to improve the status of women by offering training in appropriate skills and organizing cultural lectures and symposia.

There are a number of social service agencies whose task it is to remedy social problems, many of which are created by the process of social development itself. The Government takes the view that poverty and deprivation are not necessarily due to the failure of individuals to meet their own needs. Most of these problems are a result of broader external conditions in society as a whole, and will not solve themselves. Public and private interventions are necessary to improve the conditions of the individual and the community. The social service agencies will continue to pay attention to the development of Saudi society, to assist in improving the standard of living, and to take steps to redress some of the social imbalances which have inevitably become more pronounced during a period of rapid economic change.

In addition to these social services, there is a compulsory occupational insurance scheme, covering provisions for sickness and retirement, for employees in both the public and private sectors.

The Government also created the General Organization for Social Insurance (GOSI), in 1969. GOSI is responsible for protecting workers from poverty in cases of incapacity, old age and work injuries. It is in charge of the Government's Social Insurance Law, which covers 5.8 million workers.

### Self-Reliance

In all the social service programs, there is an emphasis on helping people to help themselves, wherever possible. The Government's objectives are:
– to extend the scope of integrated social development activities with other service providers and citizen groups in order to meet the basic needs of disadvantaged groups and individuals;
– to emphasize the social responsibility of the population for improving the standards of local communities and poor districts within cities through private sector activities;
– to assist the population in improving their real standard of living by their own efforts and without reducing incentives to work;

- to extend social service programs to all parts of the Kingdom and to all eligible persons;
- to encourage family solidarity and support the desired socialization of children;
- to provide care for clients requiring institutionalization if it is impossible to deliver sufficient care in the family setting.

The Government can create the conditions for social development, just as it has created the conditions for economic diversification, but it has always been King Fahd's view that, for the fulfillment of the Kingdom's aspirations, it is essential that Saudi citizens understand the objectives of the development programs and become, through their personal involvement, committed to the Kingdom's goals.

Such commitment in the social area may take many forms. It may appear as active participation in the Kingdom's cultural life (through, for example, authorship), or as an enhanced appreciation of the Kingdom's cultural traditions (by, for example, greater use of the Kingdom's libraries and museums), or in a changed perception of the value of types of work which may previously have been accorded low social status.

The Saudi Government has been and will remain committed to its investment in social development in order to ensure that children and young people in the Kingdom are given the fullest opportunity to develop their potential and become responsible and productive citizens.

## INFORMATION SYSTEMS

King Fahd, perhaps more than any of his predecessors, has recognized the importance of an effective system for disseminating information. Whether in terms of communicating Government policy within the country or in terms of presenting the Kingdom's viewpoint outside the country, professional expertise in the techniques of modern mass communication is essential. The need for such expertise is particularly acute at the level of international affairs where competing versions of the truth and conflicting value systems can distort the judgment of allies and foes alike.

The Ministry of Information is responsible for all information services, including radio, television and publications. The Ministry provides information and news to the public through a network of radio and television broadcasting stations, and through the publication and distribution of books and other material.

The Ministry initiates and undertakes information campaigns in cooperation with other Government agencies, covering different fields such as health, eradication of illiteracy, fire risk and traffic safety instructions.

The Ministry of Information has 38 local publication offices and there are eight centers for local and seven centers for foreign information.

**Radio**

In 1932, King Abdul Aziz set up his own private radio network in the Kingdom, primarily to enable him and his officials to keep themselves informed of events.

In the full sense of public broadcasting, transmissions began in the Kingdom of Saudi Arabia in 1948 – from a small station in Jeddah. This was followed three years later by a station in the Holy City of Makkah. These two stations, which were on the air for no more than fourteen hours a week, broadcast recitations from the Holy Quran, the sayings of the Prophet, news and cultural programs and some music.

From these relatively modest beginnings, the Saudi Radio Broadcasting Service emerged. In 1964, the Riyadh Broadcasting Station and the Call of Islam Station (based in the Holy City of Makkah) began transmissions.

In the discharge of his duty as the Guardian of the Holy Places and the Kingdom's role as the center of the Islamic world, King Fahd, following the precedent of his predecessors, has employed radio to strengthen Islam within and outside Saudi Arabia. In 1973, the Kingdom began short wave and high frequency broadcasting in Bembari, Bengali, English, French, Indonesian, Pharsi, Somali, Swahili, Turkestan, Turkish and Urdu. By 1999, the number of radio broadcasting stations had reached 25. These broadcast programs through the following six main radio broadcast services:

1. The General Programs Service: This station concentrates on transmitting live programs, like news, conferences, national occasions, prayer and pilgrimage rituals. It transmits for twenty hours a day.

2. The Second Programs Service: This station concentrates on transmitting popular programs, varieties, analyses, ritual of prayers from the Holy City of Makkah and sports competitions. It transmits for eighteen hours a day.

3. The Islamic Call Service: This station serves the Islamic Call, conveying the message of Islam to the whole world, presenting Islamic thought and its achievements in the history of human civilization, defending the issues of the Islamic nation and presenting the importance of Islamic heritage. This service started under the name of "Voice of Islam".

4. The Holy Quran Service: The service started in March 1972. Its transmission reaches all the Arab world in addition to East and South Asia and mid-African countries. It transmits for twenty-four hours a day.

5. European Program Service: This service transmits in two languages, English and French, for thirteen hours a day.

6. The Oriented Programs Service: The oriented programs started in 1950 to

introduce Islam and present the authentic Islamic doctrine in the ten local languages of the countries to which the programs are transmitted. These languages are: Bengali, Indonesian, Malaysian, Mbariya, Persian, Somali, Swahili, Turkestani, Turkish, Urdu.

There is also the Awareness Station during the Hajj season. It offers advice and informs the pilgrims of the health and social facilities available to them in the Holy Cities of Makkah and Madinah and the Holy Sites.

In addition to the above, there are twenty-three FM stations.

## Television

In 1964, King Faisal commissioned the American National Broadcasting Corporation (NBC) to construct a national television network. The first test television transmissions in the Kingdom took place in 1965 from stations in Riyadh and Jeddah.

Throughout the development of the Kingdom's television services, the Ministry of Information has ensured that only the most advanced technology has been utilized. The result is certainly the best-equipped and most sophisticated television facilities in the region.

The television complex in Riyadh stands as a fine example of this commitment to technical excellence. This complex includes the most advanced production and transmission studios, a complete film production facility, a theater (with seating capacity for 800) and, rising majestically above it all, the transmission tower, an edifice 560 feet [170 m] high, topped by a glass, jewel-shaped structure from which all of Riyadh is visible.

*King Fahd inaugurating the TV Station in the Holy City of Madinah*

*General view of Television Tower, Riyadh*

When color television was introduced, obviously a major event in the development of television services in the Kingdom, the Ministry of Information, in conjunction with the Ministry of Post, Telegraphs and Telephones, selected the French SECAM-3B system, since it was considered to be the most advanced color television system in the world.

There are currently two television channels: one in Arabic; the other in English (during which time is allocated for the transmission of news in French). Programming is a balanced blend of religious and cultural programs, entertainment and music, Arabic drama programs, non-Arabic films and serials, children's programs, and news and current affairs programs. Special programming is produced for all the major events in the Islamic calendar, especially for Ramadan and for the period of the Hajj, the annual pilgrimage to the Holy Places.

Today, there are 123 television transmission centers and 62 television centers. There are also six major TV production centers.

## Publications

Prompted by the Kingdom's general development and, in particular by the Kingdom's extensive and intensive educational program, a thriving publications industry has grown up. Daily newspapers, weekly publications, other periodicals and a wide selection of books now compete for the reader's interest. There are more than 122 publications in the Kingdom, 12 of which are daily newspapers, 23 weekly magazines and 23 monthly magazines.

The main daily publications are the following:
- *Arab News,* an English language daily newspaper with local and foreign news coverage
- *Al-Bilad*
- *Al-Jazirah*
- *Al-Madinah al-Munawara*
- *An-Nadwah*
- *Okaz*
- *Al-Riyadh*
- *Saudi Gazette,* an English language daily newspaper with local and foreign news coverage
- *Saudi Review*
- *Al-Watan*
- *Al-Yaum*

Many foreign news publications are available in the Kingdom.

The growth in the number of newspapers and periodicals published in the Kingdom has engendered an active advertising business in Saudi Arabia.

**Saudi Press Agency**

The Saudi Press Agency (SPA) is the central department for the collection and dissemination of official news of the Kingdom of Saudi Arabia. It distributes news reports to newspapers, news agencies, radio and television.

Established in 1970, SPA with the help of the development of modern communications, can now transmit its news reports twenty-four hours a day, in Arabic, English and French. In addition to the daily news, it transmits features, commentaries and analyses as part of its wide-ranging information services.

**Ministry of Information Internet Site**

Since 1998, the Ministry has maintained a web site in English on the Internet, which contains more than 3,000 "pages" of information on the geography, history and development of the Kingdom of Saudi Arabia. The site (www.saudinf.com) is enhanced by the daily updated news release section and by links to other official Saudi Government web sites.

## THE ARTS

While the Government's major priorities have been the development of the infrastructure, the education and healthcare of the people, and diversification of the economy, the arts have not been neglected. King Fahd's concern to give young Saudis the best start in life, not only in terms of a conventional educational syllabus but also in the sense of a wider appreciation of the arts, is widely recognized.

The General Presidency of Youth Welfare was established in 1974 as an agency responsible for sports, culture and social activities. It licenses and subsidizes sports and literary clubs and is responsible for the construction of sports facilities for the benefit of sports clubs and the public. It also prepares both an annual and a five-year plan for the encouragement and development of the arts.

Within the Kingdom it organizes regular competitions and exhibitions. Abroad, it arranges exhibitions of Saudi Arabian art, to provide Saudi artists with an international forum and to strengthen cultural ties with the host countries. The Presidency has organized exhibitions of Saudi Arabian art in the following Arab countries – Algeria, Bahrain, Jordan, Kuwait, Morocco, Oman, Qatar, Tunisia and the United Arab Emirates – and outside the Arab world in India, Italy, Mexico, Sweden, Turkey, West Germany and the United States of America.

The Presidency is also an active participant in the Arab Youth Festivals and Exhibitions, the Kuwait Exhibition for Formative Artists and other periodic

exhibitions in Europe, Asia and India and takes part in the Biannual Arab Exhibition which is supervised by the Arab Formative Artists' Union.

*One of Jeddah's Museums*

In 1972, a Royal Decree was issued to form the Saudi Arabian Arts Society. In 1978, the name of the Society was changed to the Saudi Arabian Society for Culture and Arts. The Society has eight branches in addition to its main office in Riyadh.

The Society is responsible for protecting and nurturing the culture of the Kingdom. Its duties are defined as follows:

1. to develop progressively the level of culture and arts in the Kingdom;
2. to look after the welfare of Saudi artists and work towards raising their cultural, artistic and social standard;
3. to sponsor talented young people and provide an opportunity for them to develop and display their talents;
4. to represent the Kingdom in all matters relating to the development of culture and arts at both Arab and international levels.

The work of the Society is managed by a number of committees:

1. The Cultural Committee

This Committee is responsible for encouraging Saudi men of letters and for raising public literary and cultural taste.

2. The Plastic Arts Committee

This Committee assists in the development of the plastic arts. It encourages Saudi artists and promotes their work by arranging exhibitions both within and outside the Kingdom.

3. The Music and Vocal Arts Committee

This Committee encourages music and singing, with special attention to the rich folk-art of poetry and song to be found in the various regions of the Kingdom.

4. The Information and Publications Committee

This Committee is not only responsible for the dissemination of all culturally related information to the Society's branch offices and to local newspapers but also maintains an archive of artistic productions and events in the Kingdom.

The Society also maintains a cultural video film and recording library and is responsible for the Kingdom's first cultural center in Riyadh, created to revive and popularize the Kingdom's cultural heritage.

In 1999, the King Fahd Cultural Center was completed. Situated in the capital, the King Fahd Cultural Center is a fine example of how King Fahd has set out to achieve modernization within the cultural traditions of the country. The Center is housed in a building which, in the grace and beauty of its design, suitably reflects the riches of the Kingdom's artistic productions, both past and present, which are to be displayed there. The building occupies an area of 11,960 square yards [10,000 sq m] and, within it are contained a theater with a seating capacity of 3,000; a library; a training theater; a restaurant; and a cafeteria; as well as the necessary administrative offices.

The Kingdom, conscious of its cultural responsibilities, has given special attention to museums and archaeological sites. There are twelve museums in the Kingdom, all well equipped and open to the public. The most important of these are the following:

• The National Museum of Archaeology and National Heritage
• The Museum of al-Masmak Palace in Riyadh
• The Regional Museum of Dammam
• The Hail Museum
• King Abdul Aziz Historical Center in Riyadh

The most important archaeological sites in the Kingdom are as follows:

• The towns of Salih (Mada'in Saleh) with their Nabataean graveyards
• The Islamic archaeological sites in Makkah and Madinah

Architecture and the plastic arts also receive considerable support from the Government, which has established several institutes built in accordance with Islamic architectural and stylistic conventions.

*Opposite: Mada'in Saleh*

The Kingdom also organizes annually one of the most important cultural

festivals in the Arab world, the National Festival of Heritage and Culture in al-Janadriyah region, Riyadh. The festival has become a crossroads where poetry, intellect, culture, art, theater, heritage and history meet.

## SPORT

The well-being, protection and development of young people in Saudi Arabia is of special concern to King Fahd who is President of the Higher Council for Youth.

The General Presidency of Youth Welfare (GPYW) has been responsible for the fast development of sport within the Kingdom.

The GPYW provides all sorts of sports facilities, such as sports centers, youth camps, sports halls, public playgrounds and club buildings with required equipment.

In 1975 there were 53 sports clubs. This figure rose to 154 in 1999, with a membership of more than 160,000. In 1999 there were 22 sports federations committees. GPYW has 13 main and 9 branch youth offices in the Kingdom.

It has established two permanent youth camps at Taif and Hail. Each camp

*King Fahd International Stadium, Riyadh*

comprises indoor sports halls, a theater, a restaurant, six 20-person capacity buildings, sixty scouts' tents, parks and various facilities.

The following projects were completed in 1999:

- 154 sports clubs
- 25 club buildings for the sports clubs
- 21 youth hostels
- 15 sports centers
- 6 indoor halls and swimming pools
- 5 public playgrounds
- 2 coastal centers
- An institute for leadership training
- A sports medical hospital
- An Olympic committee building
- GPYW building
- An international stadium in Riyadh with a capacity of 80,000 spectators
- 3 branch offices (Jeddah, Dammam and Riyadh)

The GPYW has also established complete sports cities. There are twelve in the Kingdom:

*King Fahd International Stadium, Riyadh*

- The King Abdul Aziz Sports City in Makkah
- The Prince Muhammad bin Abdul Aziz Sports City in Madinah
- The King Fahd Sports City in Taif
- The Prince Abdullah bin Abdul Aziz Sports City in Qassim
- The Prince Sultan bin Abdul Aziz Sports City in Abha
- The Prince Abdullah bin Jalawi Sports City in Al-Hasa
- The Prince Abdul Aziz bin Masaad bin Jalawi Sports City in Hail
- The Prince Saud bin Jalawi Sports City in Khobar
- The Sports Center in Tabouk
- Jizan Sports City
- Al-Mujma'ah Sports City
- Al-Baha Sports City

In the northeast of Riyadh is the King Fahd International Stadium, one of the largest and widely regarded as one of the most beautiful sports stadia in the world. The Stadium occupies an area of 600,000 square yards [500,000 sq m] and accommodates 80,000 spectators. The seating has been cleverly designed to provide all spectators with an unimpeded view.

The Kingdom is an active member of the Olympic movement. The Saudi Arabian Olympic Committee was established in 1964. There are nineteen sports federations affiliated to the Saudi Olympic Committee. The activities of the Olympic Committee cover ancient Arabian sports like hunting, horse-

*Saudi National Football Team in action*

racing, shooting, swimming and international sports like volley-ball, tennis, table-tennis, cycling, running and athletics. In 1984, Saudi Arabia competed in the Olympic Games for the first time, in football and rifle-shooting.

The efforts of the Saudi athletes culminated in the success of the Saudi National Football Team in 1984 when the team won the Asian Football Cup. The Saudi Youth Football Team also won the Third Asia Cup in 1988 in Thailand and the World Youth Cup in Scotland in 1989.

In school sports, the Kingdom's team won the gold cup in the tournament held in Tunis in 1986, the 25th Asia Games held in Saudi Arabia in 1986, the Second and Third International Friendship Games held in Muscat in 1989 and 1991 and the 28th Asia Cup held in the United Arab Emirates in 1992.

The Kingdom currently caters for more than twenty different sporting activities.

## THE ROLE OF WOMEN IN SAUDI ARABIAN SOCIETY

The position of women in Islamic society in general and in Saudi Arabian society in particular is a complex and frequently misunderstood issue. It is certainly true that Muslim and Western views of the role of women show sharp cultural differences but the stereotype of Muslim women, as uneducated, with no rights and with no opportunities is a caricature born of ignorance or malevolence.

The Holy Quran gave women economic and social rights long before such rights were attained by Western women. From the beginning of Islam, women have been legally entitled to inherit and bequeath property, holding their wealth in their own names even after marriage, without obligation to contribute that wealth to their husband or their family. The important role played by the wives of the Prophet Muhammad, peace be upon him, in the course of his ministry sorts ill with the view that Islam in any way undervalues the female half of humanity.

It is nevertheless true that, under Islam, a woman is enjoined to behave modestly in public and that, as in the West until recently, is generally expected to give a full commitment to making a family home – a home within which, incidentally, she enjoys a preeminent role. Such expectations are rather different from those now widely required of women in the West, just as the stability of family life and the security of women in

> **SAUDI WOMAN APPOINTED TO KEY UN POST**
> New York, 26th October 2000
>
> UN's Secretary General Kofi Annan has appointed Dr Thouraya Obaid, from the Kingdom of Saudi Arabia, to a key post at one of the UN's agencies. "I feel happy about appointing Dr Thouraya Obaid, a Saudi, to the post of Executive Director of the UN's Population Fund," said Kofi Annan. He noted that Thouraya Obaid is a prominent figure, fully conversant with the UN and its activities in the field of population and organization of family affairs.
>
> "Thouraya's role in the field of women's rights and her efforts to improve the health status of women are undeniable," he said, and added: "Dr Thouraya is also concerned with enlightenment on the dangers posed by the AIDS virus."
>
> Dr Thouraya has an outstanding record in the field of sociology and human studies. Her previous work at the UN's Department of Social Affairs has demonstrated her great concern with the social topics pertaining to the role of the UN in the field of population and the organization of the family.
>
> *Source: SPA*

Islamic society differs markedly from the conditions which women now face in Western society.

This said, it would be a mistake to think that the role of women in Saudi Arabian society is confined to home-making. The development of the Kingdom of Saudi Arabia has brought with it increasing opportunities for women in both education and employment. In 1960, the Government of the Kingdom of Saudi Arabia undertook the introduction of a national education program for girls. By the mid-1970s, about half of Saudi Arabian girls were attending school. Five years later, education was available to all Saudi girls. By 1980, there were six universities for women.

Under King Fahd, there has been further encouragement to women to take an active role in public as well as in private life. In terms of employment, women now play an active role in teaching, medicine, social work and broadcasting.

# THE EXPANSION OF THE HOLY MOSQUES IN MAKKAH AND MADINAH

*"Spending on the Holy Places will be unlimited
in accordance with their status in our hearts as Saudis and
in the hearts of Muslims throughout the world."*
KING FAHD

EACH YEAR, IN one of the great assemblies of humanity, some two million pilgrims gather in the Kingdom of Saudi Arabia to perform pilgrimage (Hajj).

The origin of this tradition goes back into the distant past, to pre-Islamic times, when God instructed the Prophet Abraham to build a house, the Kaaba, in Makkah and the Archangel Gabriel gave Abraham a Black Stone, thought to be a meteorite, which is set in the northeast corner of the Kaaba.

Towards the end of the fifth century, the Quraysh, a tribe which had settled in the Makkhan valley, took control of the Kaaba. The Quraysh prospered in trade and the prestige of the Kaaba brought many Arabs to the city on the annual Hajj. Yet, the Prophet Abraham's message of the One God was gradually forgotten and pagan idolaters violated the sacred Kaaba. Only a few visionaries kept the faith, until the Prophet Muhammad, peace be upon him, born circa 570 AD, returned from the hijrah in 629 AD to destroy the pagan idols in the Kaaba. The Mosque and the city then prospered as the center of Islam's remarkable spread.

The role of the monarchy in serving the Holy Places and facilitating pilgrimage has always been of paramount importance to the Saudi Royal Family. During his reign, King Fahd's father, King Abdul Aziz, made clear in no uncertain manner that attacks by brigands on pilgrims would not be tolerated and, within available resources, every effort was made to ensure the safety and comfort of pilgrims.

In King Fahd's reign, this tradition has been maintained and, with the benefit of increased revenues, a program of expansion and refurbishment on an unprecedented scale has been implemented. Of all the projects with which

*Holy Mosque in Makkah*

King Fahd is personally identified, none has been closer to his heart than the expansion of the Holy Mosques in Makkah and Madinah and to emphasize the monarchy's commitment, and his own, to this responsibility, in 1986 King Fahd adopted the title of Custodian of the Two Holy Mosques in preference to the title of His Majesty.

## THE EXPANSION OF THE MOSQUE IN THE HOLY CITY OF MAKKAH

The religious center of the Holy City of Makkah is the Holy Mosque (Al-Masjid Al-Haram) and the well of Zamzam, located inside. The present Haram, meaning "sanctuary", dates from 1570 AD, and takes the form of a central quadrangle surrounded by stone walls. Around the inner sanctuary is a marble pavement, the El Mataf. The holiest shrine of Islam, the Kaaba, is situated at the heart of the Holy Mosque's central courtyard.

The tradition of expanding the Holy Mosque dates back to 638 AD when the increasing number of conversions to Islam led the second Caliph Umar bin al-Khattab to develop the site.

When King Abdul Aziz established the modern Saudi State, one of his primary concerns, like that of the early Caliphs, was his role in overseeing the well-being of the pilgrims undertaking the annual Hajj. Aware that the Holy Mosque could not support the growing numbers of worshippers, he initiated a refurbishment and expansion program. In 1988, King Fahd laid the foundation stone for the third Saudi expansion of the Holy Mosque in Makkah and so initiated an expansion of the Holy Mosque which in scale and grandeur was unprecedented. Work began in 1989.

*Opposite: Kiswah, the cloth covering of the Holy Kaaba*

There were many difficulties to be overcome. The work had to be carried out with minimum disruption to the movement of pilgrims and the normal life of the city of Makkah. The area designated for the expansion contained a number of utilities (water, electricity and telephone services) which had to be removed and replaced elsewhere without interrupting supplies, disrupting the commercial activities of the city or impeding the progress of pilgrims. The extension of the Holy Mosque had to be joined to the existing structure in such a way that the existing structure was undamaged and the old and new structures merged seamlessly with each other.

The development of the Holy Mosque site has incorporated an expansion of the western wing of the existing Mosque, and a subsequent enlargement of

*Holy Mosque in Makkah*

the building to hold more than a million worshippers during the Holy Month of Ramadan, and during Umra and Hajj. The expansion project includes over 71,750 square yards [60,000 sq m] of prayer area on the enlarged roof, in addition to another almost 103,000 square yards [86,000 sq m] in the surrounding plaza. Two towering minarets have been added to complement the seven existing whitened stone structures, the latest additions carefully matching the former in architectural style. An elaborate new entrance and eighteen other gates

have also been built. Other exquisite decorative work, specially commissioned by King Fahd, adorns a series of 3 domes running parallel to the main gate structure and close to 500 marbled columns on the ground and first floors.

*King Fahd, with Crown Prince Abdullah and Prince Sultan, laying the foundation stone marking the start of the expansion of the Holy Mosque in Makkah*

New prayer halls on the ground and first floors are complete and ready to accommodate the millions who now make the journey of a lifetime to the Holy City of Makkah, and a sophisticated broadcasting network has been installed to cope with the additional requirements. Indeed, the safety and comfort of the Hajjis has become a major concern for the authorities, necessitated by their sheer volume in recent years. The newly laid floor tiles were made of specially developed heat-resistant marble, and further to ensure the comfort of worshippers the whole structure is cooled by one of the world's largest air-conditioning systems.

To facilitate the movement of worshippers to the newly developed roof area of the Holy Mosque during the busiest seasons, additional escalators have been incorporated alongside a number of fixed stairways in the northern and southern sides of the building. To accommodate the escalators, two buildings were constructed. Each building had two sets of escalators. These, added to the escalators installed elsewhere in the Holy Mosque, bring the total number of escalators to 56, with the capacity to handle 105,000 people an hour.

In order to reduce traffic congestion around the Holy Mosque, the development project has involved

*Escalators in the Holy Mosque*
*in Makkah*

the construction of a new tunnel for vehicles in the vicinity of Alsouk Alsagir.

Free car parks, with a 12,000-vehicle capacity, have been provided for pilgrims so that they may leave their cars and travel from the car parks to the Holy Mosque by bus or taxi in ten to twenty minutes, depending on the volume of traffic. Pedestrian routes and tunnels have also been carefully planned and laid out to ensure the safety of the worshippers.

Other improvements resulting from King Fahd's generous patronage have included a newly laid drainage system. (Flooding and drainage problems had beset the Holy City of Makkah and its Holy Sites since the pre-Islamic period.)

## THE EXPANSION OF THE PROPHET'S MOSQUE IN THE HOLY CITY OF MADINAH

The Holy City of Madinah is a pilgrimage city second only to the Holy City of Makkah, and is the city to which the Prophet Muhammad, peace be upon him, and his followers migrated in 622 AD (the hijrah).

According to Islamic tradition, when the Prophet Muhammad, peace be upon him, made the hijrah, with the first Muslim community, his first act on arrival in the Holy City of Madinah was to locate a suitable piece of land for the enclosure that was to become his Holy Mosque. The Mosque was erected as a combined effort by all the Muslim followers of the Prophet, and its basic design is said to have survived ever since as a model for all subsequent Mosques.

The Prophet's Mosque contains the tomb of the Prophet Muhammad, peace be upon him, and is therefore one of Islam's most sacred shrines. (The first two caliphs, Abu Bakr and Umar, are also buried there.)

The Mosque was rebuilt by the third Caliph, Uthman, in 649–50 AD, using stone to replace the early wooden structure, and the site was later expanded

*King Fahd laying the*
*foundation stone for the*
*extension of the Prophet's*
*Mosque*

greatly by the Umayyad Caliph al-Walid in 707 AD. Much of the early structure was destroyed by the great fire of 1256 AD, however, and the oldest parts of the Mosque standing today reflect successive waves of Ottoman building work.

*Prophet's Mosque in Madinah*

The expansion and development plans formulated by King Fahd for the Prophet's Mosque in the Holy City of Madinah were just as ambitious as those for the Holy Mosque in Makkah. Before the expansion was implemented, although the Prophet's Mosque in Madinah received each year approximately the same number of worshippers, its area was little more than one tenth of the Holy Mosque in Makkah. King Faisal had added some areas for prayer on the western side of the Prophet's Mosque where pilgrims could pray out of the glare of the sun but these arrangements were temporary and insufficient to meet the ever-growing need.

Determined to provide the Prophet's Mosque with space and facilities commensurate with its importance as of one of Islam's two holiest sites, King Fahd gave orders for what must be the greatest Mosque expansion program in the history of Islam.

*Right and opposite: King Fahd signs on the last crescent of the last minaret in the expansion of the Prophet's Mosque*

The project was launched by King Fahd in 1985. Before the expansion could begin, it was necessary to prepare the area on which the extensions were to be built. This operation alone involved a Herculean effort. Almost 400 buildings had to be demolished. Because the site was holy and the engineers were determined to avoid any possibility of damage to the existing Mosque, explosives were not employed. Instead, the supporting posts of each building were weakened and then ripped out by bulldozers. The resultant rubble, estimated to have been 654,000 cubic yards [500,000 cu m], was used to landfill areas on the outskirts of Madinah in preparation for further expansion of the city.

The land designated for the expansion of the Prophet's Mosque, even when cleared, was far from ideal and, before building could commence, it was necessary to pile-drive some 8,500 steel-encased stakes to a depth of between 100 and 160 feet [30–50 m] into the ground down to the bedrock in order to ensure the extensions would be able to withstand any eventuality and would be strong enough to support an additional floor if, at a later date, such a further development is deemed necessary.

By the middle of 1990, the main building had been finished and, by April 1994 the entire project had been completed. The total area, including the ground around the Mosque, now stood at 478,803 square yards [400,327 sq m], of which King Fahd's expansion accounted for 460,000 square yards [384,000 sq m]. The area could now accommodate in excess of one million worshippers at the busiest times.

A unique feature of the expansion project was the development of the twenty-seven main plazas. Each plaza is now capped by a state-of-the-art sliding dome, which can be rapidly opened or closed according to the weather and can be used in unison or separately as required. Elaborately carved stone friezes decorate the domes, and the plazas have been paved in decorative geometrically patterned marble tiles. The project also necessitated the building of six additional minarets, the most powerful visual sign of the Mosque, each 354-foot [105 m] construction crowned with a 4-ton gold-plated crescent.

The development of the surrounding open areas and the seven newly constructed entrances ensure the smooth passage of pilgrims into the Prophet's Mosque. Indeed, the designers of the entire project have masterfully considered every eventuality of the existing and future capacity of the Mosque, and all this within the strictures of the existing architectural pattern. The building extensions have therefore been fitted out with a suitable number of staircases and escalators. The designers have added an extension to the roof area for praying purposes, whilst also allowing for the possibility of adding another floor to accommodate worshippers in the future.

Like the splendidly redeveloped Holy Mosque in the Holy City of Makkah, the Prophet's Mosque is now fully air-conditioned. The comfort of worshippers has been further enhanced, however, by an ingenious method of natural ventilation. A series of domes, 27 in number, have been installed. These domes can be opened or closed, according to weather conditions. In the inner courtyard, twelve enormous mechanically operated teflon umbrellas, six in each court of the Mosque, have been developed by King Fahd's architects to protect from and withstand the high temperatures.

The Prophet's Mosque project also includes provision of extensive car

**PUBLIC TELEPHONE SERVICES**
To enable pilgrims to contact home in the course of their pilgrimage, the Kingdom has provided, in Makkah al-Mukarramah, al-Madinah al-Munawwarah and Jeddah, 791 international communications cabins, 2,580 public telephones and 92 offices providing fax and telex services.
*Source: MOI publication*

*Mechanically operated teflon umbrellas in the inner courtyard of the Prophet's Mosque*

parking facilities and the construction of a new dual carriageway, the Bab Alsalam Road, linking Madinat Alhujaj on the western side of the Holy City of Madinah to the site of the Mosque. A series of service tunnels, drainage systems and supply networks now also criss-crosses the area. In fact, the magnitude of support services made it necessary to construct a vast basement complex in which to accommodate the service equipment and wiring needs, as well as various other maintenance works.

The reconstructed main gate leading into the Mosque site, the new King Fahd Entrance, is situated on the northern side, and is topped with a profusion of domes and minarets on both sides. The exquisite decorations and architectural touches here and elsewhere are in complete harmony with earlier building work on the site, and

they feature wonderfully crafted golden grilles, cornices, pillars, brass doors and marble works, as well as special ornately carved pigeonholes for the Holy Quran.

Further enhancements include a public address system operational throughout the Mosque and surrounding areas; a closed circuit television system as part of the safety measures; an advanced fire-warning and fire-fighting system; a cold water drinking system; the provision of adequate washing facilities; a backup electrical system to be used in the event of any problem with the main electrical system; and extensive free parking facilities.

The renovated Prophet's Mosque in the Holy City of Madinah inspires awe in all who visit. As King Fahd himself so eloquently expressed it:

**PROVISION OF DRINKING WATER**
To the north of Mina, the Kingdom has built a roofed reservoir with a capacity of 1,308,000 cubic yards [1 million cu m] – the largest such reservoir in the world. In total there are 18 major water reservoirs serving the holy sites.

The water-bottling plant in the south east of Arafat is able to produce 14,400 bottles an hour. On King Fahd's instructions, this water is distributed free to pilgrims.
*Source: MOI publication*

*Interior view of the Prophet's Mosque*

*"With the help of God, the Government and people of Saudi Arabia have been able to turn dreams into reality. Who could have believed that the expansion of the Prophet's Mosque would equal the area of the city of Madinah in ancient times and that we would accommodate such huge numbers of worshippers and visitors?"*

## FURTHER EXPANSION PROJECTS

The wholehearted commitment of King Fahd and the Saudi Royal Family to their acknowledged special responsibility for preserving Islam's Holy Mosques in the Holy Cities of Makkah and Madinah has effectively ensured that more Muslims than ever before are now able to make the annual pilgrimage. Moreover, the spectacular development of the Kingdom's airport and hotel facilities has kept pace with the work at the Two Holy Mosques, ensuring the further well-being and comfort of pilgrims.

The development and enhancement of the Two Holy Mosques has ensured that the Holy Cities of Makkah and Madinah are able to cope with the millions who make the annual Hajj, as well as the hundreds of thousands of pilgrims who visit the Kingdom every month in order to perform the minor pilgrimage (Umra). And we should note that the expansion projects have not been solely confined to the Two Holy Mosques. Other Holy Sites have also benefited from King Fahd's generous patronage.

An all-encompassing master plan for the development of the myriad of Holy Sites in the Kingdom has been charted by the Ministry of Municipal and Rural Affairs. The plan effectively calls for the wholesale transformation and modernization of services in Mina, Muzdalifah and Arafat in the coming decade. The development plan will naturally aim to retain the traditional characteristics of the Holy Sites, as has been accomplished to great effect at the Mosques in the Holy Cities of Makkah and Madinah.

> After its most recent expansion, the Namira Mosque in Arafat, where pilgrims perform both noon and afternoon prayers on Arafat Day, can now accommodate 300,000. The Mosque is equipped with its own broadcasting network.
> *Source:* Kingdom of Saudi Arabia, 100 Years in the Service of Islam and Muslims, *The Islamic Center for Information and Development*

> Other major Mosques on the holy sites are al-Khayf Mosque, with a capacity of 45,000; the Mosque in the area of Muzdalifa which can accommodate 8,000 people; and the Quba Mosque in al-Madinah al-Munawwarah, the first Mosque built under Islam which, after the expansion commissioned by King Fahd, can accommodate 20,000 people.
> *Source: MOI publication*

## PROVISION OF FACILITIES AND ASSISTANCE FOR ALL PILGRIMS

A primary purpose of the expansion of the Two Holy Mosques was to meet the needs of the ever-increasing numbers of pilgrims. Below are the figures for the numbers of pilgrims arriving in the Kingdom from abroad between 1970 and 2000, showing their mode of travel.

*Pilgrim camps in Arafat*

The total number of pilgrims performing Hajj in 2000 was 1,733,785 (Ministry of Hajj Information Committee, March 2000). This figure includes pilgrims from inside as well as those from outside the Kingdom.

Each year, the Kingdom harnesses all its resources to facilitate the pilgrimage to the Holy Places. Minutes of the weekly council meetings, chaired by King Fahd or his deputy, show a preoccupation with the Hajj and a determination to spare no effort or expense in making the Hajj as safe and secure as possible.

King Fahd's concern for the welfare of pilgrims is evident at a personal level, as much as in the vast expansion projects. There are innumerable instances where King Fahd has intervened personally to help pilgrims in the performance of the Hajj. In April 1999, a group of 162 guest pilgrims left the Kingdom on

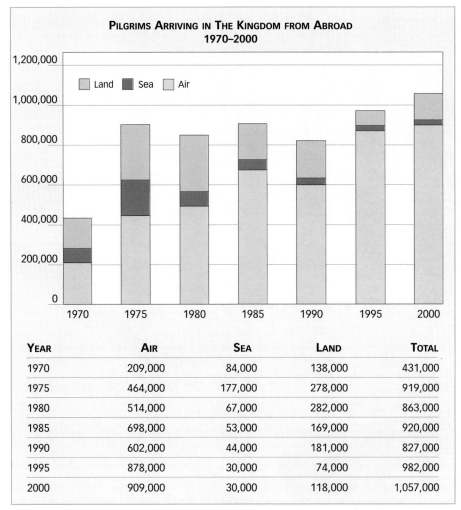

| YEAR | AIR | SEA | LAND | TOTAL |
|------|-----|-----|------|-------|
| 1970 | 209,000 | 84,000 | 138,000 | 431,000 |
| 1975 | 464,000 | 177,000 | 278,000 | 919,000 |
| 1980 | 514,000 | 67,000 | 282,000 | 863,000 |
| 1985 | 698,000 | 53,000 | 169,000 | 920,000 |
| 1990 | 602,000 | 44,000 | 181,000 | 827,000 |
| 1995 | 878,000 | 30,000 | 74,000 | 982,000 |
| 2000 | 909,000 | 30,000 | 118,000 | 1,057,000 |

In 2001, there were 1,363,992 pilgrims from abroad performing Hajj, bringing the total number of pilgrims for 2001 to 1,804,800.

completion of their Hajj which had been financed at the personal expense of King Fahd. Again in 2000, King Fahd issued instructions that some 1,500 Muslims (amongst them, 160 from Europe and the United States and a further 300 from Kosovo) should be invited to perform Hajj at his own expense.

The Madinah-based King Fahd Complex for Printing the Holy Quran is further evidence of King Fahd's conviction that it is his duty to assist the pilgrims who visit the Kingdom. In a determined program to make the word of Islam as accessible as possible, for the Hajj in 2000, King Fahd instructed that every pilgrim should be given a copy of the Holy Quran on completion of the Hajj rituals.

# DEVELOPMENT OF THE SAUDI ARABIAN ECONOMY

## BACKGROUND

THE LIFE OF King Fahd is not about the exploitation of the Kingdom's vast oil resources; it is predominantly about how the ensuing revenues have been managed and deployed. Nevertheless, because of the crucial role oil has played and continues to play in the story of the Kingdom, it is not inappropriate to recount the key facts in the discovery of "black gold" and the development of the Kingdom's oil, gas and petrochemical industries.

The history of oil in the Middle East and the Arab world goes back many centuries during which seepages of oil and tar were used for a multitude of purposes. A mission of German experts visited Iraq in 1871 and reported plentiful supplies of oil. In 1907, another mission said Iraq was a veritable "lake of petroleum". In Iran, oil was found in quantity in 1908. The major Iraqi field was discovered at Kirkuk in 1927 and began producing oil in commercial quantities; oil flowed abroad in 1934. In 1932, petroleum was discovered in Bahrain.

In 1923, a New Zealander, Major Frank Holmes, acting on behalf of a British syndicate, the "Eastern and General", obtained the first Saudi Arabian oil concession from King Abdul Aziz, an exclusive concession to explore for oil and other minerals in an area of more than 30,000 square miles [77,700 sq km] in the Al-Hasa region. The concession, at a bargain price of £2,000 per annum to be paid in gold, came to nothing. The Eastern and General Syndicate was unable to persuade any oil company to invest sufficient funds for exploration and, after paying the £2,000 for two years, they ceased to fulfil their part of the agreement. The King waited for three years and then, in 1928, revoked the concession. From the viewpoint of Major Frank Holmes and his London-based syndicate, this episode must represent one of the world's greatest lost opportunities.

In 1930, King Abdul Aziz was faced with a substantial fall in revenues, resulting from a drop in the number of pilgrims caused by the worldwide recession. The King invited a wealthy American businessman and philanthropist, Charles R. Crane, to visit the Kingdom. Crane had already shown an eagerness to meet the King. In the course of Crane's visit, it was agreed that he should send a mining engineer to conduct a survey of Saudi Arabia to assess the Kingdom's water, mineral and oil resources.

In 1931, the engineer Karl Twitchell arrived in Jeddah. Twitchell was a civil and mining engineer, with Middle East experience, having worked for Crane in the Yemen. After an extensive survey of many months, Twitchell submitted his report to the King. A key finding was that the geological formations in the eastern region around Dhahran strongly indicated the presence of oil.

While Twitchell's survey was proceeding, Socal, the Standard Oil Company of California, which had sent two geologists to Bahrain, was becoming increasingly interested in the oil potential of the mainland of Saudi Arabia.

In 1933, Twitchell arrived in Jeddah with a Socal representative, Lloyd Hamilton. Despite some impressive competition from the Iraq Petroleum Company, Hamilton succeeded in negotiating a concession for exclusive rights to oil in the eastern region. The agreement which had a 60-year life (later to be extended for a further six years) received royal assent in July 1933. Thus, the Kingdom broke what had been virtually a British monopoly of oil concessions in that part of the world.

Initial exploration produced disappointing results but in 1935 a well drilled in Dhahran found indications of oil in commercial quantities. The following year, Socal, now operating through its subsidiary the Californian Arabian Standard Oil Company (Casoc), put into effect Article 32 of the 1933 agreement and sold one-half of its concession interest to the Texas Oil Company.

Oil production began in 1938, by which time the vast extent of the oil reserves was becoming apparent.

With this confirmation of the commercial viability of the oil reserves, another supplementary agreement was signed on 31st May 1938, adding six years to the 60-year life of the original agreement. This second instrument, known as the Supplemental Agreement, enlarged Socal's concession area by almost 80,000 square miles [207,200 sq km]. It also included rights in the Saudi Government's half interest in the two neutral zones shared with Iraq and Kuwait.

In 1944, the Californian Arabian Standard Oil Company was renamed the Arabian American Oil Company – Aramco.

From the late 1940s through the late 1950s, relations between the Saudi Government and Aramco went smoothly. It was not until the 1959–60 unilateral reductions in petroleum prices by the major petroleum companies in the area of the Gulf that relations began to change. These unilateral cuts were an influential factor in prompting the creation of the Organization of Petroleum Exporting Countries in 1960.

It was inconceivable in the political and economic context of the second half of the twentieth century that so important a national resource as oil, representing as it did most of the country's national income, should remain under the ownership of foreign companies. In 1973, the Saudi Arabian Government took a 25% stake in Aramco. In 1974, this share was increased to 60% and in 1980 it was amicably agreed that Aramco should become 100% Saudi-owned, with the date of ownership back-dated to 1976.

At the same time, and of equal importance, the Saudi Arabian Government was implementing a consistent policy of Saudization, replacing foreign expertise and labor with Saudi nationals as far as possible. In this context, it is interesting to quote a newspaper account of a major step in this process, published by the *New York Times* (6th April 1989):

*At a quiet dinner a few days ago, the last American to preside over the world's largest oil company handed over power to its first Saudi boss. The Saudi, a man who started working there more than 40 years ago as an office boy, earned engineering and management degrees as he climbed up the ladder.*

*The transfer of the Arabian American Oil Company from the American John J. Kelberer, to the Saudi Ali Naimi, took place at Hamilton House, named after an American lawyer who negotiated the first agreement that opened this kingdom to American oil companies 56 years ago and led to the formation of Aramco, as the company is known to the world.*

*While the formal transfer of power was low-key, in the Aramco tradition, the event was one of great moment both in Saudi and international terms.*

Thus the oil of the Kingdom which had lain for so long beneath Saudi Arabia's deserts and which then for decades had been exploited by foreign interests, became at last a national resource controlled and managed by those under whose soil it lay.

## OIL IN THE KINGDOM TODAY

In terms of production the Kingdom of Saudi Arabia is easily the largest single oil producer. The figures for 1999 show that, with a daily production of 8.6 million barrels, the Kingdom of Saudi Arabia is 800,000 barrels a day ahead of the United States and almost 2.5 billion barrels a day ahead of the Russian Federation.

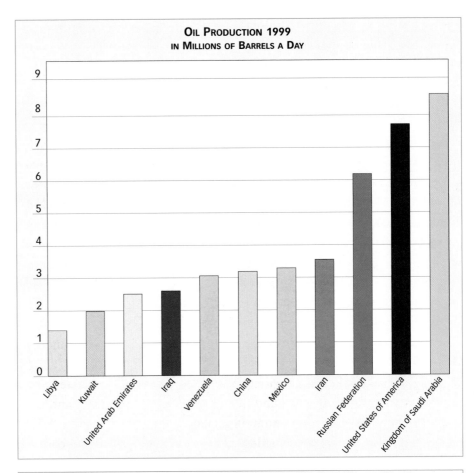

**OIL PRODUCTION 1999**
**IN MILLIONS OF BARRELS A DAY**

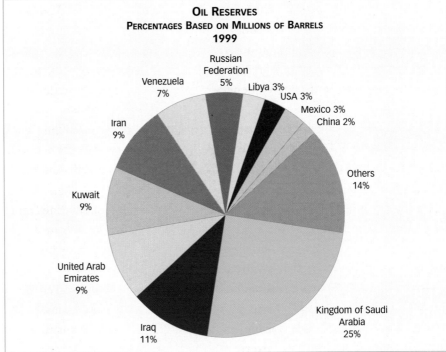

**OIL RESERVES**
**PERCENTAGES BASED ON MILLIONS OF BARRELS**
**1999**

In terms of reserves, the Kingdom holds 25% of the world's proven oil reserves.

Clearly the Kingdom of Saudi Arabia holds a dominant position in the oil market. How the Kingdom, under King Fahd, has used that position and how the media in general have presented the Kingdom's policy on oil is worthy of fuller discussion.

## THE KINGDOM'S OIL POLICY

Under King Fahd, the Kingdom has maintained an entirely consistent policy of attempting to manage the oil market so that the interests of both producers and consumers are fairly balanced. These are not just words. In determining the optimum price for oil, King Fahd has recognized and promulgated throughout his reign the following truths:

- Oil is a finite energy resource which should be managed and not left entirely to the vagaries of the market.
- Too high a price for oil damages the economies of oil-consuming countries and encourages efforts to find alternative sources of energy.
- Too low a price for oil damages society in oil-producing countries, can seriously undermine efforts to develop and diversify oil-reliant economies and can encourage waste in energy-consuming societies.

From the earliest years, the Kingdom of Saudi Arabia has shown a considerable degree of sophistication in its attitude to the oil market. From 1974, the Kingdom has continuously used its influence to try to impose some degree of stability on the oil market. It has consistently shown an understanding of the economic needs of consuming nations, as well as those of its fellow producers. (Indeed, by accepting the dollar as the currency for oil payments, Saudi Arabia has even shared the consequences of dollar inflation and the devaluation of the money paid for oil.)

At this point we should perhaps consider what has happened to the price of oil over the last three decades if we take inflation into account. When the oil-consuming nations complain about the price of oil, they forget that, even at US$25–$30 a barrel, oil is far from being at a historically high level.

The chart overleaf shows the price of crude oil in a gallon of gasoline from 1968 to March 2000, in real terms (i.e. adjusted for inflation). Of course the price paid by the consumer (the price at the pumps) has risen steeply but that is because of taxes, not because of the price of oil.

The chart also shows that the Kingdom of Saudi Arabia has not been entirely successful in stabilizing the price of oil. There are many reasons. The Organization of Petroleum Exporting Countries (OPEC), the main instrument through which Saudi Arabia can exert its influence on the oil market, does not

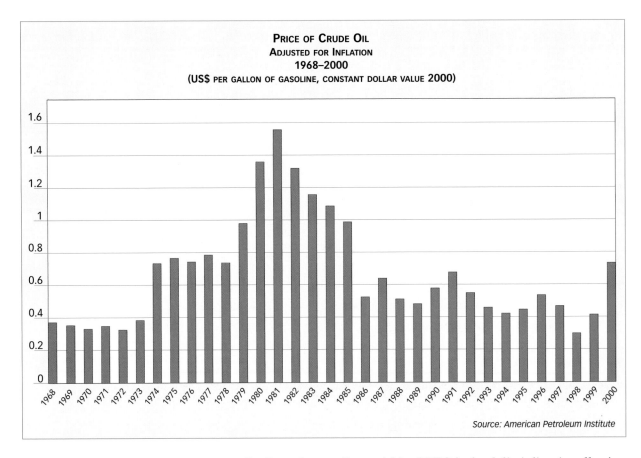

PRICE OF CRUDE OIL
ADJUSTED FOR INFLATION
1968–2000
(US$ PER GALLON OF GASOLINE, CONSTANT DOLLAR VALUE 2000)

*Source: American Petroleum Institute*

represent all oil producers. Even within OPEC lack of discipline in adhering to agreed quotas has undermined the Kingdom's ability to keep the price of oil within the range it believes to be fair to both producers and consumers. There have been political events, preeminently conflicts in the region, which have outweighed any possible effort to control the oil price. Nevertheless, the record shows, over and over again, that, when the price has plummeted or soared, it is the Kingdom of Saudi Arabia that has done its best to ameliorate the situation.

In contrast, in general, the oil-consuming nations have shown little appreciation of the need for fairness to oil producers as well as consumers. When the price has fallen to absurdly low levels (e.g. US$10 a barrel), thereby threatening the economic life not only of countries such as Saudi Arabia but all the developing nations where Saudi funds are helping to improve economic conditions, the consuming nations have simply enjoyed the benefits of cheap energy, encouraged by Western media praise for the market mechanism that has humbled the oil producers. When, on the other hand, the price of oil has risen, then suddenly the oil-consuming nations find their voice and use it to express considerable reservations about market mechanisms and to urge management of the oil market to bring the price down. The high price is

If you decided to replace the oil in a standard barrel with mineral water, it would cost approximately US$200 to fill it.
*Source: Author's calculations*

widely presented as a threat to the global economy; whereas the threat posed by the low price to the oil producers is seemingly of little account.

This is not the only aspect of the attitude of the oil-consuming nations that is less than fair. Governments in the oil-consuming nations are fond of attributing increased fuel costs to the oil producers. In terms of what the individual consumer pays at the pumps, such attribution of blame is highly misleading.

On occasions, some of the governments of consuming nations

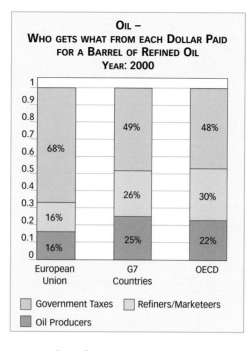

seem to act like ruthless middlemen, pressing the producer to accept the lowest possible price and the consumer to pay the highest possible price. This may be acceptable in the souk, although even there the trader has to ensure he does not entirely alienate the producer, the consumer, or both. But in the management of oil, such behavior smacks of narrow short-term political expediency.

It is against this background that, over the last two decades, King Fahd has sought to elevate the oil price issue above the level of national self-interest. The Kingdom has of course expressed concern when the oil price has fallen to absurdly low levels; but it has also argued strongly for measures to bring the oil price down when that price has risen out of the range which the Kingdom and most serious analysts believe to be fair to both producers and consumers. It has always been King Fahd's view that, in the exploitation of a finite resource as precious as oil, international and global considerations, as well as national needs, should be taken into account. It is damaging to the world economy to have major rises or falls in the price. This fact alone suggests that rather than presenting the producer/consumer relationship as one of conflict, it would be more constructive to recognize it as one of interdependence. It must also be true that, as the world's reserves of oil diminish, and the value of that diminishing resource increases, agreement between the producers and consumers on how best to manage this economic process would seem to be highly desirable. Such an approach would surely be preferable to a "free market" which presumably would simply mean that the producers should extract the maximum price from their remaining oil reserves, regardless of the political

*Ras Tanura Refinery*

or economic consequences for the consumers – much as the consuming nations have quite happily taken advantage of excess supply in the 1980s and 1990s to reduce the oil price as far as possible.

In passing, it is perhaps worth adding that the "free market" philosophy, espoused by some of the non-OPEC oil producers in the 1980s and 1990s, is self-evidently inappropriate in the context of a resource such as oil. The oil market cannot be free of governmental decisions which are politically motivated and have little or nothing to do with market mechanisms. For example, as we have seen, the level of tax imposed by governments on oil companies is no less a determining factor of the price of oil than is the decision of a producer to increase or decrease production. Both can be "external" factors which dramatically affect the "supply and demand" equation. The notion that it is

possible for government policy to have no bearing on the decisions of oil companies or on the oil market is either naive or disingenuous. The decision of a government with substantial oil export revenues not to cooperate with OPEC may well be politically astute, but it has little to do with *laissez-faire* economics. More importantly, management of the oil market raises global considerations, stretching decades ahead, which the "free market" approach simply does not accommodate but which governments, with a responsibility for the well-being of future generations, must assuredly address.

The real question is this. Will the main consumers, the industrialized nations, persist in seeing oil as simply another commodity to be obtained from its source at the lowest possible "market" price – or will they recognize that, in an increasingly interdependent world, the interests of producer and consumer, while not identical, must in the end be brought together in the interests of the global economy?

In terms of the economy of the Kingdom of Saudi Arabia, oil will continue to play a key role. The Kingdom's development plans have used the oil revenues to diversify the Saudi Arabian economy, expanding the non-oil industrial sector and the agricultural sector. It remains, nevertheless, true that oil will continue to represent the major sector of the economy. In 1999 official estimates of Saudi Arabian oil reserves topped 262,000 million barrels; proven gas reserves were estimated at 204.5 trillion cubic feet [5.8 million cu m]. Even these estimates are considered conservative by many who have suggested that oil reserves could be as high as 315,000 million barrels. It is therefore inevitable that in this new century the Kingdom of Saudi Arabia will continue to derive most of its income from the black gold that lies within its territory.

It is also inevitable that the Kingdom's role in the politics and economics of the Middle East, and indeed, on the wider international stage, will grow in importance, as the smaller oil reserves of other countries become more difficult and more expensive to exploit – or, finally, are exhausted.

## Impact of Fluctuating Oil Revenues on Saudi Arabia's GDP

Developed countries look for stable growth in their economies and measure changes in gross domestic product (GDP) in low, single figure percentages. More substantial changes are likely to cause serious economic and social dislocation. Because the Kingdom's GDP is heavily dependent on oil revenues and because the price of oil, despite the Kingdom's efforts to stabilize it, has fluctuated wildly in the course of King Fahd's reign, Saudi Arabia has had to accommodate within its planning and development program, the most dramatic swings in GDP.

The table and chart below show the Kingdom's GDP from 1984 to 1999, broken down by oil sector and non-oil sector.

To see more clearly what has happened, we can look at the two main sectors of the economy separately.

The non-oil sector shows a more or less steady picture of growth. This reflects the commitment of the Saudi Government to expand the non-oil sector, diversifying out of oil.

It is when we look at the oil sector (see page 78) that we see the extraordinary fluctuations in revenue with which the Kingdom has had to contend. These columns show actual falls in annual revenue from oil in some years of 10%, 15%, 20%, even 30%.

| YEAR | Oil Sector | % CHANGE | Non-Oil Sector | % CHANGE | TOTAL | % CHANGE |
|---|---|---|---|---|---|---|
| 1984 | 132,556 | | 214,869 | | 347,425 | |
| 1985 | 96,958 | −26.9% | 213,073 | 0.8% | 310,031 | −10.8% |
| 1986 | 67,461 | −30.4% | 200,385 | −6.0% | 267,846 | −13.6% |
| 1987 | 70,443 | 4.4% | 201,557 | 0.6% | 272,000 | 1.6% |
| 1988 | 69,116 | −1.9% | 207,793 | 3.1% | 276,909 | 1.8% |
| 1989 | 90,746 | 31.3% | 213,334 | 2.7% | 304,080 | 9.8% |
| 1990 | 148,053 | 63.2% | 236,940 | 11.1% | 384,993 | 26.6% |
| 1991 | 167,525 | 13.2% | 267,512 | 12.9% | 435,037 | 13.0% |
| 1992 | 186,524 | 11.3% | 265,774 | 0.6% | 452,298 | 4.0% |
| 1993 | 158,364 | −15.1% | 276,201 | 3.9% | 434,565 | −3.9% |
| 1994 | 157,722 | −0.4% | 284,014 | 2.8% | 441,736 | 1.7% |
| 1995 | 175,201 | 11.1% | 295,951 | 4.2% | 471,152 | 6.7% |
| 1996 | 212,629 | 21.4% | 307,746 | 4.0% | 520,375 | 10.4% |
| 1997 | 214,021 | 0.7% | 325,499 | 5.8% | 539,520 | 3.7% |
| 1998 | 140,513 | −34.3% | 330,247 | 1.5% | 470,760 | −12.7% |
| 1999 | 173,848 | 23.7% | 338,506 | 2.5% | 512,354 | 8.8% |

*Data Source:* Achievements of the Development Plans, 1970–2000, *Ministry of Planning*

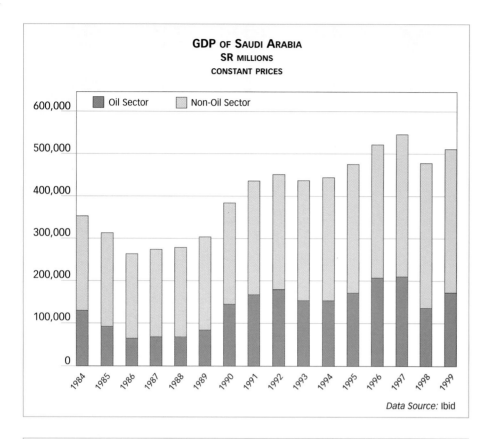

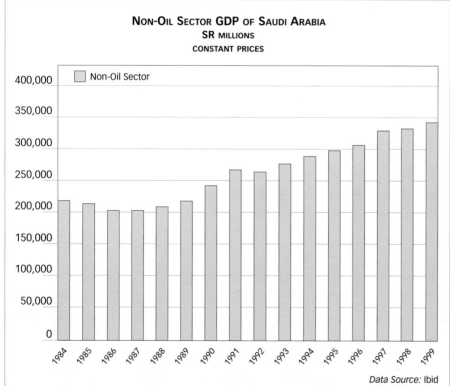

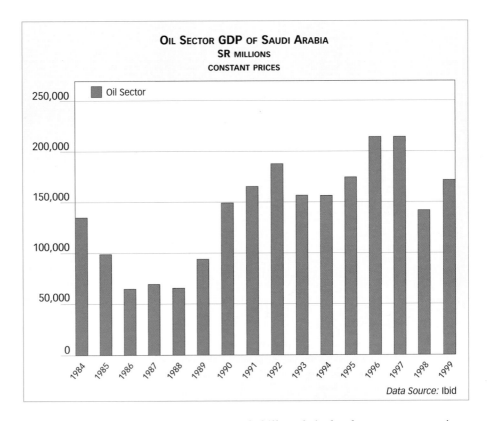

It has taken a remarkable degree of skill and, indeed nerve, to sustain a coherent development program through a period of such severe swings in GDP and it is a tribute to King Fahd's vision and tenacity of purpose that, whatever the economic circumstances, he has never been deflected from maintaining those policies, derived from Islam, that have infused his thinking. (Just as those Western commentators who predicted that the influx of foreign workers would cause social instability, so those who predicted that savage fluctuations in the oil price would cause economic dislocation have been proved wrong.)

That said, the dangers of relying on a single source of revenue which is subject to such dramatic price fluctuations are obvious and clearly justify King Fahd's determination to use the Kingdom's resources to diversify the economy.

# DIVERSIFICATION OF THE ECONOMY

## AGRICULTURAL DEVELOPMENT

THE STORY OF the Kingdom's policy towards agriculture under King Fahd is a particularly interesting one because it provides an insight into several aspects of his developmental philosophy. Saudi Arabia, a country consisting largely of desert terrain, with modest natural ground water resources and subject to extremes of temperature, is scarcely ideal for agricultural development. And yet, despite these less than favorable initial circumstances, Saudi Arabia has managed to develop the agricultural sector of the economy over the last three decades to an extraordinary degree.

While industrial diversification may have been an obviously sensible strategy for a revenue-rich, oil-dependent developing country, investment in the agricultural sector, given the inimical climatic conditions, was a less self-evidently justified strategic choice. Nevertheless, the development of agriculture has been given a high priority by the Government throughout the development plans and has played a major role in the national strategy to diversify the economic base. It is King Fahd's view of the society he wished to build which explains the Government's sustained commitment to agriculture.

At the end of 1985 almost half of the Kingdom's population was still living in rural areas and a significant proportion of total Saudi employment was in agriculture. Apart from the strategic significance of increasing domestic food production for a growing population, the development of agriculture fulfilled other important roles. King Fahd foresaw that the Kingdom's most daunting challenge in the twenty-first century would be to provide employment for a young and fast-growing population. Agriculture generated employment both within the sector itself and in closely related agro-industries.

At least as important, agricultural development could raise income levels and improve rural living standards for both settled and nomadic communities alike. It is a running theme throughout King Fahd's policy statements that the benefits that the Kingdom enjoys should be spread throughout all sections of Saudi society, and development of agriculture has been seen as one way to achieve this goal.

King Fahd has also been eager to see some moderation in the urbanization of the population and he well understood that development of the agricultural sector would have a positive influence on the population balance, helping to prevent population drift to urban centers. In ensuring that all sections of society benefited from the Kingdom's prosperity, investment in agriculture was seen as a way of taking the benefits out from the cities to the people rather than drawing the people into the cities away from their homes.

Finally, agricultural development was seen to have a role in maintaining the ecological balance through combating desertification.

So we can see that, apart from its contribution to the diversification of the economic base and to import substitution, the investment in agriculture has been motivated by a number of political, social and environmental considerations, all aimed at creating a particular kind of society.

In implementing the Government's agricultural policy, the Ministry of Agriculture and Water plays a key role, blending State support and guidance with the encouragement, as far as possible, of self-reliance in the agricultural community.

The Ministry takes direct responsibility for irrigation and drainage projects if they are beyond the means of local farming communities, and, through the Arable Land Distribution Scheme, identifies land suitable for reclamation and allocation to Saudi citizens for agricultural applications.

The agricultural sector has achieved a complete revolution based on the most up-to-date scientific technology which has been applied to farming methods, irrigation, and animal and fishing resources.

This unique revolution stemmed from a clear philosophy concentrating on agricultural self-development. The State has been responsible for drawing up policies and setting aims, supporting and guiding the private sector, and following up private sector activities; while the private sector itself has implemented all stages of productive operation without State interference, or unhealthy competition among individual or corporate members of the private sector.

Arising from this philosophy, and as a result of subsidies and incentives, the great transformation from a traditional to a modern agricultural system has been accomplished, at the level both of individual farmers and of large agricultural companies. In addition, the Kingdom has seen the development and modernization of research and agricultural training centers, running in parallel with the rapid development and expansion of agricultural productivity. In the

*Agriculture in the Kingdom*

course of King Fahd's reign, Saudi Arabia has been able to attain self-sufficiency in one of the world's major strategic crops: wheat. In 1978, the Kingdom's wheat production amounted to 3,000 tons. By 1999 it had increased to 1.8 million tons.

While the Kingdom has concentrated on self-sufficiency, it has not neglected its wider obligations. In line with King Fahd's commitment to overseas aid, Saudi Arabia has supported the World Food Program in its fight against global food inequalities. Its efforts and contribution in this field are widely recognized, be they through local or regional or international funds or through bilateral aid.

To cope with the ambitious plans for agricultural development, the General Organization for Grains Silos and Flour Mills (GSFMO) was established in 1972. The main goals set for the new Organization were as follows:

- To establish and operate a comprehensive industry for the storage of grains, production of flour and forage.
- To introduce other processing activities related to grains.
- To promote the Organization's products at home and abroad.
- To purchase grains and maintain adequate reserves to draw on in case of emergency.
- To bear in mind the goals of the Government's agricultural policy.

(*Source:* King Fahd bin Abdul Aziz, *Saudi Desert House Agency, 2000*)

The GSFMO was successful in setting up grain silos in all areas of concentrated wheat production. As a result, farmers found it easy to market their

*Agricultural terrace, Baha*

*Wheat field in Baljurashi*

crops without having to pay freight for taking their harvest to far-away markets. To ensure the smooth sale of the harvest, the Organization set a policy of buying it at incentive prices. This policy has helped to attract new farmers and large-scale agricultural companies to invest in wheat-growing. To cope with its expanding operation, the Organization has more than ten branches in all parts of the Kingdom.

Below we give a brief summary of agricultural developments in the Kingdom.

## Expansion of Cultivated Land

The cultivation areas in the Kingdom have doubled over the last two decades. In 1975, cultivated land in the Kingdom of Saudi Arabia was no more than 150,000 acres [60,700 hectares]. The figures for 1998 show that there are now more than 12 million acres [4,885,000 hectares] under cultivation and a further 13 million acres [53 million hectares] that could be prepared for cultivation.

## Wheat Production

The total wheat produce of the Kingdom of Saudi Arabia in 1975 did not exceed 3,000 tons; in 1999, the Kingdom's production reached 1.8 million tons, representing an astronomical rise in wheat production in the Kingdom. The Kingdom has achieved self-sufficiency in wheat production.

## Dates

Dates are one of the richest and oldest alimentary products in the Kingdom. There are 13 million date palms in the Kingdom, producing about 400 types

**SAUDI DATES DISTRIBUTED TO THE NEEDY IN SYRIA**
Riyadh, 3rd December 2000

The World Food Program, an affiliate of the United Nations, today received a shipment of 1,000 tons of Saudi dates to be distributed to drought-stricken rural areas in Syria. The shipment is the third within an amount of 4,000 tons allocated by the Kingdom, in addition to US$250,000 to the support program.
*Source: SPA*

of mainly high quality dates. Date production has risen from 240,000 tons in 1970 to 650,000 tons in 1999, an increase which has enabled the Kingdom to export to neighboring countries – in addition to the large quantities it offers as aid to the World Food Program which in turn distributes it to countries in need of this major source of nutrition.

### Red Meat

There has been an increase in projects involving the raising and fattening of sheep and cattle, which have had important implications in terms of the need for the cultivation of fodder, subsidized by the Government. These developments have contributed to the fulfillment of the country's requirements for good quality meat. In 1970 meat production amounted to 7,000 tons. This figure had increased to 160,000 tons by 1999.

*Agricultural wealth in Saudi Arabia*

### Fruit and Vegetables

The Kingdom of Saudi Arabia produces a variety of essential vegetables, including potatoes, both for local consumption and for export to neighboring States. Vegetable cultivation is carried out on modern agricultural principles of controlled environment; and the operations of preparation and packing of produce employ the most modern techniques, as required for modern markets. By the end of 1997, the Kingdom produced about 2,600,000 tons of fresh vegetables, including tomatoes, watermelons, potatoes and cucumbers. Production of fruits exceeded 1,150,000 tons.

### Milk and Dairy Products

In 1975, there was no significant milk or dairy production in the Kingdom of Saudi Arabia. Total production supplied 5% of the local demand; in 1985 the Kingdom was not only meeting the self-sufficiency limit of milk and dairy products and their derivatives but was also exporting part of its production to neighboring countries. In 1997 the Kingdom's production of dairy products amounted to 816,000 tons.

### Poultry

In 1975, the poultry industry in the Kingdom of Saudi Arabia was unable to meet even 10% of local demand; by 1985 the Kingdom had exceeded self-sufficiency in egg production and was exporting to neighboring countries. In

1999 the volume of egg production was 139,000 tons. As for the production of poultry for eating, the Kingdom is now more than self-sufficient.

## Sea Food

The Government has given special attention to this sector along all its Arabian Gulf and Red Sea coasts. Following a number of studies, it has provided various means of support and incentives to small fishermen, facilitating the purchase of boats equipped with modern fishing gear and offering effective marketing facilities.

Aware of the importance of fish, the State formed a company with a capital of SR 100 million, the Saudi Fisheries Company, in which, in addition to the State, some 16,000 citizens hold shares. This company has successfully built its private fleet and provides a large variety of fish and prawn for local and export markets. In 1999, 56,000 tons of fish were caught.

## State Aid to Farmers

Since the agricultural sector makes a major contribution to the diversification of income resources, and in view of the importance of encouraging farmers to continue working the land, the Government has adopted a policy of generous farming subsidies including interest-free loan offers and aid to agricultural investment and production projects. The Government offers aid to the value of 50% of the cost of agricultural machinery and equipment imports, as well as for seeds, fertilizers and fodder. It also contributes to the cost of insecticides and air transport of milch cows from abroad. The Saudi Agricultural Bank and other governmental trust funds offer interest-free loans in order to finance investments and operations in various agricultural projects. In 1999, the Agricultural Bank provided 6,628 loans, to a total value of SR 903 million. The Government also offers free arable land to farmers and agricultural companies; has a subsidy policy for wheat and date prices; and has imposed a customs tax to protect the production of eggs for consumption.

## Agricultural Companies

The key to the success of the Kingdom's efforts directed at agricultural development has been its encouragement of the private sector to build up and establish agricultural companies, whether public corporations or large private limited companies. In the last few years, large public corporations have been established for various agricultural purposes, with capital varying between three hundred and five hundred million Saudi Riyals each. Among these are the following:

• The National Agricultural Development Company (NADEC) is based in Riyadh and has a capital of SR 400 million. The State owns 20% of the company's share, with the rest owned by 127,000 Saudi shareholders.

*Agriculture in Saudi Arabia*

- The Eastern Agricultural Development Company (STADCO) is based in Dammam and has a capital of SR 300 million and 30,000 Saudi shareholders.
- The Hail Agricultural Development Company (HADCO) is based in Hail with a capital of SR 300 million and 57,000 Saudi shareholders.
- The Bisha Agricultural Development Company has a capital of SR 500 million.
- The Al Baha Investment and Development Company has a capital of SR 150 million.
- The Saudi Fisheries Company is based in Dammam and has a capital of SR 100 million. The State owns 40% of the company's shares, with the rest

owned by 8,500 Saudi shareholders. It has achieved tangible success in efficiently providing the local market with clean fish and exporting a variety of its produce.

- The Fisheries and Marine Life Company – the Saudi Fisheries Company owns 63% of its capital.

The success of these companies in fulfilling their objectives is evident from the increase in the local agricultural productivity of wheat, fodder and milk, as well as in the processing and packaging of dates, and cattle breeding and fattening. Further evidence of these companies' dynamism is seen in their future plans for diversification of agricultural production, the development of food industries and the adoption of modern marketing techniques.

**Agricultural Research Stations and Centers**

As a result of its awareness of the importance of research and its responsibility for achieving the best results, the Ministry of Agriculture and Water has established a number of centers and stations, which through experimentation, and economic and analytical studies, aim to employ the most modern means for the development of agricultural and animal resources. Saudi personnel are being trained in these centers and stations in order to raise their efficiency and the level of their qualifications. The results of all such research is being published and distributed among farmers and other relevant institutions in order to share the ensuing benefits.

**Training**

In view of the importance of training human resources for the preparation of technical staff highly efficient in different agricultural fields, the Ministry of Agriculture and Water has established several training centers in numerous agricultural regions (e.g. Riyadh, al-Qassim, al-Hofuf and Jizan) to train officials from the Ministry and farmers and their children. Also, Ministry officials and

*Pastures in Saudi Arabia*

some farmers are being sent for training at international centers and universities which have particular specialities so that, on their return, they can apply their knowledge in the Kingdom, after adapting it to the agricultural needs and conditions of Saudi Arabia.

### Forests and Grazing Land

The Government has undertaken many procedures for the protection and conservation of forests and grazing land and has built twenty nurseries in different areas to produce the necessary seedlings for the development and expansion of forests. It has planted tree barriers in the form of defensive lines to stop creeping sands, and has used trees for similar purposes alongside the main roads outside the cities in the eastern region.

Natural grazing land accounts for approximately 75% of the land in the Kingdom of Saudi Arabia. This has led the Ministry of Agriculture and Water to establish a center specializing in the study of the development and protection of pastures, as a basis for increasing animal resources.

### National Parks

The Kingdom of Saudi Arabia, through its vastness, enjoys a diversity of good natural scenery ranging from mountains covered by a variety of flora including trees and wide plateaux with attractive plants in spring through to beautiful

*Al Jabal Forest, Baha*

green oases in the middle of the desert, distinguished by their wild fauna, and the rich coastal regions of the Red Sea and the Arabian Gulf.

The Government of Saudi Arabia has recognized the importance of protecting these natural resources which are for the enjoyment of present and future generations. With this in mind, it has established parks, like the National Park of Asir on the large mountainous and hilly landscape of Asir around the city of Abha. There are also studies and designs in preparation for the establishment of modern parks in Riyadh, Al-Hasa, Al-Baha and elsewhere.

## Agriculture Today

The development of the Kingdom's agriculture is, in some ways, the most exciting of all the developmental programs. At a time when desertification is a major issue amongst environmentalists and one which, with global warming, is becoming an issue of primary international concern, the Kingdom is channelling resources into turning the desert into agriculturally productive land. The scale of the task is enormous but anyone who has seen the great circles of wheat growing in the desert between Riyadh and Jeddah will realize that the Kingdom's commitment is more than equal to the challenge. The Kingdom of Saudi Arabia is now self-sufficient in many types of agricultural produce and is, in many cases, able to export.

All these developments in the agricultural and environmental field have been close to King Fahd's heart and in 1997, in recognition of the Kingdom's role in agricultural development, the achievement of food security and the Kingdom's contribution to combating hunger and poverty in developing countries, King Fahd was awarded the International Agricultural Gold Medal by the Food and Agricultural Organization (FAO).

## Supply of Potable and Irrigation Water

Water resources are scarce in Saudi Arabia. It is a desert country lying within the continental zone where temperatures are high in summer and low in winter. It is also characterized by low annual rainfall. The scarcity of water was the reason behind many tribal conflicts until King Abdul Aziz recognized that provision of water was essential for the stability of his newly unified country. In the early 1930s, he recruited international experts to conduct geological surveys for underground water. He also decided to build dams to retain rainwater for irrigation and drinking after purification.

Under King Fahd, the need for water has increased dramatically as agriculture, industry and the population have expanded. No expense has been spared to meet demand for this most essential resource. The Ministry of Agriculture and Water is responsible for the provision of water from various sources. There are currently four major programs for water provision in the Kingdom.

### Desalination

The first water desalination unit was established in the Kingdom in 1928 when King Abdul Aziz ordered the establishment of a desalination unit under the name of "Kandasa" for provision of drinking water for Jeddah. In 1970, the desalination station was set up in Jeddah.

Today Saudi Arabia produces more potable water from the sea than any other country. In 1974, a Royal Decree was issued for the establishment of the Saline Water Conversion Corporation (SWCC). According to its regulations it was set up to enhance the Kingdom's natural water sources. The Corporation began by producing a few thousand cubic yards [meters] of desalinated water to meet regional needs. But within a short period, it expanded its operations to produce electricity at the desalination plants. Under the SWCC, the production of desalinated water increased more than 100-fold, while the power production also registered a greater than 80-fold increase within two decades.

The Kingdom has two types of desalination plants:

• One-function plants (produce only desalinated water).
• Dual-purpose plants (produce both desalinated water and electricity).

The dual-purpose plants produce 20% of the Kingdom's total electricity production.

Desalination plants on the Red Sea coast are the following:
1. Asir
2. Al Birak
3. Duba
4. Farasan Island
5. Haql Al-Madinah Al-Munawwarah
6. Jeddah
7. Al-Lith
8. Makkah
9. Al-Qunfudhah
10. Rabigh
11. Al-Shuaiba
12. Al-Shaqiq
13. Taif
14. Umm Laj
15. Al Wajh
16. Yanbu

Desalination plants on the Arabian Gulf coast are the following:
1. Al Jubail
2. Al Jubail-Riyadh
3. Al Khafji
4. Al Khafji Express
5. Al Khobar

(*Source:* A Country and a Citizen for a Happy, Decent Life, *MOI Publication*)

The Jubail desalination plant is the biggest water desalination station in the world. For transportation of the desalinated water inside the Kingdom, the SWCC has set up pipelines that stretch more than 1,240 miles [2,000 km]. A report by the Ministry of Agriculture and Water noted that the production of desalinated water is expected to exceed 800 million gallons [3,028 million litres] per day, while the generated power is expected to exceed 5,000 megawatts. Pipelines will extend for more than 2,485 miles [4,000 km] while the number of water reservoirs will increase to 166, with a total capacity of more than 12,160,000 cubic yards [9,300,000 cu m] of desalinated water.

*Jubail desalination plant*

In order to improve performance and reduce cost as well as to develop modern methods for the desalination of water and the generation of power, the SWCC established a research and development center in Jubail in 1987. The research center includes five basic laboratories that are equipped with the most modern devices and experimental stations. The SWCC has given top priority to the process of training, with particular emphasis on the Saudization of jobs. In 1999, the SWCC was awarded the International Desalinating Agency Prize, in recognition of its achievements.

*Abha Dam*

Statistics show that the rated capacity of desalination plants in the Kingdom has grown from 5.1 million gallons [19.3 million litres] per day (mgd) in 1970 to 572.6 mgd [2,167 million litres] in 2000. The quantity of water supplied by the desalination plants has risen from 4.6 mgd [17.4 million litres] in 1970 to 458.1 mgd [1,734 million litres] in 1999, representing an average annual growth rate of 17.4%.

**Subterranean Water Projects**

The Ministry of Agriculture and Water has established several large and self-contained projects to extract subterranean water in order to provide the population of the Kingdom in different areas with good quality water. The largest of these are the water project in the city of Riyadh and the Jeddah water project feeding the city of Jeddah. If the other self-contained water projects covering different towns and villages and Bedouin centers are included, the Kingdom can now boast that pure water is available to every home in all corners of Saudi Arabia. Given the growth in demand over the last three decades this is an outstanding achievement and is indicative of the Government's total commitment to providing all essential services to every corner of the Kingdom.

**Dams and Reservoir Projects**

In order to exploit rain and flood waters as efficiently as possible, the Ministry has concentrated on building several dams in various areas. Before 1975, there were 16 dams; the number had increased to 190 by 1999. These dams contribute to the increase of subterranean water reserves and the provision of potable water, as well as helping to protect plantations and some villages against the flooding which previously threatened them as a result of sudden torrential rises in the level of water.

The biggest dam is the King Fahd Dam in Bisha Valley with a capacity of 425 million cubic yards [325 million cu m]. Other dams include: Wadi Najran with a capacity of 111 million cubic yards [85 million cu m]; the dam of Wadi Jizan with a capacity of 98 million cubic yards [75 million cu m]; Wadi Taruba, Wadi Ekrimah and Wadi Yanbu, all with a capacity of 39 million cubic yards [30 million cu m] and the dam of Wadi Fatima on the outskirts of the Holy City of Makkah with a capacity of 26 million cubic yards [20 million cu m].

## Recycling of Purified Sewage Projects

These projects recycle purified sewage water for agricultural and industrial use. The first project was established in the city of Riyadh and saves about 261,600 million cubic yards [200,000 cu m] of purified water a day. Similar projects are planned for al-Qassim and al-Dammam.

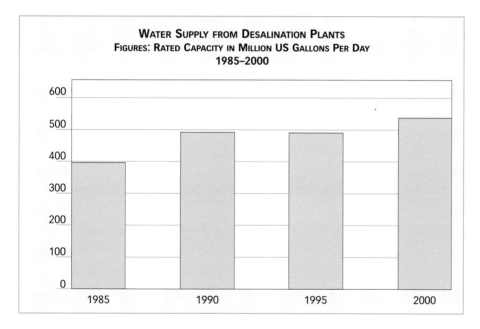

## INDUSTRIAL DEVELOPMENT

While the foundations for the industrial development of the Kingdom were laid before Crown Prince Fahd became King, the vigor with which the program of industrialization has been pursued is largely attributable to King Fahd who, both as Crown Prince and King, has always seen industrialization as the best way to reduce the Kingdom's dependence on oil.

To achieve this end and to reduce the Kingdom's need for imported goods, the Saudi Government has encouraged the development of a wide range of

*Industrial facility*

manufacturing industries. During the period 1970 to 1999, the number of operating factories increased from 199 factories, employing 13,865 workers to 3,163 factories, employing 291,621. Capital investment also increased, from SR 2.8 billion in 1970 to SR 231.2 billion in 1999. In 1999 alone, ninety-one new factories opened. (*Source:* Achievements of the Development Plans, 1970–2000, *Ministry of Planning*)

The Government has provided a range of incentives to encourage the private sector to participate in the Kingdom's industrial effort. Eight industrial estates provide private Saudi manufacturing companies with the necessary infrastructure and services at a very low cost. Credit facilities on generous terms are available for such enterprises.

A good indication of the Government's determination to expand the industrial base of the economy and a measure of the Government's success are the loans disbursed by the Saudi Industrial Development Fund (SIDF). SIDF, which was set up in 1974, is a Government agency charged with the responsibility of providing a source of funds to private sector industries and public utility companies. The total loans approved for industrial projects, from its creation until 1999, amounted to SR 36.4 billion. These loans have helped in the establishment of some 1,668 industrial projects, such as building materials, cement, chemicals, foodstuffs, minerals and other essential products – and export of the surplus products. (*Source:* Ibid)

Behind these figures lies King Fahd's sustained strategy of reducing Saudi

Arabia's dependence on oil. It is a daunting task. Saudi Arabia possesses 25% of the world's oil reserves and, therefore, the economy must remain oil-based in the foreseeable future. Nevertheless, by judicious use of the oil revenues, the Government of Saudi Arabia is expanding the industrial base and other economic sectors, and gradually reducing the degree of dependence.

The expansion of non-oil activities brings with it the acute need to make best use of manpower at all levels. Saudi Arabia has a small population relative to the size of its economy. Much of the economic expansion during the construction of the Kingdom's infrastructure necessitated the use of expatriate labor. Developments in education and training are a clear indication that, just as the Government is reducing dependence on oil, so it is determined to reduce dependence on foreign labor, especially in the areas of science and technology.

The SIDF has played a key role in creating local Saudi industrial enterprises and the employment opportunities which they present. The wide range of locally manufactured goods now available in the Kingdom attests to the success of the SIDF's contribution.

## Saudi Arabian Basic Industries Corporation

The Saudi Arabian Basic Industries Corporation (SABIC) is an example, *par excellence*, of the practical results of the Kingdom's blend of long-range planning, long-term major investment and the judicious use of public and private sources of finance.

SABIC was established by Royal Decree in 1976, with a capital of SR 10 billion – its task to set up and operate hydrocarbon and mineral-based industries in the Kingdom of Saudi Arabia. The Public Investment Fund provides long-term loans to SABIC on highly concessional terms. The balance of SABIC's capital requirements comes from SABIC's joint venture partners. In addition, SABIC can make use of normal commercial loans. With these sources of finance, SABIC is able to undertake industrial projects considerably in excess of its own authorized capital.

The main features of the first phase of the industrial program launched by SABIC were:
- 5 ethylene-based petrochemical complexes with a total annual capacity of 1.6 million tons of ethylene;
- 2 chemical-grade methanol plants with a total annual capacity of 1.25 million tons;
- 1 urea plant with an annual capacity of 500,000 million tons;
- 1 iron and steel plant at Jubail with an annual capacity of 800,000 tons;
- expansion of the Jeddah Steel Rolling Mill to produce 140,000 tons per annum. (*Source:* Modernity and Tradition: The Saudi Equation, *Knight Communications*)

Implementation of SABIC projects began in 1979. In that year, SABIC concluded four joint venture agreements with foreign companies. By the end of 1999 SABIC had established sixteen basic, downstream and support industries, having annual production capacities of about 27.67 tons [25.1 million metric tons] of products like petrochemicals, plastics, fertilizers, metals, industrial gases. The sixteen industries are the following:

1. Jeddah Steel Rolling Company (SULB)
2. Saudi Iron and Steel Company (HADDED)
3. Saudi Methanol Company (ARRAZI)
4. Al-Jubail Fertilizer Company (SAMAD)
5. Saudi Yanbu Petrochemical Company (YANPET)
6. Al-Jubail Petrochemical Company (KEMYA)
7. Saudi Petrochemical Company (SADAF)
8. National Methanol Company (IBN SINA)
9. Arabian Petrochemical Company (PETROKEMYA)
10. Eastern Petrochemical Company (SHARQ)
11. Saudi Arabian Fertilizer Company (SAFCO)
12. National Chemical Fertilizer Company (IBN AL BAYTAR)
13. National Plastic Company (IBN HAYYAN)
14. National Gases Company (GAS)
15. Saudi European Petrochemical Company (IBN ZAHER)
16. Arabian Industrial Fiber Company (IBN RUSHD)

(*Source:* Achievements of the Development Plans, 1970–2000, *Ministry of Planning*)

SABIC's major role in the development of petrochemical and mineral-based industries in Saudi Arabia is clear. Less obvious, but perhaps more important, is the function SABIC fulfills in providing a mechanism for the

*Saudi Yanbu Petrochemical Company (YANPET)*

acquisition by Saudi citizens of the managerial, professional and technological skills required to control and expand a modern industrialized economy. In 2000, 75% of SABIC's workforce were Saudi nationals.

In 1998 SABIC was ranked the second largest Saudi company and held 313th place among the 500 largest companies in the world.

In 1992, SABIC had profits of just under SR 2 billion. In 2000, SABIC posted a net profit of SR 3.63 billion, a dramatic increase of 113% on the 1999 figure of SR 1.707 billion. SABIC also announced record sales revenues of SR 24.6 billion in 2000, a very substantial increase on the previous year's SR 19.18 billion. (*Source: Saudi Press Agency news release*)

These figures attest to the remarkable achievements of an organization that holds a central position in the Kingdom's program of industrial diversification.

In the field of industrial and marketing cooperation, SABIC has a 20% share in each of the Aluminium Bahrain (ALBA) and Gulf Aluminium Rolling Mill Company (GARMCO). It also owns one third of Gulf Petrochemical Industries Company (GPIC), 25.7% of Bahraini-Saudi Aluminium Marketing Company (BALCO) and 20% of United Gulf Company for Industrialization.

*SABIC's Industrial Policy*

The following notes on SABIC's industrial policy were supplied by the management of SABIC:

SABIC's policy and strategies are directly derived from its planned objectives. Having been established as one of the principal vehicles for diversifying the Saudi economy, SABIC's strategies were drawn along three basic lines of action.

The first is to make use of the comparative advantages of local industrial production by utilizing and adding value to available natural resources ... Hence, the setting up of basic industries that are based upon hydrocarbon and mineral resources.

The second is to construct related downstream and supporting industries, thus contributing to the expansion of the Kingdom's industrial base, and at the same time providing investment opportunities for private capital either directly in SABIC's industries or in related industries and services.

The third line of action is to participate in training and building Saudi technical and managerial capabilities in industrial planning, implementation, operation, maintenance and development.

Now, with SABIC's projects moving from the construction and implementation phase to that of actual production, there have emerged the elements of efficient, safe and profitable operation of industries – together with the most important requirement for the continued development of SABIC as a successful commercial enterprise, and as a corporate vehicle for marketing its products.

In this direction, SABIC is careful to enter the petrochemical markets as a worldwide producer worthy of its name:

> *Seeking the best and most appropriate qualities in its products;*
> *Pursuing serious, fair and honest competitions in its business dealings; and*
> *Endeavoring in a gentlemanly way, and within its direct interests, to work for the*
> *benefit of both the consumer and world industry as a whole.*

(*Source:* Modernity and Tradition: The Saudi Equation, *Knight Communications*)

### Industrial Cities

In its efforts to broaden the industrial base of the Saudi Arabian economy, it was obvious that the Kingdom should take advantage of its copious hydrocarbon energy resources.

The industrial cities at Jubail and Yanbu have played a key part in the Kingdom's determination to develop hydrocarbon-based and energy-intensive industries. The Royal Commission for Jubail and Yanbu, established in 1975, has created the basic infrastructure for these two cities, often described as the jewels in the Kingdom's industrial crown.

*Night view of petrochemical industries in Jubail*

In an effort to follow a balanced regional development objective, the Ministry of Industry and Electricity has established eight developed industrial cities, with various utilities and services necessary for the establishment of factories, at Riyadh, Jeddah, Dammam, Qassim, Al-Hasa and Makkah. By 1999, these industrial cities covered a total area of 49 million square yards [41 million sq m], and had cost more than SR 2 billion. Currently, phase three of the second industrial cities in Riyadh, Qassim and Hofuf is being implemented. Development work on four new industrial cities in Madinah, Asir, Jouf and Tabouk has also started.

### Other Aspects of Industrial Diversification

Inevitably, any consideration of the Kingdom's industrial diversification program centers on the establishment and development of large-scale State-owned industrial companies engaged in oil refining and petrochemical production.

But there is another sector, smaller but in terms of employment and in terms

of the future, of considerable significance. There are some 2,000 general manufacturing companies licensed by the Ministry of Industry and Electricity, and some 20,000 light-industrial workshops licensed by the municipalities.

*Night view of basic industrial district in Yanbu*

Another feature of King Fahd's strategy in seeking industrial diversification is the type of industrial projects which are appropriate to Saudi Arabia's geography and demography. Although Saudi Arabia is vast in size, the population of the Kingdom is small, and, despite the reduction in numbers of immigrant workers in recent years, it remains true that the economy still requires a large foreign workforce to complement the indigenous population. It is not therefore appropriate for the Kingdom to encourage the development of labor-intensive industries. Rather, it favors the introduction and expansion of high-technology industrial ventures with a high productivity/worker ratio, which will provide suitably trained Saudi citizens with well-paid and challenging occupations.

Because of Government policy and support, the non-oil industrial sector has increased in both size and efficiency of operation and can now claim to have achieved output-per-worker figures which are amongst the highest in the Arab world.

The table overleaf gives statistics on the number of operating factories in the Kingdom with the total capital and total manpower from 1985 to 1999.

| YEAR | NUMBER OF OPERATING FACTORIES (CUMULATIVE FIGURES) | TOTAL CAPITAL OF OPERATING FACTORIES (SR MILLION) (CUMULATIVE FIGURES) | TOTAL MANPOWER OF OPERATING FACTORIES (CUMULATIVE FIGURES) |
|---|---|---|---|
| 1985 | 1,298 | 96,451 | 145,299 |
| 1986 | 1,401 | 127,858 | 155,567 |
| 1987 | 1,496 | 131,519 | 163,689 |
| 1988 | 1,583 | 132,962 | 168,010 |
| 1989 | 1,676 | 135,190 | 174,723 |
| 1990 | 1,800 | 150,072 | 183,011 |
| 1991 | 1,897 | 152,167 | 189,737 |
| 1992 | 2,013 | 154,204 | 197,355 |
| 1993 | 2,153 | 156,266 | 204,405 |
| 1994 | 2,647 | 215,800 | 213,039 |
| 1995 | 2,725 | 217,000 | 221,070 |
| 1996 | 2,831 | 218,800 | 224,877 |
| 1997 | 2,952 | 221,000 | 228,380 |
| 1998 | 3,072 | 228,900 | 285,200 |
| 1999 | 3,163 | 231,233 | 291,621 |

*Source:* Achievements of the Development Plans, 1970–2000, *Ministry of Planning*

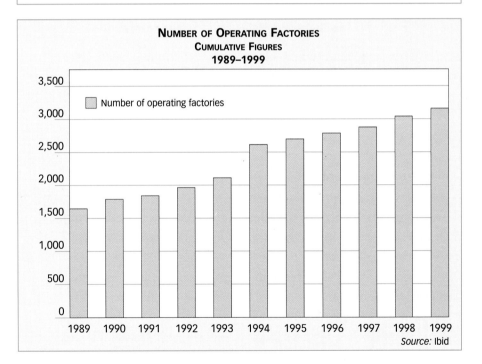

Source: Ibid

## Industrial Development, the Present and the Future

The Fourth Development Plan (1985–90), the first published during King Fahd's reign, gave a clear and succinct description of the industrial sector of the Saudi economy.

Industrial development of the Kingdom is of comparatively recent origin and essentially comprises three components:

First, are the SABIC (Saudi Arabian Basic Industries Corporation) enterprises, which comprise mainly the downstream hydrocarbon industries and, to a lesser degree, the heavy metals industry. These industries are capital- and energy-intensive, utilizing raw material feedstock from the oil and gas industries, and their petrochemicals output is primarily for export. The production plants are technologically very advanced, and the controlling companies are usually joint ventures with foreign partners who have varying degrees of control, but never above 50%. These industries are normally referred to as the "basic" industry sector.

Second, is the large group of factories licensed by the Ministry of Industry and Electricity (MIE) and best described as the "formal" manufacturing sector. Most of these enterprises are privately sponsored and eligible for Saudi Industrial Development Fund (SIDF) loans. Their output is geared primarily to the domestic market, which is very open and competitive. A range of investment incentives is available to companies, following a screening procedure; for example, sites with low-tariff energy and utility services, industrial estates, SIDF loans, preferential purchases by State organizations, training grants and, in some cases, tariff protection.

The third group can be referred to as the "informal" manufacturing sector, and is composed largely of labor-intensive small workshops in repair and small-scale production activities. These workshops require neither an MIE license nor its screening procedure, but do require a license from the municipalities and registration as companies with the Ministry of Commerce. Furthermore, the Ministry of Industry is not responsible for monitoring their activities. The financing needs of this sector relate mainly to working capital requirements such as raw material, rather than premises and equipment. Finance comes mainly from the owners of the workshops, and this can be supplemented by grants from the Saudi Credit Bank, if the owner has completed GOTEVT vocational training.

The Seventh Development Plan (covering the years 2000–2005) indicates the Government's future intentions for the continuing development of the country's economy:

Improving the utilization of economic resources owned by the Government, and increasing the capability of the associated equipment, and giving priority to the economic perspective when using these economic resources, and providing for the participation of the private sector in the following ways.

1. Making water a fundamental element and an important measure in evaluating economic capacity in Government and private sector projects.

2. Continuing to explore for and develop natural resources such as mineral and marine wealth.

3. Horizontal and vertical expansion in the petrochemical industry and derivatives of gas and petrol, through the private sector or through mixed (public/private ownership) companies.

4. Increasing the capacity for the refining of petroleum products as much as possible.

## The Private Sector

It is clear that although the State must continue to play a key role in the Kingdom's economy, the Saudi Government is eager to see the private sector assume increasing responsibility for the country's economic development.

The Kingdom of Saudi Arabia follows a free trade policy, believing that such a policy and the competition it encourages is the most effective way of utilizing resources efficiently, of employing those resources to meet the changing needs of society, and of providing consumers with the greatest degree of choice.

This policy has led the Government to encourage the private sector of the economy to become as efficient and competitive as possible. Fledgling Saudi industries need help (in the form of grants, soft loans, or, in some instances, even protective tariffs), but the longer-term aim is to generate a private industrial sector capable of facing local and fair foreign competition, of meeting the Kingdom's own industrial needs as far as practical and, indeed, of exporting Saudi goods to other Arab States and beyond.

As part of this economic strategy, the Government is progressively privatizing public organizations, encouraging both domestic and foreign investment in the Kingdom's industrial sector.

The clearest indication of the Kingdom's future policies for the private sector is provided by the Seventh Development Plan and the fifth plan to be published in the course of King Fahd's reign.

### The Third Strategic Principle

Continuing with the policy of opening up areas to the private sector so that it may carry out many social and economic functions, on condition that this will result in a real benefit through reduction in costs, enhanced performance and employment of citizens. This policy may be pursued in the following ways:

1. Continuing to implement a privatization policy, which follows an appropriate schedule and arranging the situation so that it is in tune with the requirements of privatization to ensure that the privatization targets are met.

2. Expediting the review of all systems relating to the activities of the private sector, with the aim of simplifying procedures and eliminating difficulties.

3. Paying attention to the domestic tourism industry by preparing and encouraging the private sector to invest in this field.

4. Simplifying the process for the establishment of more joint stock companies.

5. Developing the currency exchange market and providing greater opportunity for domestic and foreign investment.

6. Encouraging and helping investors to explore for and exploit mineral resources through the production of basic equipment, enriching the knowledge base and offering easier financing for mining projects.

7. Continuing to encourage cooperative societies and domestic charitable organizations to set up social and economic projects such as running health centers and hospitals, centers for the rehabilitation of the handicapped and private clinics, and establishing charities.

8. Encouraging commercial banks to increase their facilities for production projects and to take a greater interest in small projects.

9. Working to increase the effectiveness of projects and cataloging them in order to acquaint citizens with investment opportunities in the production sector.

10. Enhancing the potential of the private sector and preparing it to deal adequately and effectively with the possible consequences of international developments.

11. Encouraging the establishment of national financial companies for domestic financial investment.

12. Improving the competitive value of Saudi domestic products in order to meet the sharp increase in competition in regional and international markets.

13. Encouraging citizens to save, and introducing channels to collect and invest small savings, in the following ways:

 a) Expanding the role of the media in highlighting the importance of saving.

 b) Encouraging commercial banks to introduce effective means and systems to collect small savings.

 c) Encouraging the establishment of a savings bank to act as a model for other savings banks in the future.

 d) Continuing to protect price stability in order to protect the value of savings.

14. Offering more channels to attract the savings of citizens.

15. Encouraging the private sector to make greater investments in the field of education and training.

16. Encouraging the private sector to make an effective contribution to the development of the regions.

## Mineral Resources and Mining

Geological surveys and mineral exploration have revealed that, in addition to the vast oil reserves, the Kingdom of Saudi Arabia possesses large deposits of various minerals, including bauxite, copper, gold, iron, lead, silver, tin and a number of non-metallic minerals.

The most important deposits discovered are the following:

- Al-Jalamid phosphate
- Al-Sawawin iron ore
- Al-Khnaiguiyah zinc
- Al-Hajar, Zalm and Ad-Duwaihi gold
- Jabal Sayid copper
- Al-Zabirah bauxite
- Harat Kishb and Harat Rahat basalt
- Yanbu clay

(*Source:* Achievements of the Development Plans, 1970–2000, *Ministry of Planning*)

In line with King Fahd's policy in other sectors of the economy, the Saudi Government has been eager to train Saudi nationals to play the fullest possible part in the exploitation of the Kingdom's mineral wealth.

In March 1997, in order to coordinate projects and promote efficiency in the mining industry, the Saudi Arabian Mining Company (MAADIN) was created, with an initial capital of more than $1 billion. The company is responsible for regulating mineral exploration and overseeing its progress. Mining projects wholly or partly owned by the Government will be consolidated and restructured in the commercial sector. MAADIN will also provide sufficient basic infrastructure for mining projects located in more remote areas. MAADIN has obtained exploration licenses for the gold deposits in Wadi Bidah, Al-Hajar, Ad-Duwaihi, Samran, Sheban, Zalm and Hamdah, for phosphate ore in Wadi Al Sarhan and Turaif, for magnesium in Zargat, Jabal Abt and Jabal Al Rukham, for zinc in Al Khnaiguiyah, as well as licenses for exploration of industrial metals in Jabal Sodah. (*Source:* Ibid)

## Diversification

When the oil revenues began to flow in earnest, Saudi Arabia was still undeveloped. Even in 1975, Riyadh itself was little more than a few streets, with an open sewer running through the town. If we think back to that time, given the climate of the Kingdom, the nature of the terrain and its sheer size, given the distribution of the population and its nature, agrarian, nomadic and mercantile, the prospect of developing a diversified economy seemed more like a dream than a potential reality. To achieve such a diversification, it was necessary to put a number of prerequisites in place. An infrastructure capable of supporting industry and commerce had to be built; the population had to be educated; above all the people had to be persuaded that, God willing, with their help, the dream could be fulfilled.

The organizational skills required (which found expression in the series of Five-Year Plans) were of the highest order – but most striking of all was the vision of King Fahd who marshaled the vast resources of the Kingdom to bring this transformation about.

In the beginning, inevitably, there was heavy reliance on expatriate labor at all levels but, from the start, it was clear that King Fahd foresaw a time when Saudi citizens would be able to take full responsibility for their own country. To this end, King Fahd gave education the highest priority. Saudi citizens were given every encouragement to pursue their studies through school and, whenever beneficial, finance to study at the best universities abroad. At the same time, funds were provided to expand the Kingdom's own universities so that, as soon as possible, the majority of Saudi young people would be able to take their education to the highest level within the Kingdom.

## Saudization

In recent times, the program of Saudization (replacement of foreign labor by Saudi nationals) has accelerated. To some extent, the surge in revenues engendered by the oil price increase of 1979–80 tended to foster false expectations amongst the population. The gradual realization that the "boom" period could not continue indefinitely encouraged the Saudi workforce to adopt a more realistic and, in the longer run, much healthier attitude to the role they can and must play within the Saudi Arabian economy, both in the public and private sectors.

This change of attitude would have occurred in due course even if the oil price had not fallen. By the end of the Third Development Plan (which ran from 1980 to 1985), most of the Kingdom's infrastructure was in place. Industrial sectors such as construction were inevitably facing a very considerable contraction. The rationale behind all the Kingdom's development plans has been to create a diversified economy, with thriving agricultural and industrial sectors, manned and managed by Saudi citizens. It is therefore fair to say that diminished revenues have simply hastened a process which was an essential element in King Fahd's long-term strategy.

It is also the case that the influx of foreigners, so necessary for the building of the Kingdom's infrastructure and the development of its industrial and agricultural base, brought with it some social strains. The Kingdom of Saudi Arabia is a strictly Muslim country, with a society based on the pure form of Islam promulgated by Imam Muhammad bin Abdul Wahhab more than 200 years ago. The millions of expatriate workers arriving in Saudi Arabia came from many different countries with diverse cultural backgrounds. The expatriates faced the problems of adjusting to Saudi society and there were those in the Kingdom who feared that Saudi society itself could be diluted by the influence of alien cultures. These fears proved groundless.

**Future of the Saudi Economy**

In terms of the immediate future, budgetary constraints have necessitated a clear formulation of strategic priorities. For the Government, the highest priorities are likely to be defense, education and health. At the same time, the Government is looking to the private sector to play a much greater role in the industrial and agricultural development of the Kingdom (see **The Private Sector**, page 102). The infrastructure is in place and the groundwork has been completed for the development and the expansion of Saudi Arabia's economy. There will be an increasing reliance on private sector investment to achieve further advances.

In the longer term, much will depend on oil. As we have seen, there has already been a remarkable diversification in the country's economy, but it must be true that the Kingdom's oil and gas reserves remain its greatest natural asset and its largest single source of revenue.

The Kingdom of Saudi Arabia possesses a quarter of the world's known recoverable oil reserves. Other exploitable oil fields in other parts of the world will, no doubt, be found and existing or even new alternative forms of energy may be developed but it seems certain that, in the course of the first decades of this century, the oil reserves of many countries, currently net exporters, will be exhausted. It is to be hoped that, as this happens, the decreasing number of producing nations and the increasing number of oil-importing nations will develop a sane, global economic policy which will be fair to both sides and will make best use of a dwindling energy resource. King Fahd's view of how the world's oil resources should be managed will eventually prevail.

Whatever the case, the Kingdom's revenues from oil are likely to rise again. Precisely how that increased revenue will be deployed cannot be determined now, but we can be certain that the same principles which have governed the Kingdom's Development Plans will be brought to bear in formulating new plans for the maintenance of Islam, for the enhancement of the quality of life of Saudi Arabian citizens, and for the continued development of the Kingdom's economy.

## THE BUILDING OF MODERN CITIES

The last three decades have seen the most extraordinary transformation of the Kingdom's cities and towns. To some extent, the expansion of the cities and towns was an inevitable consequence of the determination to diversify the economy, but the manner in which the transformation has been effected is largely attributable to the vision of King Fahd.

Visitors to the Kingdom over the last thirty years have been stunned by the way in which plans which seemed highly ambitious, if not impractical, on one visit have been implemented by the next. Streets are suddenly lined with trees. Buildings that would do credit to any modern city arise. The area of cities has expanded so quickly that landmarks which were on the edge of the city in 1980 are now considered part of the city center. Shopping malls as good as any in the West burgeon. The prestigious headquarters of major corporations soar skywards. In the main cities, restaurants offer cuisine from every part of the world to the highest standard.

Here we give a brief description of some of the Kingdom's main cities in the hope that some of the vision and dynamism which have effected the transformation will shine through.

## Administrative Regions

For administrative purposes, the Kingdom of Saudi Arabia is divided into thirteen regions.

## Riyadh

Riyadh, which lies in the central region, is the capital city of the Kingdom of Saudi Arabia and now rivals any modern city in the world for the splendor of its architecture. Broad highways sweep through the city, passing over or under each other in an impressive and still growing road network. The name Riyadh comes from the plural of the Arabic word "rawdhah" meaning a place covered with gardens and trees and indeed trees now bedeck the broad streets and avenues.

| REGION | LOCATION OF REGIONAL HQ |
|---|---|
| Riyadh Region | Riyadh City |
| Makkah Region | Makkah City |
| Madinah Region | Madinah City |
| Qassim Region | Buraidah City |
| Eastern Region | Dammam City |
| Asir Region | Abha City |
| Tabouk Region | Tabouk City |
| Hail Region | Hail City |
| Northern Border Region | Arar City |
| Jizan Region | Jizan City |
| Najran Region | Najran City |
| Baha Region | Baha City |
| Al-Jouf Region | Skaka City |

Of all the Kingdom's developmental achievements, Riyadh is perhaps the most obvious and accessible to the foreign visitor. From the moment he lands at the King Khalid International Airport, itself a marvel of design wedding the traditional Arab style with the best of modern architecture in a happy marriage of spacious practicality, the traveler is aware that he has reached a city that must be counted one of the wonders of the twentieth century.

The history of Riyadh and its growth from a relatively small settlement into a great modern city is inextricably involved with the rise of the House of Saud. With Riyadh as the capital of the Saudi Arabian Kingdom which King Abdul

*University Avenue, Riyadh*

Aziz founded, it was inevitable that the city would grow. By 1955, all Ministries and Government offices had been moved to or established in Riyadh. In the same year, a Royal Decree was issued raising the status of the municipality of Riyadh to that of mayoralty. Its scope of responsibility was greatly enlarged and its resources increased to enable it to cope with its growing size and population.

Today, apart from its importance as a seat of Government and as a thriving commercial center, Riyadh is also a center of Arab diplomacy. It is the venue for many international Arab meetings and is the site of the Diplomatic Quarter, an area built specifically to accommodate all embassies and their staff.

In the midst of this extraordinary growth, its history has not been forgotten. Preservation orders now ensure the survival of the Musmak Fort which King Abdul Aziz scaled in 1902, a fitting reminder of a turning point in the history of the city and, indeed, the Arabian Peninsula.

Riyadh was chosen as Capital of Arab Culture for the Year 2000, following nominations by the Arab Culture Ministers and a recommendation from UNESCO within the International Cultural Accord to choose a cultural capital for every culturally homogeneous geographical region in the world. The selection was in recognition of the Kingdom's cultural renaissance, particularly in Riyadh.

As noted in earlier sections, the Saudi cultural movement is developing all the time, with support from King Fahd. There are many cultural activities and developments in Riyadh. Places like the King Fahd National Library, the King Fahd Cultural Complex and the cultural centers in the Diplomatic Quarter help to give Riyadh its unique cultural character. Riyadh has become the meeting place of the intelligentsia, literary and cultural personalities in the Arab world through the National Guard Festival of Heritage and Culture and through the King Faisal International and Charitable Prize.

The best indicator of Riyadh's rapid growth is its area. Sixty years ago, it was only 3.3 square miles [8.5 sq km]. Today it is 695 square miles [1,800 sq km] in area, including a number of open areas in its new suburbs. The population of Riyadh has also grown remarkably. In 1918, the population of the capital was 19,000. The population passed the 2 million mark in 1985 and reached 3,400,000 in 1999. Currently (2001) it is about 4,300,000.

*King Abdul Aziz Public Library*

King Fahd has charged the Municipality of Riyadh with a number of

*King Faisal Charitable Foundation*

construction projects which it has implemented with evident enthusiasm. These are the following:

- Carrying out its routine organization and planning responsibilities by beautifying the city and keeping it clean.
- Establishing a large number of public gardens, parks and green landscaped areas, with fountains, artificial waterfalls and streetlamps.
- Planting islands in the middle of streets and providing a source of water for irrigation of parks and gardens.
- Establishing more than 100 children's playgrounds in various parts of the city.
- Establishing a number of parks and gardens to outstanding technical specifications.
- Establishing several commercial markets in various parts of the city, in order to bring the services closer to the inhabitants, hence reducing traffic in the city center.
- Building a number of multi-story car parks, in order to reduce the number of cars parked on the streets. (*Source:* This is Our Country, *MOI Publication*)

*King Saud University in Riyadh*

### Education

In addition to an increase in the number of primary, intermediary, secondary and private schools, a number of adult education centers for eradicating illiteracy have been established in Riyadh.

Other educational centers are the following:

- Girls' Education College
- Imam Muhammad bin Saud Islamic University
- King Abdul Aziz Cultural Center
- King Abdul Aziz City for Science and Technology
- King Abdul Aziz Military Academy
- King Faisal Air Force College
- King Khalid Military College
- King Saud University (the first university to be set up in the Arabian Peninsula) (*Source:* Ibid)

### Health

Riyadh contains a number of internationally recognized hospitals. The hospitals have been set up and administered by a number of governmental bodies. There are also a number of private hospitals.

The Ministry of Health is responsible for the following hospitals:

- Hospital for Chest Diseases
- Hospital for Infectious Diseases

- Obstetric and Pediatric Hospital
- Prince Salman Hospital
- Riyadh Central Hospital

*Imam Muhammad bin Saud Islamic University*

The Ministry of Higher Education and King Saud University administer the King Abdul Aziz and King Khalid University Hospitals.

The Ministry of Defense and Aviation administers the Armed Forces Hospital and the Flying Hospital.

*King Fahd Medical Center*

*Water Tower, Riyadh*

The National Guard administers the King Fahd Hospital. The Public Security Directorate Hospital provides healthcare to public security personnel and their families.

In addition to the above, there are the following:

- The King Faisal Specialist Hospital, which covers fifty-two different medical specializations and has a medical research center associated with it
- The King Khalid Eye Hospital
- The King Fahd Medical City
- The National Hospital, belonging to the Social Security Organization

*Water*

Riyadh's water resources are summarized below:

**Dams:** Five dams have been built near Riyadh to store rain and storm water for human consumption and also to increase supply of underground water. These dams, with a total storage capacity of 15.7 million cubic yards [12 million cu m], are:

- Wadi Hanifa Dam
- Hair Dam
- Laban Dam
- Namar Dam
- Olab Dam

**Salboukh Water Project:** This consists of 16 wells, with a daily capacity of

78,500 cubic yards [60,000 cu m], together with a filtration plant, cooling towers, precipitation tank, a desalination plant and an electricity plant.

**Wasei Water Project:** This consists of 62 wells, with a daily capacity of 261,600 cubic yards [200,000 cu m]. Located 68 miles [110 km] from Riyadh, it comprises integral pumping station, pipelines, overhead and ground tanks, a filtration plant and an electricity plant.

**Bowaib Water Project:** Located 40 miles [65 km] from Riyadh, it consists of 18 wells, with a daily capacity of 104,600 cubic yards [80,000 cu m].

**Jubail Desalination Pipeline Project:** Two pipelines have been built from the desalination plant in Jubail to Riyadh, covering a distance of 290 miles [466 km] and with a total capacity of 210 million gallons [795 million litres] a day.

*Transport and Communications*

Riyadh is also a major transport and telecommunications center, because not only is it the capital city of the Kingdom, it is also located in the center of the national road network, linking it with the north, south, east and west of the country. One of the main roads is the King Fahd Road, built through the city from the north to the south.

Riyadh is linked with Dammam by a railway line starting at King Abdul Aziz Port in Dammam and ending at the Customs area in Riyadh.

The Ministry of Post, Telegraphs and Telephones has completed a number of large-scale telecommunications projects using satellites and coaxial cables.

*Road network in Riyadh*

There are 124 automatic telephone exchanges and 951 lines for coin-operated telephones, as well as post and telephone offices in all parts of the city.

### Industrial Area

The industrial city established in Riyadh is proof of industrial development in the capital. The industrial city covers a total area of 539,443 square yards [451,028 sq m] and contains the largest factory in the Kingdom, employing 1,000 people, working in shifts.

Another industrial city has been set up, plots of land have been distributed and most factories have started production.

### Riyadh Zoo

The Riyadh Zoo dates back to 1957, when it comprised animals presented to the late Kings Abdul Aziz, Saud and Faisal. It was reopened in 1987, after a comprehensive development project. It covers an area of 160,000 square yards [134,000 sq m] and is designed to allow animals open spaces as well as places to sleep at night. It has 40 species of animals. It also contains gardens, rest areas, children's playgrounds, fountains, artificial lakes and other services.

### Major Modern Landmarks

During the period of rapid development, a number of major modern landmarks have been built in the city.

- **King Khalid International Airport**: Located 21 miles [35 km] from the city center, it is built on an area of 87 square miles [225 sq km] and serves 15 million passengers annually. It was designed and equipped to play its part in the city's overall modernization process.
- **The Gulf Bridge Flyover**: This is a three-level bridge, connected to the city's busiest traffic routes. It is 2,400 yards [2,200 m] long and 30 yards [27.5 m] wide and, with its attached tunnels and crossings, is regarded as one of the major landmarks of Riyadh.
- **The Television Complex**: The large television tower, rising 577 feet [176 m] into the air, can be seen from all parts of the city.
- **King Fahd International Stadium**: Established in 1988, it is characterized by its tent-shaped design and a translucent, highly durable and fireproof cover designed to provide maximum weather protection for the spectators.
- **The Foreign Ministry Complex**: With its innovative design, marble-clad walls, floor decorated with fine Arabic calligraphy and surrounded by green gardens and fountains, it houses various departments of the Ministry.
- **The Qasr-al-Hukm Area Development Project**: Qasr-al-Hukm is the office of the governor of Riyadh region. It is located in the center of the city. The project aims to develop the area, but at the same time preserve its historical

monuments, such as Al-Masmak Palace. The Project has included the establishment of commercial and cultural centers, car-parking areas and other facilities.

*The Holy Kaaba in the Holy City of Makkah*

- **King Abdul Aziz Historical Center**
- **National Museum**

## The Holy City of Makkah

The Holy City of Makkah, which lies inland 45 miles [73 km] east of Jeddah, is set in a rugged landscape consisting mostly of solid granite, with rocks sometimes reaching 980 feet [300 m] above sea level. Makkah is enclosed by the Valley of Abraham, which is surrounded by two nearby mountain ranges. The northern range comprises the Al-Falaw and Quagian mountains, while the southern range consists of Abu Hudaidah Mountain to the west, Kuday to the south and Abu Qubais and Khindimah to the southeast. (*Source:* Ibid)

Makkah was the birthplace of the Prophet Muhammad, peace be upon him, and was the city to which he returned after the migration to Madinah in 622 AD. Makkah is the holiest city on earth to Muslims. Five times each day, the world's one billion Muslims, wherever they may be, turn to the Holy City of Makkah to pray. And at least once in their lives, all Muslims who are not prevented by personal circumstance, perform the Hajj, the pilgrimage to

Makkah. Thus each year, the Holy City of Makkah is host to some two million hajjis (pilgrims) from all over the world.

The Holy Mosque in Makkah houses the Kaaba, in the corner of which is set the Black Stone which marks the starting point for the seven circuits of the Holy Mosque which every hajji must complete.

*Education*

Since the emergence of Islam, Mosques have always been regarded as a place of both worship and learning. The Holy Mosque in Makkah has long been the great place of learning. Students were organized in groups where they were taught subjects ranging from interpretation of the Holy Quran to the laws of Shariah and the Prophet's Tradition, by scholars. As the number of students exceeded the capacity of the Holy Mosque, scholars and teachers began organizing classes in their homes. These classes became known as the Katatib in Makkah. Schools were later established by rich Muslims from inside and outside Makkah.

Alsoultiya was the first school to be established, in 1873. The first evening school was Al-Najah, founded in 1931.

In 1925, King Abdul Aziz issued a special directorate to supervise Makkah's education system and later that of the other parts of the Kingdom.

Education in the Kingdom has grown steadily. The number of boys' schools in Makkah and its suburbs, in 1997, was 215 primary schools with 63,679 students, 95 intermediate schools with 27,949 students and 36 secondary schools with 16,096 students. There is also the King Fahd Comprehensive School and Hera Advanced School.

Makkah also has a number of schools for girls and a number of private schools.

There is only one university, the Umm-Al Qura University, the Kingdom's seventh oldest university, established in 1981.

*Health*

Because of Makkah's special status as the Holy City, healthcare is not confined to the city's inhabitants. It also includes comprehensive services for pilgrims during the Hajj and Umra.

Health services in Makkah include the following:
- Ajyad Hospital
- Al-Nour Hospital
- Hera Hospital
- King Abdul Aziz Hospital
- King Faisal Hospital

Health services in the Holy Places include the following:
- Arafat General Hospital

- Jabal Al-Rahma Hospital
- King Abdul Aziz Bridge Hospital
- Mina General Hospital
- Mina Temporary Hospital
- Namirah Hospital

There are also a number of health centers in Makkah and the Holy Places.

### Water

Water resources in Makkah consist solely of underground water in sedimentary silts covering the beds of major valleys in the region. Makkah also gets desalinated water from the Al-Shuaiba plant on the Red Sea coast, with a daily capacity of 148,500 cubic yards [113,500 cu m].

### Roads

A major part of the ringroad around the Holy Haram was completed in 1986 at a cost of SR 1,724,171,000. The project included drilling through Abu Qubais Mountain and building two tunnels, each 650 yards [596 m] long and 12 yards [11.4 m] wide. Two further tunnels were dug through Al-Saba-Banat Mountain, each 195 yards [178 m] long and 12 yards [11.4 m] wide and two flyovers in Ajyad were built. Two tunnels were also built through Qala'at-Ajyad Mountain, each 392 yards [359 m] long and 12 yards [11.4 m] wide. Flyover ramps and ordinary ramps were also built. There are also two more tunnels through the Hindi Mountain and a road link from Shi'b Ali to Shi'b Aamir.

The second phase of the project, at a total cost of SR 3,760 billion is intended to complete the required tunnels and roads to facilitate the flow of traffic for pilgrims.

There are six roads linking Makkah with Jeddah, Taif, Riyadh, Madinah, Al-Lith and Yemen. These roads have been designed to meet the transport requirements of pilgrims, passengers and goods.

### Communications

The Ministry of Post, Telegraphs and Telephones has introduced a special "Pilgrims' Postal Service" which sends post to forty-three Islamic States during the Hajj season. Modern electronic equipment and systems sort, frank, pack and send out the mail.

### Municipality

The Municipality of Makkah has carried out projects for the development and improvement of the city, including road asphalting, supporting walls, flyovers, streetlamps and open landscaped areas, expansion of roads and squares and maintenance of lighting.

*Prophet's Mosque in Madinah*

## The Holy City of Madinah

Madinah is located in the northwestern part of the Kingdom, to the east of the Red Sea and lies 277 miles [447 km] north of the Holy City of Makkah. It is surrounded by a number of mountains, Al-Hujaj, or Pilgrims' Mountain to the west, Sala to the northwest, Al-E'er, or Caravan Mountain to the south and Uhud to the north. It is situated on a flat mountain plateau at the junction of three valleys. As a result, there are large green areas amidst a dry mountainous region.

Madinah is the second holiest city in Islam. It was to Madinah that the Prophet Muhammad, peace be upon him, and his followers, faced by the hostility and persecution of the Makkan merchants, departed in 622 AD – and, when the citizens of Madinah asked the Prophet to live amongst them and to arbitrate in their affairs (an invitation taken to mean rejection of polytheism and submission to the will of the one God, Allah), it was in Madinah that the Islamic era began.

### Education

From the beginning of Islam Madinah has been a center of Islamic thought. Since the reign of King Abdul Aziz, the Saudi Arabian Government has continued to develop Madinah's cultural role by investing in education, public libraries, the Islamic University and the King Fahd Holy Quran Printing Complex.

Today, for boys, there are 210 primary, 109 intermediate and 45 secondary schools and an intermediate teacher training college. For girls, there are six kindergartens, 255 primary, 97 intermediate and 54 secondary schools and 10 teacher training colleges.

### Health

Madinah's healthcare facilities extend not only to the residents, but also to visitors and pilgrims. In addition to temporary health centers, which open during Hajj, and a number of healthcare centers, Madinah has 15 hospitals, including:
- King Fahd Hospital
- Obstetric and Pediatric Hospital
- Badr Charitable Hospital
- Hospital for Infectious Diseases
- Hospital for Chest Diseases
- Eye Hospital
- Medical Care Hospital
- Psychiatric Hospital
- General Hospital

### Water

Madinah gets its water from two sources: artesian wells and desalination plants. Average water consumption is 222,400 cubic yards [170,000 cu m] a day, of which 40% comes from artesian wells and the rest by pipeline from a desalination plant in Yanbu.

The Madinah water tower at Quba'a is a local landmark, elegant in design and with a surrounding landscaped area.

### Roads

Roads link Madinah to other cities and villages in the region. The following are examples of the most important roads:
- The Makkah–Madinah expressway, 261 miles [420 km] long and connecting to the Jeddah–Madinah expressway. It includes twenty-seven overhead intersections, serving a large number of villages along its route. It consists of six lanes, three in each direction, plus a central reservation 22 yards [20 m] wide and a service road on each side, 12 yards [10.9 m] wide.
- The Madinah–Badr-Jeddah road, 311 miles [500 km] long. This runs southwest and leads to the city of Yanbu and the west coast.
- The Madinah–Riyadh Expressway, 620 miles [1,000 km] long and passing through the central area of Qassim.

*Madinah–Tabouk road*

- The Madinah–Tabouk road, 620 miles [1,000 km] long and running north-wards to link up with the road leading to Jordan and Syria.

  Main roads and ringroads have been built around Madinah to allow traffic to avoid the city.

  Madinah airport lies 7.5 miles [12 km] northeast of the city.

### Communications

The Ministry of Post, Telegraphs and Telephones provides services for pilgrims and visitors. There are more than 96,540 automatic telephone lines, 42,000 mobile telephone lines and 400 public and private telex machines.

### Municipality

To ensure that every part of Madinah has its own green open spaces, a program of landscaping and garden construction has been undertaken. More than sixty gardens have already been built, with lighting, children's playgrounds and decorative structures.

The municipality of Madinah has also preserved and maintained the historical sites which relate to the events of the early days of Islam. These are the following:

- The Prophet's Mosque, which serves as the spiritual and physical heart of Madinah.
- The Mosque of Quba'a, the first Mosque "founded on piety". Under the orders of King Fahd, this Mosque has been expanded from an area of 1,555 square yards [1,300 sq m] to 6,000 square yards [5,000 sq m].
- The Sayyid Al-Shuhada, or "Master of Martyrs" area, including the Uhud and Al-Rumat mountains where the battle of Uhud took place between Muslims and the pagans.

- The Al-Qiblatain Mosque, where God ordered the Prophet Muhammad, peace be upon him, to start praying in the direction of the Holy Mosque in Makkah.

There are also a number of other Mosques in Madinah, occupying a special place in the history of Islam.

## Jeddah

The Red Sea port of Jeddah is a bustling, thriving city. Its location on the ancient trade routes and its status as the seaport and airport for hajjis visiting the Holy Cities, have ensured that Jeddah is the most cosmopolitan of all Saudi Arabia's cities.

By the end of the 1970s, the population of Jeddah was estimated to be close to 1 million. By 1986, the estimated population was 1.4 million. With an estimated growth rate in excess of around 16%, the population by 1993 was likely to have passed the 2 million mark.

The extraordinary growth of Jeddah, demanded by the Kingdom's development programs, has been achieved in a remarkably short period. (The expansion of the seaport's capacity is a case study of what can be achieved if the will, the management and the resources are available.) At the same time, aesthetic considerations have not been ignored. Jeddah now boasts some of the most beautiful examples of modern architecture in the world. Tree-lined avenues and the generous distribution of bronze sculptures attest to the success of the city's beautification program.

*Arabic calligraphy inspired by a verse from the Holy Quran*

### Education

There are 256 primary, 129 intermediate and 61 secondary schools for boys. For girls, there are 206 primary, 97 intermediate and 66 secondary schools.

The King Abdul Aziz University is also located in Jeddah. It was the third university to be established in the Kingdom and now has ten colleges.

### Health

Jeddah has a total of 85 State and private hospitals and clinics. The most important ones are the following:
- King Fahd Hospital
- Jeddah Central Hospital
- The Eye Hospital
- Obstetric and Pediatric Hospital
- The Quarantine Hospital

- King's Port Hospital
- Al-Shatie Hospital
- Obstetric, Maternity and Child Care Center
- Al-Thagr Hospital
- Red Sea Hospital
- King Khalid Hospital and Medical City, affiliated to the National Guard
- King Fahd Armed Forces Hospital

There are also 28 private hospitals and 108 private clinics, some of which are run by Saudi Arabian Airlines.

*Water*

Providing adequate water for Jeddah was a major problem for the city for many centuries. Jeddah was supplied with water from Wadi Fatima, east of Jeddah. Water was collected from six springs at Wadi Fatima and then transferred to fixed tanks near Abu Shuaib to be filtered, before being carried by pipeline to a reservoir 6 miles [9 km] from Jeddah.

The rapid expansion of Jeddah and the increasing population made it important to find new water resources. It was decided to bring water from Wadi Khalis, 60 miles [97 km] north of Jeddah.

In 1969, the Kingdom started using the latest techniques of saline water conversion. In 1970 a dual-purpose desalination plant was built in Jeddah. This produces 5 million gallons [18.9 million litres] of desalinated water and 50,000 kilowatts of electricity. Jeddah's increasing water consumption led to expansion projects, until daily production reached 88.5 million gallons [335 million litres] and 840 megawatts of electricity.

*Roads and Transportation*

A program for building an integrated road network, serving both the new and old areas of the city, has been completed. The program included building the north–south road which links up with the Kingdom's national road network and the east–west roads which link with the city's internal roads. There are

broad bridges, highways, ringroads, arterial roads, roads through residential *A view of Jeddah*
areas and some seventy-four flyovers built at intersections.

The Public Transport Company's buses serve many of the city's residents.
There are also air-conditioned buses running between Jeddah, Makkah, Taif
and Madinah.

*Jeddah's Corniche*

The King Abdul Aziz International Airport was the first international airport to be built in the Kingdom. The Airport is built on an area of 40.5 square miles [105 sq km] and is divided into three air terminals: the domestic terminal, the international terminal (used by 40 international airlines) and the pilgrims' terminal. The pilgrims' terminal has been built to resemble an Arab tent and has won an international award as an example of innovative, advanced engineering. The Airport has been built to handle ten million passengers annually.

Jeddah Islamic Port is the largest port in the Kingdom for the transportation by sea of passengers and goods. As Jeddah expanded, the Port played an essential role in handling million of tons of material. The Port was fully reconstructed to include forty quays able to handle all sorts of goods, as well as pilgrims arriving by sea.

*Communications*

Jeddah is a major telecommunications center because of its commercial, industrial and cultural importance and its role in providing services to the pilgrims. There are in excess of 320,000 telephone lines.

*Municipality*

The redevelopment of Jeddah has taken place under a phased plan focused on maintaining the city's traditional patterns of architecture and, at the same time, improving, refurbishing and providing better lighting for the city.

There are now more than 335 public parks in Jeddah. The total length of tree-lined streets is more than 230 miles [370 km]. There are more than 66,000 lampposts in the city and there are wholesale markets for vegetables, fruit, sheep and cars.

Jeddah's Corniche, or sea front, is one of the city's most important achievements and is a major attraction for visitors to Jeddah. The Corniche was built in three parts: the northern coast, the southern coast and Sharm Ubhor.

The northern part was built first, to serve as a park for the city's residents. It was carefully landscaped to take advantage of the nature of the terrain and allow the best possible views of the sea and the way sunlight is reflected on it. Seats were scattered along the Corniche to provide comfortable resting and viewing places.

The southern part was built next, after filling the shallow ravines up to 22 miles [35 km] to the south.

Sharm Ubhor, to the north of the city, is characterized by its deep water. The Corniche has been extended to run parallel to the south beach of Sharm Ubhor to accommodate numerous picnic sites.

The General Presidency of Youth Welfare contributed to the project by building a Youth Welfare Center at Al-Ruwais. There are also parks, children's playgrounds, restaurants, drinking kiosks and recreation areas.

*Left: Ubhor Beach, Jeddah*
*Overleaf: A Mosque in Jeddah*

*King Fahd Fountain, Jeddah*

One of the most distinctive nighttime sights of Jeddah is the fountain presented by King Fahd to the city. The King Fahd Fountain is the tallest fountain of its kind in the world, the water gushing from sea level to a height of 850 feet [260 m].

Decorative signs have added to Jeddah's beauty. These include Arabic lettering, in particular verses from the Holy Quran, and signs describing the nature of the places where they stand. Signs are designed and put in place only after careful appraisal of the place itself and the surrounding environment so that they form a natural part of the landscape.

## Taif

Taif is located on the eastern slopes of the Al-Sarawat mountains, 5,600 feet [1,700 m] above sea level. It is 55 miles [88 km] from the Holy City of Makkah, 99 miles [160 km] from Jeddah and 560 miles [901 km] from Riyadh. Its cooler temperatures have made it a traditional summer resort for the Holy City of Makkah and Jeddah and, in the summer months, the seat of Government is moved from the dry heat of Riyadh to the more equable climate of Taif.

Taif was one of the first cities to embrace Islam (less than a decade after the

Hijra) and is one of the richest archaeological areas in the Kingdom, famous for having been the site of the Okaz Souk, where Arab poets were wont to hold poetry competitions.

Until 1951, Taif's area was a modest square mile [2.5 sq km]. This area has increased considerably since then, reflecting the general growth of cities in the Kingdom. The State distributed plots of land to citizens free of charge, and the ensuing program of building quickly led to the expansion of the city area. Taif has now become a major economic center, particularly for agriculture and trade.

*Education*

Taif has 34 primary schools, 43 intermediate schools and 4 secondary schools for boys and 13 primary schools, 28 intermediate schools and 3 secondary schools for girls. A branch of Umm Al-Qura University is also based in Taif.

*Water*

Because of its geographical position, Taif is rich in underground water reserves and there are also a number of wells scattered in the outskirts of the city. Water is also brought to the city from the Wadi Araba, 62 miles [100 km] from Taif. In addition, a pipeline from the Al-Shuaiba plant on the Red Sea supplies desalinated water.

*General view of Taif*

*Main street, Taif*

## Roads

Taif is connected with other cities and other regions by a number of asphalt roads, the most important of which are the following:

- Taif–Makkah road, 53 miles [85 km]
- Taif–Riyadh road, 560 miles [900 km]
- Taif–Abha road, 390 miles [630 km]

## General Services

There are 9 general hospitals, 54 post offices and 16 telegraph and telex offices. There are also more than 235 Mosques and five Eid Prayer Mosques.

## Tourist Areas and Resorts

Taif is the center of a number of nearby tourist areas and resorts, including:

- Al-Shefa: one of the Kingdom's most beautiful resorts and only 20 minutes' drive from Taif. 17,000 trees are planted on 21 islands on the road.
- Al-Hada: well-known for its natural beauty, Al-Hada lies 12 miles [19 km] from Taif. More than 60,000 trees have been planted there.

There are about 400 parks in Taif city. These include the following:

- The Municipal Park: comprising 12 parks crossed by "Park Streets", the biggest public park, covering a total area of 469,000 square yards [392,000 sq m]. The parks have been decorated with fountains and other structures.

- Red Shaeeb Park: comprising 19 parks, with a total area of 19,140 square yards [16,000 sq m].
- Al-Radf Park: one of most popular open spaces in Taif, it comprises 18 parks with a total area of 17,460 square yards [146,000 sq m]. At the center of the park is the Eid Prayer Mosque.
- The Green Belt Park: located on the Al-Hada to Al-Shefa road to the east of the city, it comprises 15 parks with a total area of 15,200 square yards [127,000 sq m].
- Al-Nasim Park: includes 18 parks, some of which have been designed in the form of mountain terraces. Here is the home of the Taif Municipal Club.
- Jabajib Dam Park: situated on a hill overlooking Al-Hada Mountain from the south, this park consists of two parks separated by a lake, 8,400 square yards [7,000 sq m] in area, formed by the accumulation of storm water.

Taif also has a number of gardens. The most important ones are the following:

- King Fahd Park: the biggest and most important garden in Taif, attracting a record number of visitors. With a total area of 209,300 square yards [175,000 sq m], it contains children's playgrounds and a lake. The lake boasts an artificial waterfall flowing from one of the hills. There is a Mosque, four large fountains, a graveled road and a lighting system.
- Al-Sadad Garden: a family garden, specially designed to provide a quiet place for family recreation.

*King Fahd Park, Taif*

- Hawiya Public Garden: situated in the suburb of Al-Hawiya, the garden has an area of 90,000 square yards [75,000 sq m].
- Khalediah Mountain and Sariat Al-Motamar Gardens: two mountain gardens, separated by an area planted with trees. These two mountain gardens have a total area of 70,600 square yards [59,000 sq m] and are located to the east of the King Fahd Garden.
- Arabian Peninsula Garden: this garden is located in the district of Qamaria and has the shape of the Arabian Peninsula. It has an area of 44,250 square yards [37,000 sq m] and contains children's playgrounds and decorative structures.

The Taif Zoo has some forty different kinds of animals from various parts of the world, in addition to local rare animals and birds.

### Archaeological Monuments

Taif is rich in archaeological monuments dating back to different pre-Islamic eras. These include ancient writings and drawings; the Souk of Okaz, which played an important role in the history of Arabic poetry; several pre-Islamic fortresses; the Al-Abbas and Alkou Mosques; a number of fortresses built by the Ottomans; and the ancient Wadi Ekrima Dam, with some of its stones bearing ancient inscriptions.

## The Industrial Cities of Jubail and Yanbu

The two industrial complexes, built at Jubail on the Arabian Gulf and Yanbu on the Red Sea by the Royal Commission for Jubail and Yanbu, are the key to the Kingdom's national industrialization plans. These two industrial cities provide the basis for the Kingdom's program to develop hydrocarbon-based and energy-intensive industries. The massive investment in these industrial cities was provided in order for the Kingdom to gain access to the world's petrochemical markets. This route to industrialization exploits the Kingdom's natural advantages in terms of cheap energy and cheap raw materials for petrochemical manufacture.

On 9th September 1975, a Royal Decree was issued, establishing a Royal Commission for Jubail and Yanbu and giving it full responsibility for the planning, construction, operation and administration of all the facilities and utilities required to transform Jubail and Yanbu into modern industrial cities. The commission has an independent budget and special powers to enact administrative and financial laws and regulations. The President of the Commission is King Fahd, who assumed this responsibility in his capacity, at the time, of Crown Prince and Deputy Premier.

Development of basic industries in Jubail and Yanbu is the responsibility of Saudi Basic Industries Corporation (SABIC) and Saudi Aramco.

*Yanbu east–west pipeline construction*

In the context of enhancing the private sector's contribution to the national economy, including the privatization of some activities undertaken by Government agencies responsible for industrial development, the Council of Ministers' Resolution No. 57 has been issued stating the establishment of a Saudi Joint Stock Company for Services at Jubail and Yanbu industrial cities.

## Jubail Industrial City

The infrastructure of the industrial city of Jubail extends to an area of 397 square miles [1,030 sq km]. At the end of 1999, the population was estimated to be around 101,000. It is envisaged that by the year 2010, the city will accommodate 290,000 inhabitants.

### Civil Works

By the end of 1999, Jubail was ready to accommodate more basic, secondary and support industries. Vast areas of land were levelled, filled-in and compacted. Residential districts have been established to accommodate administrators, engineers and workers. So far, 11,416 residential units have been built, of which about 7,449 housing units have been constructed by the private sector. Other infrastructure facilities such as water, sewage, electricity, road, medical and education facilities have also been completed.

The total capacity of the water desalination plants, operated by the Royal Commission and the Saline Water Conversion Corporation, is 578,000 cubic yards [442,000 cu m] per hour. The length of the primary water network is currently 486 miles [782 km] and the capacity of the sanitary and industrial waste-water treatment plant is 148,700 cubic yards [113,700 cu m] per day. This includes the industrial waste-water plant with a capacity of 54,540 cubic yards

*King Fahd inaugurating Al-Fanateer Hospital, Jubail*

[41,700 cu m] per day and the sanitary treatment plant with a capacity of 94,170 cubic yards [72,000 cu m] per day. The network of sewage pipelines extends to 403 miles [648 km].

The Royal Commission has installed an electricity grid network 795 miles [1,279 km] in length. SCECO-East is responsible for power supplies. A network of 60,000 telephone exchange lines with a total length of 230 miles [370 km] has also been completed and currently 22,163 telephones are in operation.

There are 488 miles [786 km] of main and express roads. An airport has been built which includes 5,560 square yards [4,650 sq m] of terminals and other facilities. There are 23 berths in the King Fahd Industrial Port.

Medical facilities – which include two hospitals, with a 416-bed capacity, augmented by three dispensaries and clinics and two primary healthcare centers, are now in operation. Thirty-seven Mosques, apart from 10 Jamia Mosques, have also been constructed.

The industrial college of Jubail has been built for the training of Saudi manpower. The college is able to train 1,200 people a year. In 1999, 816 students graduated from this college. Education for both boys and girls is well catered for, including 19 kindergarten, 15 primary schools, 5 intermediate schools, 4 secondary schools and 1 school for non-Saudis.

*Industrial Development*

There were seventeen basic industrial plants operating in Jubail by the end of 1999. All of these plants are capital-intensive by nature. It is estimated that by the year 2010, these industries will provide 107,000 new jobs. Currently they utilize natural gas, which was previously flared off without any economic return. The gas will continue to be utilized as fuel and as a primary input in the steel, aluminum, plastic and fertilizer industries.

The industries at Jubail can be divided into three categories:

Basic industries: these are undertaken by SABIC and Saudi Aramco. Seventeen basic industrial plants have already been completed and are currently in operation. A further eight are in the study and planning phase.

Secondary industries: these industries are established by the private sector and depend on products from basic industries. Sixteen plants are currently in operation, three other projects are under construction and another eighteen projects are in the study and planning phase.

Supporting and light industries: these plants are established and operated by the private sector and manufacture products which are needed by other industries or by housing projects during the construction stage or for operations and maintenance activities. Currently there are 100 such plants in production at Jubail, 29 plants are under construction and another 42 plants are in the study and planning phase.

## Yanbu Industrial City

Yanbu Industrial City and its modern residential facilities cover an area of 31 square miles [80 sq km]. By the end of 1999, the city was able to accommodate 72,740 residents. It is envisaged that by the year 2010 the city will have a population of 150,000.

Construction work for Yanbu has been completed to accommodate the basic and secondary industries.

*Civil Works*

The following infrastructure projects had been completed by the end of 1999.

Workers' residential areas including housing and recreation facilities and 11,177 family housing units have been constructed.

The city has a storage capacity of 523,000 cubic yards [400,000 cu m] of potable water and water for industrial purposes; a potable water distribution network of about 330 miles [530 km]; a sewage treatment facility able to process some 35,300 cubic yards [27,000 cu m] a day; industrial waste treatment plants able to handle 31,390 cubic yards [24,000 cu m] a day; and a sewage network of 330 miles [530 km]. The Royal Commission has also set up desalination plants with a total capacity of 523,000 cubic yards [400,000 cu m] an hour.

In addition, electric power generation capacity has been increased to 423 megawatts. An electrical distribution network, 346 miles [557 km] in length, has also been laid.

A 342-bed hospital and four dispensaries have been completed.

An airport with a 2-mile [3.2 km] runway and 4,800 square yards [4,000 sq m] of terminals and facilities has been completed.

A road network of 279 miles [449 km] has also been laid.

The following facilities have been established and are now fully operational:

- A telephone network of 30,000 telephone lines (now transferred to the Ministry of Post, Telegraphs and Telephones).
- Twenty-two berths in the industrial port have been completed.
- Sixteen Mosques, as well as 9 Jamia Mosques, have been built.
- Five elementary, 13 primary, 4 intermediate, 2 secondary schools and 1 international school have also been established.
- Yanbu Industrial College has been built to accommodate 1,000 students. By the end of 1999, 618 students had graduated.

*Industrial Development*

The industries at Yanbu industrial city are divided into three categories:

Basic industries: these industries are undertaken by SABIC and Saudi Aramco. Eight basic industrial plants have been established and are now in operation. One new plant is under construction and one plant is in the study and planning phase.

Secondary industries: these industries are established by the private sector and depend on the basic industries. Eleven plants are in operation, two plants are under construction, one plant is in the study and planning stage.

Supporting and light industries: these plants are established and operated by the private sector and manufacture products which are utilized by other industries or the housing sector during the construction stage or for operation and maintenance activities. There are currently 33 plants in operation, three plants under construction and another two in the study and planning stage.

**Abha**

Abha lies in the Asir region, in the southwest of the Kingdom, 7,200 feet [2,200 m] above sea level. It overlooks the steep slopes of the Sarawat mountains to the west and the coastal plains of Tihama and the densely forested Al-Sodah mountains. To the south and southwest lie the mountains and plateaux of Al-Qara'a and Al-Jarrah and to the east and north are agricultural plateaux and plains. Abha is approximately 5.4 square miles [14 sq km] in area. With a growth rate of 4%, the population stands at 160,000.

The headquarters of the Asir Governorate is based in Abha, its jurisdiction

*A tourist site in Asir region*

covering an area of 154,450 square miles [400,000 sq km], inhabited by over one million people.

## Education

In 1936, the Al-Saudia Primary School in Abha was the first school established in the Asir region.

Today for boys, there are 17 primary and intermediate and 4 secondary schools, 1 teacher training college, 3 Holy Quran teaching schools and the Al-Noor Institute in Abha. There are also 24 primary, 4 intermediate and 2 secondary schools for girls, in addition to a health institute, a Holy Quran school, a needlework center and a nursery and a kindergarten.

The Imam Muhammad bin Saud Islamic University in Riyadh has set up an Islamic Law College and an Arabic Language and Islamic Law College in Abha. The King Saud University in Riyadh has also set up a teacher training college, a school of medicine and a women's teacher training college.

## Health

Abha has the following health facilities:
- Asir Central Hospital, with 574 beds
- The Tuberculosis Hospital, with 100 beds
- The Psychiatric Hospital, with 50 beds
- Abha General Hospital, with 300 beds
- Four primary health centers
- Four private dispensaries
- Malaria and Bilharziasis Prevention Center

*Abha Dam*

## Water

The growth of the city has led to an increase in water consumption in Abha. In addition to abundant underground water, there are a number of dams in various locations in Asir. Among these is the Abha Dam, with a storage capacity of 3,139,000 cubic yards [2.4 million cu m].

Desalinated water is also supplied by the Al-Shaqiq desalination plant on the Red Sea.

## Roads and Transport

Abha, in the southern part of Saudi Arabia, is a focal point on the road network and, through the network, is joined to every other part of the Kingdom. The most important road connections are the following:

*Tunnel on Abha–Baha road*

*Children's playground, Abha*

- Taif road, 350 miles [562 km] long
- Jizan road, 124 miles [200 km] long
- Khamis Misheit–Najran road, 236 miles [380 km] long
- Jeddah coastal road, 454 miles [730 km] long
- Wadi al-Dawasir road, 217 miles [350 km] long

There is also the Tihama chain of various mountain descents, crossing the rugged highlands and separating the coast from the inland areas.

Abha airport is the Kingdom's fourth airport, in terms of volume of air traffic. In 1978, the airport was expanded to include runways to accommodate large Jumbo jets and aircraft maintenance workshops.

### Municipality

In 1977 a detailed development plan for Abha was drawn up and it had been implemented by 1983. The city's tourist areas have been developed to attract summer visitors. Comprehensive asphalting, paving, lighting and landscape projects have been carried out, appropriate to Abha's status as the capital of the Asir region. Modern meat, fruit and vegetable markets were built and an industrial area was set up to include maintenance, repair and manufacturing workshops.

### Parks and Gardens

Because of Abha's beautiful location, a number of parks have been established to attract summer visitors. All these parks form part of the Asir National Park, completed by the Ministry of Agriculture and Water in 1980 and covering an area of over 1 million acres [450,000 hectares]. The Asir National Park includes six areas, encompassing the most important landmarks and geographical features. It also provides a natural habitat for animals, birds and plants native to the Kingdom.

There are also other parks, among them the Al-Jarra, Al-Sahab, Wadi Al-Mahalah and Al-Saqf parks. The city also has a number of gardens.

*Other Services and Activities*

The General Presidency of Youth Welfare has set up a sports city in Abha, including a stadium, an indoor gymnasium and other sports facilities. In

addition, there is a youth hostel, a youth training center and administrative centers for sports and cultural clubs. A branch of the Saudi Society for Culture and Arts is located in Abha.

The Ministry of Information has set up a color television station, a TV transmission center and a radio station transmitting on medium wave and FM.

Because of the abundance of water and fertile soil, agriculture is the main occupation in Abha but there are also industrial and commercial activities in the region.

## Baha

The Baha region is in the southwest of the Kingdom, 7,054 feet [2,150 m] above sea level. Its western border is only 12 miles [20 km] from the Red Sea. The 931 villages in the Baha region are often located very close to each other, with distances not exceeding a half mile [1 km].

The total population of the Baha region is estimated at 332,157, with an annual growth rate of 5%.

*Education*

There are 168 primary, 61 intermediate and 29 secondary schools including morning, night and religious Shariah schools for boys.

For girls, there are 250 primary, 107 intermediate and 49 secondary schools, in addition to 10 teacher training institutes, an intermediate college, 4 kindergartens and 3 nurseries.

*Health*

The King Fahd Hospital was the first hospital in Baha, built in 1981. The Hospital was built after a visit by King Fahd, who ordered the necessary finances to be allocated to the building of a hospital. The Hospital now has 355 beds.

There are currently eight hospitals in Baha. Among these are the following:

- The Baljurashi Public Hospital
- The Galwah General Hospital
- The Convalescence Hospital
- The Physiotherapy Center
- The Mendaq Hospital

*Al-Baha Descent*

There are also 81 health centers, 8 developed health centers, a health institute for boys, 2 obstetric centers, a center for medical education and training and separate centers for preventing bilharziasis and malaria.

### Roads

Baha is connected to the surrounding villages through a network of roads linked to important locations. These include the following:

- The Baha–Al Aqiq-Jarab road, 57 miles [92 km]. Baha airport is 22 miles [36 km] from Al Aqiq.
- The Baha–Al Hojrah road, 67 miles [108 km], running westward and meeting the coastal road leading to Makkah.
- The Taif–Abha-Jizan road, 468 miles [753 km], considered one of the most important roads, connecting three regions. This road is characterized by hundreds of bridges and tunnels. It took eleven years to complete and cost SR 1.602 million.
- The Taif–Baha road, also known as the Tourist Road, serves a large number of villages.
- The Makkah–Jizan road, also known as the Coastal Road, links Baha with the Red Sea through the mountainous Baha Descent, and is one of Tihama's twelve known mountainous descents.
- The Baha Descent starts at the town of Baha and extends 15.5 miles [25 km] to Al-Mikhwat village. It passes through a very rough and steep slope covering a distance of 1,560 yards [1,425 m]. It has 64 bridges and 34 tunnels. The descent serves 42,000 inhabitants by facilitating travel between Baha, Jeddah and Makkah.

### Tourism

Because of its unique location, with beautiful scenery and moderate weather, a comprehensive development plan for the promotion of tourism in the Baha region has been prepared.

Other towns in the region have also developed their tourist facilities. There are plans for constructing large national parks and a model tourist village in the region.

### Economic Activities

Baha is well known for its traditional markets which are set up for one month each year. Agriculture, trade and service facilities for tourists are the main economic activities in Baha. Because of its fertile land, a large number of agricultural products are grown in the region, including barley, wheat, corn, potatoes, grapes and clover, which is used in feeding cattle. Attention is also being given to livestock farming of sheep, cattle, goats and poultry.

The trade sector includes wholesalers, retail groceries and services in connection with tourism.

*Al Baha Motel Frantel*

## Buraidah

Buraidah and its twin town, Unaizah, are located in the Qassim region at the center of the Arabian Peninsula, on the left edge of the Wadi Al-Rummah. The distance between Buraidah and the Arabian Gulf to the east is almost equal to the distance between Buraidah and the Red Sea to the west. It stands on a plateau, which slopes slightly from west to east, with some depressions between the hills and sand dunes. Some of these depressions are very fertile agricultural land as a result of underground water which can be extracted from soil covered with limestone and gypsum.

Because it is surrounded by stretches of sand and has low rainfall, Buraidah has a desert climate. It is hot in summer and cold in winter, with relatively low humidity.

There are a large number of Bedouin settlements in the Qassim region, giving Buraidah an above average population growth rate. The population stands at 184,000.

### Education

Before the first school was built in Buraidah (the Al-Tanzimiah School, opened in 1937) education was confined to Mosques, where a number of religious scholars taught reading and writing texts of the Holy Quran and the Prophet's Sayings.

Following the development of education in the Kingdom, the first secondary school in the Qassim region was opened in Buraidah.

Today there are 40 primary, 13 intermediate and 3 secondary schools for boys. There is also the military school; the technology college and the commercial secondary school, both affiliated to the General Organization for Technical Education and Vocational Training; the Al-Noor Institute for the Blind; the Quran College and the Social Sciences College, both affiliated to Imam Muhammad bin Saud Islamic University; the College of Agriculture and Veterinary Medicine (affiliated to the King Saud University); the Holy Quran Memorization school and literacy and adult education schools.

For girls, there are 51 primary, 6 intermediate and 2 secondary schools, 2 teacher training institutes, 5 kindergartens and a nursery, a women's

*Coffee pot sculptures, Buraidah*

college, a sewing center, a Holy Quran Memorization school and literacy and adult education schools.

### Health

The hospitals in the town of Buraidah are the following:
- King Fahd Specialized Hospital (574 beds)
- Buraidah Central Hospital (320 beds)
- The Gynecology, Obstetric and Pediatric Hospital (130 beds)
- Chest Diseases Hospital (50 beds)
- The Psychiatric Hospital (50 beds)
- Twelve primary health centers covering the entire town

### Roads

Because of its location in the center of the Arabian Peninsula, Buraidah is linked to all parts of the Kingdom via the comprehensive road network. The important roads are the following:

- The Buraidah–Riyadh road, 196 miles [317 km]
- The Buraidah–Madinah road, 342 miles [550 km]
- The Buraidah–Hail road, 186 miles [300 km]
- The Buraidah–Unaizah road, 15 miles [25 km]

In addition to agricultural roads linking Buraidah to agricultural areas, there are 30 major roads inside the town and 732 auxiliary roads.

Qassim airport serves the whole region and can receive all types of aircraft used by Saudi Arabian Airlines.

### Economic Activities

Buraidah is well known for its fertile land and abundant water. It contributed to the Kingdom's drive for development of wheat production which was so successful that Saudi Arabia not only achieved self-sufficiency but also produced a large surplus. Buraidah also produces more than twenty types of dates, in addition to vegetables, fruit and fodder. It has several poultry and dairy farms.

Commercial activities complement agricultural activities in Buraidah. A chamber of commerce and industry was established in Qassim to care for the welfare of traders and industrialists and to cope with the region's flourishing commercial activities.

An industrial estate was also constructed in the Qassim region, 4 miles [7 km] south of Buraidah. The estate accommodates fifty factories, which produce clay bricks, plastics, gases, synthetic sponges, aluminum and furniture. There are other factories producing cement, construction material and carbonated drinks.

### Municipal Services

The Buraidah municipality covers an area of 123 square miles [320 sq km], including the town of Buraidah and 24 villages. The most important projects carried out are the following:

- Buraidah Water Treatment Plant: constructed at a total cost of SR 49,388,000, it consists of two underground tanks with a total capacity of 209,000 cubic yards [160,000 cu m], 20 water filters with a capacity of 260 cubic yards [200 cu m] and seven pumping stations with a capacity of 817 cubic yards [625 cu m] each.
- The Camel and Cattle Market: has complete facilities for the wholesale of camels and cattle and cost SR 20,292,249.
- The Central Market: located at the center of the town, it comprises a

*Opposite: Buraidah Water Tower*

*Traditional house, Qassim*

building for selling meat and fish with canopies for the sale of fruit and vegetables, health utilities and car parks. It cost SR 13,898,749.

- Buraidah General Park: located on the Buraidah–Madinah road, it covers an area of 12 acres [5 hectares] of landscaped land and includes swimming pools, overhead water tanks, fountains, artificial waterfalls, buffet services, children's playground, basketball court, rest places and car parks. It cost SR 5,397,600.

- Improvement and Beautification: three phases of a project for the improvement and beautification of the town and its streets have been completed and work on the fourth phase has started. The three phases cost SR 144,790,995.

The King Khalid Urban Center is one of the modern urban installations in Buraidah, on land covering 32 acres [13 hectares]. It includes an open space for official and popular celebrations and two buildings. The first building has a large conference hall, three smaller halls and a spare hall, which may become an exhibition hall or a museum. The second building's ground floor is used as offices and the first floor is used as residential units. The Center also boasts a stage with room for 500 people, a rest room and a lounge. It cost SR 65,251,207.

The Prince Abdullah Sports Center in Buraidah is one of its most important landmarks. Built by the General Presidency for Youth Welfare on an area of 40 acres [16 hectares], it contains all the required facilities and playing grounds, in addition to a football stadium with a capacity of 30,000 spectators.

Buraidah Water Tower is another prominent landmark, with its wonderful design, visible from everywhere in town. The Tower is built 3 miles [5 km] from the water treatment plant and, with its landscaped surroundings, covers a total area of 12 acres [5 hectares]. The water tank on top of the Tower has a capacity of 10,460 cubic yards [8,000 cu m]. The Tower consists of three floors, the first floor linked with the tank's pipes, the second floor containing ventilation and air-conditioning equipment, employees' offices, cafeterias and service utilities and the third floor contains the main reception hall, with a balcony for viewing the town. This balcony contains four fountains, above which is a closed dome. The area around the Tower is landscaped and there is an artificial lake. A warning system in the Tower operates when water is too low or too high. The project cost SR 60 million.

## Unaizah

Unaizah is located 200 miles [320 km] northwest of Riyadh and in the southwestern part of the Qassim region. It covers an area of 870 square miles [2,256 sq km]. The region's population is 99,000, of which 68,125 people reside in the town of Unaizah.

### *Education*

Because of its position in the Arabian Peninsula and in the Qassim region, Unaizah had for several centuries occupied an important position in terms of scientific, trade and social interaction and was a cultural and commercial center.

In 1929, the Saleh bin Saleh School, opened – one of the Kingdom's first schools. It was renamed King Abdul Aziz School in 1937.

By 1997, in the town of Unaizah, there were 64 primary, 29 intermediate and 11 secondary schools for boys. There was also the College of Economics and Administration and a religious institute.

The first girls' school was opened in 1960. By 1997, there were 5 nurseries, 52 primary schools, 24 intermediate schools and 10 secondary schools. In addition there was an intermediate college, a sewing center, literacy and adult education schools and a health institute for women.

### *Health*

The following are the hospitals and health centers in Unaizah:
- Unaizah General Hospital
- Infectious Diseases Hospital
- Psychiatric Hospital
- Gynecology, Obstetric and Pediatric Hospital
- Unaizah New Hospital
- Eight primary health centers

### *Roads*

The Ministry of Communications' projects for asphalted roads, bridges and agricultural roads in the Qassim region were:

*A resort in the eastern region*

1. Connecting the towns and villages of the Qassim region by major roads and auxiliary roads to facilitate transport of agricultural products between them.
2. Linking the region's roads with the Kingdom's major road network.
3. Building asphalted and paved agricultural roads in all parts of the region, where needed.

*Economic Activities*

The agricultural sector developed rapidly in Unaizah, encouraged by the Government's program of reclaiming land, distributing it free to farmers and providing loans and support to the farmers. In addition to the five known types of wheat, Unaizah also produces barley, sorghum, clover, summer and winter vegetables and several types of fruit, including dates.

There are also a number of fish farms in Unaizah, using various methods of farming, and producing an average of 700 tons of fish annually.

Imports and exports form the major part of the trade sector in Unaizah, with retail traders moving from one village to another.

In addition to some traditional industries, like the manufacture of gold and silver jewelry, Unaizah also produces building materials, metal works and foodstuffs.

## Dammam

A decade ago, Dammam, the capital of the eastern region, was a separate city, but it was so close to Khobar and Dhahran that it took only a few minutes to travel from one city to another. Developments in the Kingdom linked the three cities into what is known as the Dammam Area, run by a single municipal administration. The population of the whole area is estimated at 350,000.

The Dammam Area is located in the eastern region, surrounded by the Arabian Gulf to the north, east and south and by the Dahna Desert in the west. The climate is generally hot in the summer and moderate in other seasons of the year, with an average annual temperature of 77 degrees Fahrenheit [25 degrees C].

The area consists of plains of sand, constantly shifted by winds, and salty expanses of land. These saline areas are made up of silt and muddy sand and completely cover the tidal area and the peninsula east of the Dawhat Zalum Gulf, better known as the Half Moon Bay. The area is rich in shallow underground water. This water has leaked into the Al-Hasa oasis, forming the famous Um Sabaa springs in Al-Hasa and the springs on Tarout Island.

### Education

There are 28 primary, 11 intermediate and 3 secondary schools for boys. For girls there are 42 primary, 10 intermediate and 7 secondary schools.

There are also women's institutes, needlework schools, literacy schools, an industrial institute, a secondary commercial school and a vocational training center.

The King Faisal University in Al-Hasa has set up two colleges in Dammam, one for medicine and medical sciences, and the other for architecture and planning. There is also an intermediate teacher training college, a mathematics and science center and for women, two science colleges and an arts college.

### Health

Dammam has a 402-bed central hospital, a 42-bed tuberculosis hospital, a 261-bed maternity and pediatric hospital, a 300-bed private hospital and a psychiatric hospital. There are also 13 primary health care centers and dispensaries.

### Water

The Dammam Area depends on underground water. Water is also provided by the Al-Azizia desalination plant, with a capacity of 248,500 cubic yards [190,000 cu m] a day.

*Roads and Transport*

Because of the urban and economic importance of the Dammam Area, a modern network of roads has been built to link the area to nearby cities and to other road networks.

The most important roads are the following:

- Dammam–Abu Hadria road, 100 miles [160 km]
- Dhahran–Ras Tanura road, 56 miles [90 km]
- Dammam–Qatif road, 14 miles [23 km]
- Dammam–Abqaiq road, 56 miles [90 km]
- The Half Moon Bay road, 22 miles [35 km]
- Dammam–Riyadh road, 236 miles [380 km]

On 11th November 1947, a 349-mile [562 km] long railway line from Dammam to Riyadh via Hofuf, Haradh and Kharj linked the eastern and central regions. The railway was completed in 1951 and was opened by King Abdul Aziz. The railway has continued to grow and its rolling-stock now comprises 43 locomotives, 58 passenger coaches and 1,562 freight wagons. There are also cranes, maintenance equipment and tools and a complete workshop for repairing and manufacturing spare parts. Two trains leave Dammam and Riyadh each day, carrying about 1,000 passengers and 70–80 freight wagons.

The General Railway Corporation has also built a customs terminal in Riyadh so that goods containers bound for the central region can be transferred direct from Dammam to customs in Riyadh to speed up clearance procedures. The Corporation has also built a second railway track from Dammam to Riyadh via Hofuf, cutting the journey time from seven to four hours.

There are several airports in the eastern region but the economic and urban developments of the last decade have highlighted the need for an international airport. King Fahd International Airport was built using the expertise of the Civil Defense International Projects Department at the Ministry of Defense and Aviation. The Airport lies 31 miles [50 km] from Dammam city and 40 miles [64 km] from Jubail Industrial City and meets the requirements of the whole of the eastern region, for both domestic and international flights. It is the Kingdom's largest airport in terms of area and facilities, covering 293 square miles [760 sq km].

With the Kingdom's rapid development, Dammam's King Abdul Aziz Seaport was expanded to become the main eastern sea outlet. It has quays to handle a wide variety of ships. Its facilities include 56 multi-purpose cranes, 8 container lifts, 524 fork-lifts, 168 mobile cranes, 28 container carriers, a quay 1,750 yards [1,600 m] long for small ships, a quay for fishing boats and an elevator for 1,500-ton ships, pollution disposal facilities, a water desalination plant with a daily capacity of 1,180 cubic yards [900 cu m] and a training center. The ship repair dock was built at a cost of SR 797 million and was opened by King Fahd on 13th March 1984.

*Economic Activities*

Economic activities in the three cities of the Dammam Area concentrate on agriculture, industry and commerce.

Cattle and poultry farms produce enough meat, milk and eggs to meet most of the area's requirements.

Dammam is one of three industrially developed cities (the other two are Riyadh and Jeddah). The State-owned oil industry has improved the living standards throughout the eastern region. Other industries include quarrying, aluminum, fertilizers, petrochemicals, fiberglass, asbestos, rubber, metal structures, chemicals, dairy products, industrial gases and air conditioners.

The King Abdul Aziz Airport and the Riyadh–Dammam railway have contributed to the development of trade and services in the Dammam Area. There are a number of first-class hotels and branches of the Kingdom's major banks.

*A Mosque in King Fahd Park, Dammam*

*Municipal Services*

The Government has given special care to the landscaping and improvement of the city and its surroundings. High priority has been given to the preservation of the city's heritage and ensuring that its architecture is compatible with its heritage.

Because of its coastal location, recreational and tourism facilities have also been developed. Beaches have been developed to include chalets, motels, camping areas and mooring for small boats. The Saudi Hotels Corporation has built a tourist area in the southern part of the Half Moon Bay beach. There are more than twenty-seven public gardens in the Dammam Area and the Eastern Province Seafront is one of the most important landscaping and recreational projects in the Dammam Area, stretching from Half Moon Bay to Tarout Island.

The biggest park in the Kingdom, the King Fahd Park, is in Dammam. Its lawns cover an area of 326,500 square yards [273,000 sq m] and its colored ceramic-covered flowerbeds cover a total area of 74,150 square yards [62,000 sq m]. The Park has 9,000 trees, 2,400 palm trees, 23,000 green shrubs and a computer-operated drip irrigation system. The Al-Khayyam restaurant, covering an area of 11,360 square yards [9,500 sq m] is the largest building in the Park. The most important building is the Mosque, designed in the shape of a dome and covering an area of 360 square yards [300 sq m]. It has a unique minaret that is 100 feet [30 m] high and is surrounded by lawns and paved areas.

In addition to various sports activities in Dammam, the General Presidency for Youth Welfare has established a coastal center at the Half Moon Bay beach, consisting of halls for various sports. It also has a 7,000-seat theater, a swimming pool, outdoor volleyball and tennis courts and a social club.

### Dhahran

Dhahran is an important city and part of the Dammam Area. It is known for three urban landmarks – the headquarters of Aramco (the world's biggest oil company), the Dhahran International Airport and the King Fahd University of Petroleum and Minerals.

The headquarters of Aramco constitutes a complete city in itself, with offices, housing, sport, recreation facilities, as well as schools and a large hospital administered by the company.

The Dhahran International Airport is a major landmark in the eastern region, with its distinguished buildings based on Islamic architecture, combined with modern construction techniques. It was the first international airport to be built in the Kingdom more than twenty-five years ago. Since then, it has developed and has its own water, electrical and sewage treatment plants, together

*King Fahd inaugurating the King Fahd Military Complex in Dhahran*

*King Fahd University of*
*Petroleum and Minerals*

with housing units and support facilities. The international terminal covers an area of 23,900 square yards [20,000 sq m] and the domestic flight terminal covers an area of 5,980 square yards [5,000 sq m]. The Airport is administered by 500 staff, in addition to 2,000 operations and maintenance workers, including engineers, technicians and laborers. The Airport has coped well with the rapid developments in the Kingdom and its area, runways and facilities have been continuously expanded to cope with the steady rise in air traffic.

The King Fahd University of Petroleum and Minerals has the following colleges:
- Engineering
- Applied Engineering
- Science
- Industrial Management
- Environment Design
- Computer Engineering

It also includes a university city, comprising academic and scientific research facilities and residential areas for the staff and students. The university city covers an area of 2.5 square miles [6.5 sq km]. It has more than 100 laboratories and a research institute. The university was the first national foundation to establish a computer center, before computers were introduced into governmental departments and the private sector. There is a comprehensive technology library containing references and sources for teaching, studying and scientific research purposes.

## Khobar

Khobar is the third city located in the Dammam Area, very close to the cities of Dammam and Dhahran. Before the discovery of oil, Khobar was a small fishing harbor, but with the development of the Kingdom's economy, Khobar became the commercial center of the Dammam Area, with many private companies choosing it for their headquarters. The Khobar Seaport has also been developed to handle small ships and passengers and is furnished with administrative buildings and warehouses.

Because of the high integration of the three cities of Dammam, Dhahran and Khobar in the Dammam Area, all social, cultural, industrial and commercial activities in the area cover all the citizens of the three cities.

## Hail

The city of Hail, some 3,215 feet [980 m] above sea level, is located in the Shammar mountain region, just west of the Al-Odairie Valley (also known as the Hail Valley).

Hail extends in the shape of a bow around the Samra'a Mountain. It is in effect surrounded by the Aja Mountain to the west, the Umm-Al-Riqab Mountain to the south and the Shamrah Mountain to the east.

Hail has a continental climate, with temperatures rising in summer and dropping in winter. Its population stands at 100,000, with a 9.9% growth rate.

A comprehensive development plan for Hail has been drawn up, to be implemented by 2005. The major objectives of the plan are the following:

1. Maximum utilization and sound management of the natural resources to achieve the highest possible growth rates, particularly in the field of agriculture and water.
2. Devising construction plans for every part of the region to streamline construction styles and trends in the light of its special development capabilities.
3. Upgrading all public services and the suitable distribution of these services to cover all parts of the region.
4. Completing the region's road network, connecting the city of Hail with its affiliated villages and, at the same time, with nearby cities and the Kingdom's main road network.

### Education

The first primary school for boys in Hail was opened in 1937. Today, Hail has 27 primary, 12 intermediate and 2 secondary schools for boys. It also has a

Holy Quran college, a teacher training institute and a night secondary school.

For girls, there are 2 kindergartens, 25 primary schools, 4 intermediate schools, 2 secondary schools, a Holy Quran college, a teacher training institute, an intermediate college and a sewing center.

### Health

There is a general hospital in Hail, with 208 beds; a pediatric section, with 70 beds; a physiotherapy unit; an obstetric section; and outpatients' clinics. Another general hospital, with 200 beds, is to be built to enhance healthcare in the region. There are also 40 dispensaries and 14 health centers.

### Roads

Hail is linked with the Kingdom's other regions through its airport, located 6 miles [10 km] away.

The most important roads in the region are the following:

- The Hail–Qassim road, 186 miles [300 km], continuing from Qassim to Riyadh (404 miles [650 km])
- The Hail–Madinah road, 336 miles [540 km], continuing to Makkah, Taif and Jeddah
- The Hail–Jubbah road, 65 miles [105 km], the first part of the Hail–Baqaah road
- The Hail–Al Khottah road, 31 miles [50 km], an asphalted agricultural road
- The Hail–Al Rawdhah road, 47 miles [75 km], an asphalted agricultural road

### Economic Activities

The Hail region's economy covers agriculture, trade, services and the beginnings of industry.

Because of fertile soil, abundant water and modern equipment, 80% of employees work in the agricultural sector in Hail. Following King Fahd's directive to achieve self-sufficiency in agriculture, the Hail Agricultural Development Company was established with a capital of SR 300 million. With Government help, the company has recorded very high levels of crop production, especially wheat. The advance of grazing lands around Hail has helped in the expansion of sheep, poultry and dairy farming.

The trade and services sector is also flourishing in Hail, leading to the establishment of a chamber of commerce and industry. There are 190 wholesale organizations, 1,700 retail shops, 529 boutiques for clothing and textiles and 151 organizations for selling industrial products.

The industrial sector has begun to develop in recent years. The municipality has factories producing fertilizer, building material, timber, lampposts, and concrete and aluminum products.

*Other Services*

There are 1,200 Mosques, 34 of which were built by the citizens.

There is a vocational training center set up by the General Organization for Technical Education and Vocational Training. A public library in Hail, with about 17,000 books, cost SR 26 million to build.

The General Presidency for Youth Welfare has built a sports center to supervise youth and sports facilities. There are also branches of all the ministries and governmental departments in Hail.

*Municipal Services*

There are ten municipalities and rural councils in the Hail region. As a result of cooperation between the municipality and its citizens, the Hail region won the first prize for cleanliness among the regions.

Below are some of the municipality's achievements:

- Building a factory for treatment of waste products to convert them into fertilizer, with a total annual capacity of 100 tons. The products of this factory are exported to other regions of the Kingdom.
- There are 30 gardens in the city of Hail and 25 landscaped areas, covering a total area of 430 acres [174 hectares]. There are also many parks.
- 19 fountains, 15 sculptures, 3 artificial waterfalls and 350 playgrounds for children have been built in the gardens.
- 10,000 lampposts have been erected in all parts of the city.
- 15,000 plots of land have been distributed to low-income citizens.
- 25 residential sites have been completed within the framework of the comprehensive development plan.
- A cultural center has been built, which includes a number of halls, a theater, a museum, a library, a conference hall, an exhibition hall and a seminar hall.

*Archaeological Monuments*

Hail is very rich in antiquities because of its links with other civilizations, before and after the birth of Islam. The most important features of antiquity are the following:

- A number of old castles and palaces in Hail dating back to the Ottoman era.
- Yatub: a site of antiquity, 27 miles [38 km] east of Hail. There are Thamudi writings and drawings on its rocks.
- Janein: a large mountain, 37 miles [60 km] east of Hail, containing a natural cave. On its walls there are Thamudi and Amharic writings and drawings of humans and animals.
- Faid: an oasis through which the Zubaida Route passed. Zubaida, the celebrated wife of Haroon Al-Rashid, established this route to serve pilgrims

*Aeref Citadel, Hail*

arriving from Iraq. The oasis contains many lakes, old wells and irrigation canals, plus the ancient Kharash Palace, which was built before Islam.

- Habashi Mountain (also called Al-Azeem, an Arabic word meaning the great site): rich in antiquities including the remains of houses, towers and graveyards dating back more than 4,000 years. Swords and other artefacts have also been discovered there.
- Al-The'ailibi: lying between Al-Azeem and Sumeira'a, it includes lines of stones extending 820 yards [750 m].
- Sumeira'a: 87 miles [140 km] from Hail and 26 miles [42 km] from Al-Azeem. There are many historical monuments in this area, the most important of which is a room 5 feet [1.5 m] above the ground. Islamic coins were also discovered inside some fired clay jars.
- Dayef: a historical site which has Cufic and Thamudi writings and drawings of humans and animals on its rocks.
- Al-Sefen: 22 miles [35 km] from Hail, has Thamudi writings and drawings, graveyards and big circular stones.

Other sites include Rockan, Al-Mu'alag, Al-Soba'an, Al-Mawiyyah, Towrah, Al-Shamli and Ghamrah. All these sites include rocks, graveyards and stones with different writings dating back some 70 centuries.

## Al-Hasa

Al-Hasa's special importance in the Arabian Peninsula dates back to very ancient times when as a crossroads of trade routes, it linked the eastern parts of the Peninsula with Persia, India and the Far East.

*Right: Ibrahim Palace, Hofuf*

*Below: Date palms*

Al-Hasa is the name given to the oasis in the south of the Kingdom's eastern region. It is the biggest oasis in the Kingdom and has fifty villages in its environs.

It is located between the Arabian Gulf coast and the Al-Dahna and Al-Daman deserts and covers an area of 965 square miles [2,500 sq km]. As a dry tropical region, it has only two seasons, a five-month long summer and a cold to moderate winter.

Al-Hasa is an agricultural area, 390 to 525 feet [120–160 m] above sea level, sloping slightly from west to east. Its population of 600,000 is spread over its four cities of Al-Hofuf, Al-Mobaraz, Al-Oyoun and Al-Omran and the fifty villages.

### Education

Al-Hasa now has 42 primary schools, 43 intermediate schools, 12 secondary schools, 4 private institutes and 5 Holy Quran teaching schools.

King Faisal University is based in Al-Hasa. Established in 1974, it is the sixth university to be founded in the Kingdom. The University has made rapid progress and now has faculties of medicine, architecture and planning, agriculture and food, veterinary medicine and animal resources, education and administrative sciences and planning. It also has a number of scientific centers affiliated to it.

## Roads and Transport

In addition to roads linking Al-Hasa's cities and villages, the region is linked to the following places by modern asphalt roads:

- Dammam, 106 miles [170 km]
- Riyadh, 205 miles [330 km]
- Khurais, 120 miles [195 km]
- Qatar, 165 miles [265 km]

All the 50 villages are connected with each other by a network of asphalted roads ranging in length from 3 to 120 miles [6–195 km].

The railway line between Dammam and Riyadh passes through Al-Hasa. There is also an airport, 7.5 miles [12 km] from the city of Hofuf.

Under the plan to develop and improve small ports, the Saudi Ports Authority is developing Al-Hasa's port of Aqir.

## Economic Activities

The economic activities of Al-Hasa consist of agriculture, industry and trade.

Al-Hasa has two million date palms. The dates are packed in a factory with a capacity of 500 tons per day, set up by the Ministry of Agriculture and Water. Rice, sorghum, citrus and other fruits are also very successful crops in this area. There are 200,000 sheep, 50,000 goats, 12,000 heads of cattle and 15,000

*Agricultural products exhibition in Al-Hasa*

camels. Poultry farms have also flourished, with over 100 million eggs and three million chickens produced annually.

The oil extraction and refining industry is the most important primary industry in the area, employing 20% of its workforce. There are two cement factories, a plastics factory, a textiles factory and a number of other industries and workshops.

As a result of the economic growth, trade has also flourished in Al-Hasa. There are many hotels and branches of State and privately owned banks, employing about 60% of the total workforce.

### Other Services

Al-Hasa has a general hospital, 8 public dispensaries and 6 private clinics.

It has 62,237 telephone lines and 105 telephone booths.

The General Presidency of Youth Welfare has set up the Prince Abdullah bin Jalawi Sports City, which has eight sports clubs.

### Municipal Services

The municipality has achieved the following:

- Property compensation and road expansion schemes and projects for building new roads in the towns, costing SR 671 million.
- Projects for the construction of new roads in some villages, costing SR 113 million.
- Asphalting, paving and lighting projects in towns and villages, at a cost of SR 594 million.
- Markets, building and garden projects, at a cost of SR 46 million.
- Two survey projects and studies for Al-Hasa's City Hall, costing SR 2.4 million.

### Anti-Desertification Project

Al-Hasa has always suffered from problems of shifting sands. The wind carries tens of thousands of tons of sand which it distributes indiscriminately over people and planted areas. Urgent methods were needed to prevent the destruction of towns and villages. Trees were planted as barriers, which prevented sands from reaching the inhabited areas. By 1984, an area of 34,000 donums was covered by seven million trees. These formed a powerful barrier against the creeping sands over an area of 71,432 donums. Parts of this area have been made into a public park.

### Irrigation and Drainage Project

This project, one of the most important agricultural projects carried out by the Ministry of Agriculture and Water, was launched because of the following geographical factors:

- The large number of springs in the oasis, producing large quantities of water, which flowed across the ground surface without being fully used.
- The desertification, which threatens to destroy these springs.
- The high saline content of the soil because of its proximity to the Arabian Gulf.
- The effect of these factors on agricultural lands, with large areas of land already wasted and other areas threatened with a similar fate.

*Irrigation and drainage project, Al-Hasa*

A scheme was launched to collect and store fresh spring water for distribution to the neighboring areas, to improve agriculture and to introduce new crops. Some 39,500 acres [16,000 hectares] of agricultural land have benefited from this scheme. The project consists of primary, secondary and ancillary collecting channels totalling 930 miles [1,500 km] in length, with a further 930 miles [1,500 km] of drainage channels and three water tanks with a capacity of 49,700 cubic yards [38,000 cu m]. There are also 1,240 miles [2,000 km] of agricultural roads and 45 bridges to facilitate transport between the various parts of the oasis.

## Jazan (or Jizan)

Jazan, also known as Jizan, is located in the southwest of the Kingdom, covering an area of 24,850 square miles [40,000 sq km]. It contains about 4,500 villages and towns, distributed among 39 emirates.

Jazan borders the Red Sea and its mountainous terrain extends for about 186 miles [300 km] from north to south and 30 to 45 miles [50–70 km] from east to west. It includes approximately 100 islands, of which Farasan is the largest and the most famous. It has three natural regions:

1. The fertile plains extending behind the coastal swamps.

   These are fertile because of alluvial deposits brought down from adjacent mountains and valleys and because of frequent floods.

2. Alhazoun district

   This is a region of rich pastures and forests and is subject to frequent flooding. There is also some agricultural land scattered in the mountainous areas.

3. The Mountain district

   This forms part of the Alsarawat mountains, the deep and jagged backbone of the Arabian Peninsula. Among the individual mountains that rise out of it are the Fifa Mountain, 11,000 feet [3,350 m] at its highest peak, and inhabited in spite of its roughness; the Bani Malik mountains; and Alreith, Gais and the Alhashr mountains, ranging between 2,000 and 6,000 feet [610–1,830 m]. Many of the slopes are terraced to support varieties of fruit trees such as banana, custard apple and plum, as well as crops such as wheat and barley.

A number of mineral springs exist in the region, the most famous of which are the following:

- The Hot Spring, located 31 miles [50 km] southeast of Jazan
- Alwagara, located north of Jazan-Alkawia street
- Albuza, located 33 miles [53 km] from Jazan city

The developmental process of the Kingdom has led to expansion of Jazan and an increase in its population.

### Education

The first primary school was opened in Jazan in 1935. With the development of education in the Kingdom, the number of schools and students has seen a sharp increase. By 1996 there were 240 primary, 126 intermediate and 49 secondary schools for boys. For girls, there were 360 primary, 124 intermediate and 52 secondary schools.

There are also teacher training institutes for women, a sewing institute, an intermediate college and literacy schools. There is also a vocational training center for technicians.

### Health

Following a directive from King Fahd, the Government expanded the specialized hospitals and made medication available to everyone. There are also a number of general hospitals, healthcare centers, disease prevention centers and two health institutes for boys and girls.

### Roads and Transport

The most important roads in Jazan are the following:

- The Jazan–Taif mountain road, passing through Abha and Al-Baha
- The coastal road passing through Algunfuza
- The Jazan–Subaya road, 25 miles [40 km] long
- The Jazan–Abu Arish road, 15.5 miles [25 km] long
- The Jazan–Alsamta road, 37 miles [60 km] long

There is also an airport connecting Jazan to other cities in the Kingdom.

Jazan port on the Red Sea is the main gateway for imports from all over the world to the southwestern part of the Kingdom. The harbor has all modern facilities, services and utilities. There are twelve commercial docks in addition to maintenance and fishing docks.

*Economic Activities*

Jazan's traditional economy was based on pearl-diving, fishing and building sailing boats. While diving is decreasing, fishing remains one of the main activities.

Jazan is also one of the Kingdom's richest agricultural regions. In line with the Kingdom's plan to develop self-sufficiency, the Agricultural Bank has helped farmers to extend agricultural plots and learn modern agricultural techniques. Jazan produces millet, wheat, barley, coffee beans, bananas, grapes, plums, lemons, oranges, tamarinds, mangoes, custard apples, papayas and various aromatic plants and flowers.

Jazan was first supplied with piped drinking water in 1947. Continued development has increased the water supply networks to 85, serving Jazan city and 267 villages.

The Wadi Jazan Dam was inaugurated in 1971 by the then Prince Fahd, Deputy President of the Council of Ministers and Minister of the Interior. The dam is 346 yards [316 m] long, 136 feet [41.6 m] high, 14 feet [4.4 m] wide at the base and 10 feet [3.15 m] wide at the top. It has a capacity of 93 million cubic yards [71 million cu m]. An electricity generation station and a water distillation station were also built at the dam.

*Jazan Dam*

*Archaeological Monuments*

The most important ancient features in Jazan are the following:

- Utr City: one of the most famous historic cities in the south of the Arabian Peninsula
- Abu-Arish Tower: an impressive and ancient monument
- Old Jazan City: only some of its walls, its tower and the remains of buildings remain
- Jahfan Mountain: located near Abu-Arish
- Jazan City Tower: the residence of many Turkish rulers and known as "wireless tower"
- Alshrja City

## Jouf

Jouf is located in the northern part of the Kingdom covering a total area of 22,560 square miles [58,425 sq km]. The region comprises plateaux, plains, valleys and fertile agricultural lands. The Jouf region has Skaka as its capital and numbers the renowned Domat-Al-Jandal amongst its towns.

The town of Skaka is located in the northern tip of the Greater Nufud Desert. There are 50 towns and villages affiliated to Skaka. The area is mountainous, with steep slopes in some areas and gradual slopes in others. Skaka has shared in the progress made in other regions of the Kingdom. A new town (New Skaka) was built near the old town, with modern buildings, asphalted roads and large commercial centers. Skaka is known for its traditional industry, especially the hand-woven carpet industry.

Domat-Al-Jandal lies to the southwest of Skaka and is located in a depression 186 miles [300 km] in length, parallel to the Saudi–Jordanian border. It consists of two sectors. The old sector is located in the depression and contains orchards and fields surrounded by mountainous slopes. The new sector is located on a plateau. To the north of this new sector are green fields, water springs and a number of archaeological sites. The town is famous for its swords, daggers, rifles, stone tools (such as hand-mills decorated with inscriptions), carved ornaments and hand-made carpets.

*Education*

The first school in Skaka was opened in 1943, with 60 pupils. There are now 77 primary, 41 intermediate and 19 secondary schools for boys. There are also 15 literacy and adult education schools, intermediate and secondary night schools, an intermediate teaching college and a religious institute.

The first girls' school was opened in 1962. There are now 60 primary, 29 intermediate and 13 secondary schools for girls, in addition to literacy centers and an intermediate college.

*Health*

The first dispensary was built in Skaka in 1937, and was later upgraded to a 200-bed hospital. There is also a psychiatric hospital, two hospitals in Domat-Al-Jandal and one hospital in Tabarjal.

*Water*

Drinking water is available in large quantities from surface and underground sources. This water meets the standards and specifications set down by the World Health Organization and is completely pollution-free.

*Roads and Transport*

The most important roads are the following:
- The Skaka–Ara'er road, 106 miles [170 km]
- The Skaka–Domat-Al-Jandal road, 32 miles [52 km]
- The Skaka–Domat-Al-Jandal–Madinah–Jeddah road, 900 miles [1,450 km]
- The Skaka–Ara'er–Riyadh road, 870 miles [1,400 km]
  Jouf airport, built in 1977, is 16 miles [25 km] from Skaka.

*Economic Activities*

With the help of the Government's program of subsidies to farmers, Jouf has become a leading agricultural region. Palm trees are the main agricultural product, with more than 230,000 trees planted as part of a Government program to boost palm planting. Other agricultural products include wheat, grapes, olives, figs, tomatoes, potatoes and other fruit and vegetables. There are also sheep, goat and poultry farms.

The industrial sector is still very young, as most inhabitants are farmers. There are dairy product plants, blacksmiths and plumbing and maintenance workshops. Stones used for building are produced from a quarry.

The commercial sector includes items like foodstuffs, clothes, cars and spare parts. Five banks have opened branches in Jouf. There are also hotels, restaurants and other facilities in the area.

*Archaeological Monuments*

The history of the Jouf region is very ancient, dating back to the days of the Assyrians. Jouf boasts many antiquities, which have been carefully studied and recorded by the Antiquities Department. These are the following:
- Zaabal Fortress (Zaa'bal Palace): situated on high ground overlooking Skaka, Zaabal Fortress is believed to have been built in the seventh century BC. The fortress is only accessible from one direction.
- Al Sa'ee Hill: the hill overlooks Skaka town and is a relic of the Palmyric-type fortress, surrounded by caves, and including an ancient temple.

*Omar bin Al-Khattab Mosque minaret in Domat-Al-Jandal in Jouf*

- Al-Rajajeel: stone pillars located 14 miles [22 km] south of Skaka, containing unknown writings. It is believed they date back to the fourth century BC.
- Al-Tuwair Fortress: a great rock on which are Thamudi writings dating back to the third century BC, and post-Islamic Arabic writings. Two sites were found near Al-Tuwair, which are believed to be a city buried under sand.
- Omar bin Al-Khattab Mosque: the Mosque is built from stones and is surrounded by the old city of Domat-Al-Jandal.
- Marid Fortress (Marid Castle): built with stones and 1,970 feet [600 m] high, Marid Fortress overlooks the old city of Domat-Al-Jandal from the south. The Fortress has a fence with openings for observation, two high towers, two deep wells and a number of floors.

There are also fossilized trees, fortresses, ceramic pots and at least one buried city.

### Najran

The region of Najran lies in the southwest of the Kingdom and is 3,970 feet [1,210 m] above sea level. The population of the region stands at 424,000, of which 70,000 reside in the city of Najran.

*Najran Fort, Najran*

*Old emirate building, Najran*

### Education

The first official school in Najran was opened in 1943. There are now 183 primary and intermediate schools, 25 secondary schools and teacher training institutes for boys. For girls, there are 157 schools and 60 literacy centers. In addition there are 7 kindergartens, teacher training institutes and a sewing center.

### Health

Najran has the following hospitals:
- King Khalid Hospital
- Najran General Hospital
- The Psychiatric Hospital
- The Tuberculosis and Fever Hospital
- Sharoura General Hospital

There are also 60 primary health-care centers, 6 health units and a branch of the Saudi Red Crescent Society.

*Najran Dam*

### Water

The Najran Valley Dam is 28 miles [35 km] from Najran and has a storage capacity of 111 million cubic yards [85 million cu m]. It is 285 yards [260 m] long and 65 yards [60 m] high and was built at a cost of SR 277 million.

### Roads

A network of roads links Najran to the Kingdom's general road system. These are the following:

- Al-Faisaliyah–Old Najran road, 4 miles [7 km]
- Airport–Al-Faisaliyah road, 14 miles [22 km]
- Sharourah–Al Wadea–Najran road, 230 miles [370 km]
- Najran–Silayel road, 216 miles [347 km]
- Ringroad, 19 miles [30 km]
- Najran–Dhahran Al-Janoub road, 70 miles [112 km]

### Economic Activities

More than half of Najran's inhabitants are engaged in agriculture. Fertile land and abundant water has made it possible to introduce several previously unknown plants into the Kingdom.

Najran is also a major trade and banking center. The main industry is construction. A fully equipped industrial city has been established, where plots have been given to factory owners to build factories that meet the requirements of the city and the region.

*Municipal Services*

A large-scale program was carried out to build parks and plant trees in the city and its surrounding areas. These include the following:

- Najran Park
- Abu Firas Al Hamadani Park
- Ghornata Family Park
- Ashbeelia Park
- Green Valley Park
- Khaled Al-Sudairi Park
- Al-Okhdoud Park
- Al-Fahad Park
- Al-Bouhtori Park
- Old Najran Park and children's playground

## Al-Ola

Al-Ola is a small town, 3,280 feet [1,000 m] above sea level, 236 miles [380 km] north of Madinah and administratively affiliated to Madinah. It is located in a fertile valley between Madinah and the Jordanian border and is surrounded by two ranges of high mountains.

The total area of Al-Ola is 23 square miles [60 sq km], inhabited by about 60,000 people. There are 52 sub-governorates affiliated to the governorate of Al-Ola. One of these, Mada'in Saleh, is renowned for its Nabataean historical monuments.

*Education*

There are 50 primary, 17 intermediate and 2 secondary schools for boys. There are also 10 primary schools, 1 intermediate and a secondary school for girls. In addition there are literacy schools for boys and girls.

*Health*

Two hospitals, one with 50 beds and the other with 100 beds, were established by the Ministry of Health.

*Roads*

The modern asphalted roads link Al-Ola to its surrounding area and to the Kingdom's major road network. These are the following:

- Al-Ola–Khaiber–Madinah road, 236 miles [380 km]
- Al-Ola–Tayma–Tabouk road, 186 miles [300 km]
- Al-Ola–Hail road, 249 miles [400 km]
- Al-Ola–Al-Wajh road, 112 miles [180 km]

*Archaeological Monuments*

Al-Ola has a special historical status, with its many antiquities, some of which date back to the era of the Prophet Muhammad, peace be upon him.

In the old section of Al-Ola, known as Al-Dirah, is the Rock Mosque, where the Prophet Muhammad, peace be upon him, prayed when he passed through Al-Ola. At the center of Al-Dirah is a high mountain, on top of which are the remains of the ancient Umm-Nasser Castle.

In Al-Hijr, there is an old railway station for pilgrims, the Haj Castle and a water wheel used to lift water from a deep well into a large pond located behind it. The site is full of inscriptions.

There are many more archaeological sites in and around Al-Ola, dating back to different historical eras.

## Tabouk

Tabouk is located in the northwest of the Kingdom and has various features which include the following:

- A southern coast, 310 miles [500 km] long. The towns of Deba, Al-Wajh and Omluj, as well as a number of villages, lie on this coast.
- Eastern plains, covering half the region's area and including the region's capital Tabouk, Tayma and a group of villages.
- A range of mountains, separating coastal and interior regions. A number of villages are located in the valleys of this region.

*Education*

The first school in Tabouk was opened in 1941. There are now 156 primary, 79 intermediate, and 31 secondary schools for boys, plus literacy and evening schools. For girls, there are 2 nurseries, 6 kindergartens, 102 primary schools, 45 intermediate schools and 21 secondary schools. There are also Holy Quran Memorization schools, literacy and adult education schools, a women's institute and a sewing center.

*Health*

Tabouk has 9 hospitals and 43 health centers. Among these are the following:
- King Khalid Hospital in Tabouk, 200 beds
- King Fahd Hospital in Tabouk, 120 beds, including a kidney dialysis unit
- Maternity and Children's Hospital in Tabouk, 60 beds
- Al-Wajh General Hospital, 88 beds
- Deba Hospital, 50 beds
- Haql Hospital, 50 beds
- Omluj Hospital, 40 beds

## Roads

*Marble sculpture, Tabouk*

The most important roads in the Tabouk region are the following:

- Tabouk–Madinah road, 419 miles [674 km] long and used by pilgrims from Turkey, Syria, Jordan and Lebanon.
- Tabouk–Halat Ammar road, 62 miles [100 km] long, links Tabouk with the Saudi–Jordanian border.
- Haql–Ras Al-Sheikh Hemayed road, 113 miles [182 km] long, serves a number of towns and villages.
- Al-Sharaf–Bir Bin Harmas road, 71 miles [114 km] long, serving the region's northern villages.
- Coastal road, 382 miles [616 km] long, linking a number of towns and villages to the Red Sea.
- Tabouk–Deba road, 111 miles [178 km] long, shortening the distance between Tabouk and the Red Sea, from four to two hours by car.
- Ringroad, 9 miles [14 km] long, reduces traffic congestion in the town.

## Economic Activities

With an abundance of water supplied from the four desalination plants on Tabouk's coast, and agricultural subsidies from the Government, agriculture

*Overleaf: A view of Omluj, Red Sea coast*

has developed in the region. There are projects for wheat production, sheep breeding, fruit production, roses and poultry and egg production.

The industrial sector is also developing rapidly, with factories for the production of pipes, cement and ironworks.

*Archaeological Monuments*

Tabouk's history dates back to 500 BC. It was known by the name of Taboo, when, with the town of Al-Ola, it was the capital of Al-Ayaneyean. The Archaeological Department has set up a museum in the town to contain all the monuments. It has also decided to protect and renovate the fortresses and historic buildings.

\*\*\*

This survey of the Kingdom's agricultural and industrial development is far from complete but it is sufficient to convey the broad strategic economic aims of the Kingdom under King Fahd and the way in which these aims have been fulfilled. In particular, the survey of cities and towns illustrates the determination of King Fahd to ensure that the benefits of development extend to every corner of the Kingdom and into the home of every citizen.

# KING FAHD AND
# POLITICAL REFORM

IN ANY DISCUSSION of political reform in the Kingdom of Saudi Arabia, we must begin by emphasizing that it is the fundamental assumption of the polity of Saudi Arabia that the Holy Quran, correctly applied, is more suitable for Saudi Muslims than any secular constitution.

This assumption must be viewed in the context of a nation which is completely Islamic. The entire Saudi population is Muslim; the only non-Muslims in the country are foreigners engaged in diplomacy, technical assistance or international commerce. If they are non-Muslims, they may practise the rituals of their religion only in the privacy of their homes. So there is no problem of ethnic, religious or linguistic pluralism or multiculturalism, such as is found in virtually all other developing countries.

Some critics of Saudi Arabia may advance the argument that, since the Holy Quran is almost fourteen centuries old, it does not meet current circumstances, is out of date and should be replaced by a newer form of constitution which would suit the needs and conditions of the modern world better. Such critics fail to recognize that the Holy Quran, which Muslims believe is the word of God, is perfectly able to cope with the events and issues of all times if rightly followed.

Other critics and, indeed, most of the Western media, take it as a premise that the best, if not the only acceptable, form of government is Western-style democracy. Such a view does a gross injustice to a system of government which has survived the test of time and which, in some ways at least, is rather more consensual than the voting systems of the West. Under the Saudi system of government, there is a highly active and highly sophisticated consultative process which provides powerful and continuous input to Government thinking, in terms of both short-term and long-term policies. The concept of the King as an all-powerful autocrat has no place in the Saudi system. It falls to the King to reconcile the interests of all sections of Saudi society and to formulate policies which, while giving the nation the best opportunity to fulfill its potential, will unite what may be on occasions quite disparate interests. It has been an outstanding achievement of King Fahd that, within the framework of the Islamic constitution and within the context of a deeply conservative religious establishment, he has been able to fulfill the ambitious development program embodied in the Five-Year Plans.

It is important to recognize that the Saudi system of government, as defined under the Basic System and the establishment of the Consultative Council, is not a move towards Western-style democracy, much less an imitation of Western-style democratic reform. It is an organic development of the consultative basis of the relationship between ruler and ruled that is inherent in Islamic tradition.

All developed societies consist of a general population and, within that population, numerous pressure and special interest groups. Under the typical Western democratic system, the population is invited every few years to express a preference for one of two or three monolithic political parties, each of which presents the electorate with a package of policies. It is scarcely surprising that such infrequent and insensitive means of participating alienate many from the entire democratic process, with the result that large numbers fail to vote at all. To compensate for what must inevitably be a fairly crude representation of people's wishes, pressure groups form which aim to influence policy between elections, as well as at them. This mechanism enriches the democratic process but brings with it the danger that such pressure groups may be able to exercise so great an influence that they distort policy, leading the Government to deviate from the mandate on which it was elected. Further distortion can arise from single-issue pressure groups which, by definition, have elevated their own cause above all others and which, by concentrating pressure on opinion-leaders and by skilful exploitation of the media, are able to exert influence out of all proportion to their numerical support and sometimes against the views of the majority of the population.

The Saudi Arabian system deals with such difficulties in a different way, a way that is a natural extension of the consultative tradition which has existed in the region for many centuries. The Majlis, or Consultative Council, provides an opportunity for every citizen to present his case, his request for help, his complaint about a grievance, his suggestion for an improvement, to a person in authority, whether that person is governor, a minister or the King. Apart from creating a climate in which everyone feels they have access to those in power, the Majlis also ensures that those in power are aware of and ultimately sensitive to the opinions and wishes of those for whom they are responsible.

Following in the tradition of his predecessors, King Fahd has, in the course of his reign, embraced and extended the Majlis. It is, perhaps, difficult for a

Westerner to grasp the ethos of the consultative process and the function it fulfills in Saudi Arabian society but such understanding is worth the effort. For those who are interested in how best to involve all citizens in an inclusive political process, it is possible that the Majlis can provide some useful pointers.

How then does the Saudi system of government operate?

## THE CABINET

The phenomenal expansion in governmental activities, along with the Government's continued effort to enhance services provided for its citizens, has necessitated some growth in the number of Ministries, departments and Governmental agencies.

In 1975, the Saudi Cabinet consisted of fourteen ministries represented in the Council of Ministers. The Cabinet formed by Royal Order No. A/236 on 13th October 1975, when King Fahd was Crown Prince, increased the number of ministries from 14 to 20. Today the Council of Ministers consists of:

- the Prime Minister, the King
- the Deputy Prime Minister, who is the Commander of the National Guard
- the Second Deputy Prime Minister, who is the Minister of Defense and Aviation
- Minister of Agriculture and Water
- Minister of Civil Service
- Minister of Commerce
- Minister of Communications
- Minister of Education
- Minister of Finance and National Economy
- Minister of Foreign Affairs
- Minister of Health
- Minister of Higher Education
- Minister of Industry and Electricity
- Minister of Information
- Minister of the Interior
- Minister for Islamic Affairs, Endowment, Dawa and Guidance
- Minister of Justice
- Minister of Labor and Social Affairs
- Minister of Municipal and Rural Affairs
- Minister of Petroleum and Mineral Resources
- Minister of Pilgrimage
- Minister of Planning
- Minister of Public Works and Housing
- Minister of Post, Telegraphs and Telephones (PTT)
- Ministers of State

The Council of Ministers meets once a week, under the chairmanship of the King who is the supreme authority in both legislative and executive affairs.

## POLITICAL REFORMS UNDER KING FAHD

In 1993, King Fahd introduced three major political developments which formed part of a carefully constructed strategy to modernize the Kingdom's system of Government within the framework of Islam and the Kingdom's traditions. These were the following:

- the formation of the Majlis Al-Shura (Consultative Council);
- the restructuring of the Kingdom's Regional Government;
- the promulgation of the Basic System incorporating the first two developments.

### The Consultative Council

The long-awaited setting up of a sixty-member Consultative Council, or Majlis Al-Shura (Royal Decree No. A/91, dated 27-8-1412) marked a significant move towards the formalization of the participative nature of government in Saudi Arabia. The announcement of the establishment of the Council, which

*King Fahd chairing a session of the Council of Ministers*

*Consultative Council building in Riyadh*

coincided with the 10th anniversary of the accession of King Fahd, and which was accompanied by details of a new Basic Law, clearly marked the first steps towards a more formal, broadly based involvement in the Kingdom's political processes.

At its inception, the Consultative Council consisted of a speaker and sixty members selected by the King. The Royal Decree establishing the Council made it clear, first and foremost, that the Council was set up and would operate:

*in compliance with [the existing system of government in the Kingdom] and in adherence to the Book of God and the tradition of his Messenger.*

In 1997 a Royal Decree was issued to amend the third article of the Shura system and accordingly the number of Consultative Council members was increased from 60 to 90.

In practice, members of the Council are able to initiate legislation and review the domestic and foreign policies of the Government. Any Government action not approved by the Council has to be referred back to the King. By 1998, the Council was well established and operating effectively.

In grasping the significance of these measures, it is important to understand that King Fahd's purpose in establishing the Majlis Al-Shura and in introducing other planned reforms was to provide an institutional framework through which the traditional form of Saudi Arabian Government, based on consultation within the context of the tenets and requirements of Islam, could be most effectively expressed in today's increasingly complex and inter-dependent world.

The reforms can, however, be seen as marking an important new chapter in the life of the Kingdom and in King Fahd's desire to hasten the pace of modernization, while remaining firmly within the religious and cultural traditions of the Kingdom.

It has been argued that, while oil wealth has transformed the economy and infrastructure of Saudi Arabia in the past three decades, the political machinery of the Kingdom had previously remained unchanged. These measures are seen by some as the start of a cumulative process facilitating the modernization of Saudi Arabian Government but the reforms do not mean that the Kingdom has moved away from its Islamic traditions. King Fahd himself stressed that his reforms were based on Islamic principles of fairness, decency and popular consultation.

Furthermore, the nature of the initial reforms should serve to reassure the religious conservatives. The Council as presently constituted has no lawmaking power, merely the right to summon and question ministers. King Fahd's choice of Speaker for the first Council – the Justice Minister, Sheikh Muhammad bin Ibrahim bin Jubeir – served to confirm notions that the reform process was intended to be gradual in pace and judicious in development. The Council's members are selected because they have proved themselves to be responsible and loyal citizens of the Kingdom.

In essence, the Consultative Council should be seen, not as a modest move towards Western-style democracy but as an organic development of the consultative processes by means of which the Kingdom has been governed since its inception, processes which arose from a tradition that goes back to the life of the Prophet Muhammad, peace be upon him.

## Regional Government

The reforms in Regional Government had the precise purpose of enhancing the level of administrative and developmental work in the regions of the Kingdom, while at the same time preserving security and order and ensuring the rights of citizens and their freedom within the framework of the Islamic Shariah.

King Fahd's decree dealing with Regional Government listed the thirteen regions and the cities in which the headquarters of each region are to be located.

Each of the regions has a Regional Governor with the rank of Minister who is responsible to the Minister of the Interior. The Regional Governor will be supported by an Under-Secretary.

Under the Regional Governor, each region will be subdivided into

"Governorates" (Group A or B Governorates) and "Centers" (Group A or B Centers). Each Group A Governorate will have a governor with a ranking of not less than 14th grade and he will be supported by an Under-Secretary of not less than 12th grade. The Group B Governors will have a ranking of not less than 12th grade. Each Group A Center will have a Chairman of not less than 8th grade; and each Group B Center will have a Chairman with a ranking of not less than 5th grade.

| REGION | LOCATION OF REGIONAL HQ |
|---|---|
| Riyadh Region | Riyadh City |
| Makkah Region | Makkah City |
| Madinah Region | Madinah City |
| Qassim Region | Buraidah City |
| Eastern Region | Dammam City |
| Asir Region | Abha City |
| Tabouk Region | Tabouk City |
| Hail Region | Hail City |
| Northern Border Region | Arar City |
| Jizan Region | Jizan City |
| Najran Region | Najran City |
| Baha Region | Baha City |
| Al-Jouf Region | Skaka City |

The Governor of each region, and his Vice-Governor, must take the following oath in the presence of the King before taking office:

*I swear, in the Name of God the Almighty, to remain sincere to my religion, to my King and my nation, and not to reveal any secret of my nation, and to preserve its interests, its regulations and to perform my duties truly, honestly, sincerely and justly.*

The primary objective of the Governor and his staff is to administer the region in line with the public policy of the State and the regulations of the system. The maintenance of public security, order and stability, and the guaranteeing of individual rights and freedoms within the framework of the Shariah and the governmental regulations are given a high priority, alongside a commitment to the social and economic development of the region.

Each region has a regional council, under the chairmanship of the Governor.

The structure of Regional Government and the composition of the regional governing bodies and regional councils provides further evidence of King Fahd's determination to increase the involvement of the citizenry in the Government of Saudi Arabia while maintaining stability and continuity. These measures should not be seen as a cautious attempt to move towards Western-style democratic institutions; rather they should be construed as logical and eminently sensible extensions of the traditional participative mechanisms that have facilitated good government in the Kingdom and that have allowed the inevitable tensions of any fast-developing society to be resolved through the emergence of a broadly based consensus.

*Ministry of the Interior building in Riyadh*

### The Basic System

The Basic System, which incorporates the arrangements for the Consultative Council and for Regional Government, established in written form both a description of the essential structure and organization of Government and, in effect, a bill of rights for the citizen.

The Basic System sets out the general principles on which the Kingdom of Saudi Arabia is founded. Article 1 clearly established the central tenets of the Kingdom:

*Article 1: The Kingdom of Saudi Arabia is an Arab and Islamic Sovereign State; its religion is Islam and its constitution is the Holy Quran and the Prophet's Sunnah. Its language is Arabic and its capital is Riyadh.*

The form of Government is monarchical (Article 5). Rule in the Kingdom depends upon and must conform to the teachings of Islam (Article 7), and this rule provides justice, consultation and equality in accordance with the Islamic Shariah (Article 8).

The importance of the family within Saudi society is heavily emphasized in Article 9:

*The family is the nucleus of Saudi society and its members are brought up in confor-mity with the Islamic creed and in obedience to Almighty God, the Prophet and the Kingdom's rulers, showing respect for the system of Government, love for the home-land and pride in its history.*

*Article 9*

*And the State sees as part of its role the enhancement of stable family relations, the preservation of Islamic values within the family, and the fullest development of the potential of all family members.*

The Basic System goes on to define the responsibilities of the State in some detail, giving special reference to the Kingdom's duties as guardian of the Holy Places, and setting guidelines for the exploitation of the State's wealth to ensure the economic and social development of the Kingdom.

Citizens' rights (to security, to self-fulfillment through education and free-dom of opportunity, and to the ownership of property) are all safeguarded. And a right to privacy is also guaranteed:

*Nobody is allowed to enter the house of another without the permission of the owners; and nobody has the right to investigate another's private affairs, except in accordance with the System.*

*Article 37*

The Basic System sets out, with remarkable clarity, the basis on which the Kingdom is governed, and the rights and obligations of both the State and the citizen. As the processes of consultation are extended, it becomes necessary to formalize the principles underlying the traditions which have enabled the Kingdom to pass through periods of extraordinary change with an equally extraordinary degree of stability.

In promulgating the Basic System, forming the Majlis Al-Shura (Consul-tative Council) and restructuring the Kingdom's Regional Government, King Fahd has demonstrated considerable political acumen and ability to effect change within a conservative society by organic evolution of existing institu-tions and traditions.

## The Issue of Human Rights

Before leaving the subject of political reform, we should give some thought to the issue of human rights. This is a subject which can arouse strong emotions and debate in which often there is rather more heat than light. Western criticism of the Kingdom of Saudi Arabia is based on the new morality of a largely secular, profoundly liberal society. The most prized moral quality of such a society is tolerance (although, on closer inspection, the tolerance seems to be rather selective).

The Kingdom of Saudi Arabia starts from a different set of premises. Saudi Arabia is a theistic, conservative society. Under Islam, there is absolute truth and a moral code for all time that transcends the moral fashions of the day.

The Western concept of human rights is dynamic. It has evolved over time, and is still evolving. A century ago, it would have been difficult to find in Europe any evidence of what some people today now insist are basic human rights. Given the evolutionary and sometimes erratic development of the Western concepts of human rights, Saudi Arabia feels no compulsion to adopt the West's latest version. Saudi Arabia has its own vision.

The United Nations Declaration of Human Rights was prompted largely by the West's revulsion at its own atrocities. Nazism and Marxism, both products of Western civilization, presided over the untimely deaths of many millions of innocent human beings. It is encouraging that the West has sought to legislate against such barbarity but it should recognize the particular historical circumstances which have prompted its current views. It should be aware of the danger of bundling together with legitimate and genuinely universal human rights, rights that are demanded by those espousing a permissive moral philosophy in a largely secular society.

Of course, every human being is entitled to life, freedom, dignity, justice and security. Such rights are universal. They are the right of people in Saudi Arabia, just as much as they are the right of people in the West. On the other hand, when, for example, someone argues that capital punishment is an abuse of human rights, we are entering the realm of opinion where it is perfectly reasonable to hold a different view. Saudi Arabian opinion is that capital punishment is the most effective way of safeguarding the most basic human right: the right to live. It places a high value on the life of the murder victim and, as evidence of that high value and as a deterrent to others, it exacts a high price from the murderer.

In practical terms, human rights are guaranteed in the Kingdom of Saudi Arabia under the Shariah. These rights have been explicitly stated in the Basic Law. For example, Article 27 reads: "The State guarantees the rights of each citizen and his family in cases of emergency, illness, disability and old age."

Article 28 imposes on the State the duty of providing "job opportunities for whoever is capable of working". Article 30 obliges the State "to provide education and fight illiteracy". Article 31 provides for universal healthcare in the Kingdom. Article 35 guarantees that "no one shall be arrested, imprisoned or have their actions restricted except in cases specified by the law". Article 37 proclaims the sanctity of the home. Article 40 declares: "The State protects human rights in accordance with the Shariah".

These obligations on the State, underpinned by Islam, provide a solid basis for the protection of human rights in the Kingdom. Of course, humans are fallible and therefore no system is perfect in practice. Where there are wrongs they should be righted; if there is injustice, there must be redress. But it is the height of cultural arrogance for a permissive, secular society to assert that its own current values are universally applicable and to criticize alternative value systems, not for the occasional errors or faults to which all human systems are subject, but as a matter of principle.

# KING FAHD AND FOREIGN DIPLOMACY

KING FAHD'S POLICY on foreign affairs has been underpinned by four easily defined principles. First, he has shown throughout his years as Crown Prince and King an unfaltering commitment to the unity of the Arab world and to the unity of the still more broadly based community of the Islamic faith. Throughout, he has maintained his belief that the things that unite the Arab and Muslim worlds are far more important than those that divide them. A brief survey of the recent history of the Middle East which includes the Iraq–Iran War and the Gulf War might seem to challenge such a view but any set-backs, however grave, have served only to strengthen King Fahd's resolve to use all means at the Kingdom's disposal to further the cause of unity. It has always been clear to King Fahd that the disputes and conflicts between Arab States have brought no benefit to the countries involved or their peoples but have certainly prevented the Arab world from playing the role and exercising the influence in international affairs to which, by political and economic status, it is, or should, be entitled.

The second underlying principle in King Fahd's foreign policy in any conflict is that peace must always be the goal – but that the only way to achieve lasting peace is through justice. In any negotiation, there must be compromise if there is to be any chance of success and in the world of *realpolitik* perfect justice is generally unobtainable but compromise must stop short of concessions which are profoundly unjust to one or other party in the dispute. This principle of foreign policy is most clearly apparent in the Kingdom's stance on the Palestinian–Israeli conflict which has occupied much of King Fahd's diplomatic energies for the last two decades.

Thirdly, King Fahd has always believed in quiet diplomacy. As a consequence, Saudi Arabia's foreign policy has often been described by outsiders as cautious. When working one's way through the minefield of Middle East politics, caution is no bad quality but this chapter will show that, on a number of occasions, the Kingdom of Saudi Arabia has taken the initiative in trying to resolve some of the most intractable problems within its area of influence and that, despite appearances, in some cases such initiatives have involved a not inconsiderable degree of risk.

Fourthly, under King Fahd, the Kingdom has shown a very real commitment to the vision of a single global community, whereby all countries and country groupings accept that they have a responsibility for all the peoples of the world and not just their own citizens. This aspect of King Fahd's policy is grounded in Islam which teaches that the responsibility of each person extends from the family to the country and from the country to all humanity. One of the practical manifestations of this policy has been Saudi Arabia's unfaltering foreign aid program which is outlined in Chapter Eleven.

In describing King Fahd's contribution at the level of international diplomacy, it will be necessary in each case to provide a little historical background.

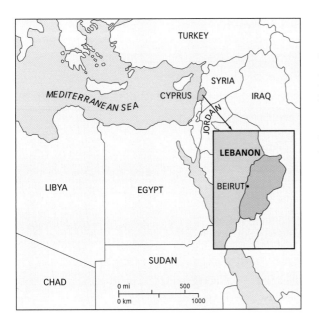

## LEBANON

Of all the countries of the Middle East, Lebanon is probably the most cosmopolitan and its politics the most difficult to grasp.

Over many centuries, Lebanon, strategically located at the eastern end of the Mediterranean, has been a thriving trading center. Muslims, the Druze, Maronite Christians and Greek Orthodox Christians have all made their homes in Lebanon. On top of these diverse cultures have been imposed the colonial influences of the Ottoman Turks (who absorbed Lebanon into their empire in the sixteenth century and retained it until the end of the First World War) and the French (who administered the country under a League of Nations mandate until 1941 when Lebanon achieved independence).

Throughout the centuries of colonial rule, the different sections of Lebanese society, with their different cultures and traditions, lived together in relative harmony, with whatever power the Turks or French were prepared to devolve distributed amongst them. After independence, this delicate but practical balance was maintained and Lebanon concentrated on developing a dynamic economy, which, through the undoubted business acumen of its people, became the banking and commercial services center of the Middle East.

Today Lebanon's population consists of a rich racial mix, containing elements from almost every country in the region. In terms of religion, Muslims constitute about three quarters of the population, Christians about one quarter. Arabic is the dominant language but both English and French are widely spoken.

The political and economic balance that enabled Lebanon to prosper after independence could not continue. The foundation of Israel in 1948, the expulsion of wave after wave of hundreds of thousands of Palestinians from their homes in Palestine into neighboring countries, have kept the region in a permanent state of disequilibrium. In the 1970s the Palestine Liberation Organization (PLO), expelled from Jordan in 1971, established themselves in Lebanon. The arrival of a large dispossessed community in a country which was already performing an extraordinary balancing act between its different religions and traditions, combined with the destabilizing effect of Israel's preemptive and retaliatory strikes against the PLO wherever they were, inevitably destabilized the country.

In 1975, violent incidents involving Palestinians and Christian Phalangists escalated into a civil war between the Muslim and Christian communities. This conflict soon led to increased Syrian involvement in Lebanese affairs. By May 1976, Syria was reckoned to have at least 40,000 troops in Lebanon.

Throughout this period, the Kingdom of Saudi Arabia deployed its diplomatic skills in order to find an equilibrium between the Lebanese factions (including the Palestinians) and the Governments of all the Arab countries involved (Syria, Egypt and Jordan) but it is scarcely surprising that the sought-for stability proved elusive.

In March 1978, following a raid on Israel by Al Fatah guerrillas based in Lebanon, Israeli forces invaded and occupied southern Lebanon which they quickly came to regard as a buffer to protect Israel's northern boundary. The United Nations Security Council approved a resolution demanding that Israel should cease hostilities and withdraw from Lebanese territory. The same resolution provided for the formation of a UN Interim Force in Lebanon (UNIFIL) to monitor Israel's withdrawal and to restore order to the country but, when the Israelis withdrew in June 1978, they handed southern Lebanon over, not to the Lebanese Government, but to the predominantly Lebanese Christian militias with which Israel had close links and a political understanding.

With southern Lebanon now effectively under Israeli control (albeit through surrogates), with continuing fighting between the Syrian forces and Christian militias in and around Beirut, further efforts by Arab countries, including Saudi Arabia, to restore Lebanon's territorial integrity and political unity were once again frustrated.

In 1982, Israeli air raids provoked the PLO into shelling northern Israel. Israel's response was a full-scale invasion of Lebanon. The Syrian forces were driven back into the Beka'a Valley but Israel's main target was the PLO. The primary tactic used by Israel was heavy and indiscriminate bombardment of Lebanese towns and cities with the intention of undermining the morale of the Lebanese people. Press reports estimated that 14,000 people were killed by the Israeli forces in the first two weeks of the invasion, 80% of whom were civilians. Throughout July and August of that year, Israel maintained a constant bombardment of West Beirut and cut off water, food, electricity and medical supplies. At the end of August, the PLO agreed to withdraw from what was left of the city.

In September, with the connivance and encouragement of the occupying Israeli forces (under the command of Ariel Sharon, Minister of Defense), Phalangist militiamen were sent into the Palestinian refugee camps of Sabra and Chatila in a "cleaning up" operation. Following the enforced departure of the PLO, the camps were now unprotected, although Israel had guaranteed the safety of the residents and the United States had agreed to use its influence to ensure Israel kept its word. According to Red Cross sources, some 2,750 refugees were butchered. Many of them were women and children. The motive of the Phalangist militiamen who carried out the slaughter was primarily bloodlust. Israel's motive had more to do with its policy of ethnic cleansing.

Efforts to resolve the political chaos in Lebanon continued but all attempts, including those of George Shultz, US Secretary of State, failed. In July 1983, the Israeli forces, suffering an increasing number of casualties inflicted on them by various hostile Lebanese factions, withdrew to south of Beirut. Lebanon was now in effect partitioned, with Israel controlling southern Lebanon (directly with its troops and indirectly through the mainly Christian militias in the area) and Beirut itself split into Muslim-controlled west Beirut and Christian-controlled east Beirut sectors.

In the first six months of 1985, Israel withdrew its forces from Lebanon. In the course of the staged withdrawal, Israel responded to attacks by Shi'ites in south Lebanon with the notorious "Iron Fist" policy which involved attacking Shi'ite villages, killing many men, women and children and detaining others on suspicion.

The Israeli withdrawal from Lebanon was widely welcomed in Lebanon but sadly taken as an opportunity to pursue factional disputes with renewed vigor. Conflict between Christian and Muslim groups continued and conflict between one Muslim group and another increased.

Following yet another outburst of fighting between Muslim and Christian groups in May 1989, an emergency summit meeting of Arab leaders was convened in Casablanca, Morocco. At this summit a Tripartite Arab Committee was set up, with King Fahd, King Hassan of Morocco and President Chadli of Algeria as its members. This high-powered Committee was tasked with finding a way to enforce a ceasefire in Lebanon and bringing about conditions in

In America, our nation's responsibility for the whole tragic incident [at Sabra and Chatila] has gone largely unnoticed. We put our own good faith behind Israel's word of honor; otherwise the PLO would never have agreed to leave. The PLO leaders trusted America's promise that the Palestinians left behind would be safeguarded. When America promised "to do its utmost" to assure that Israel kept its commitments, they took that commitment at face value. They would never have trusted an Israeli promise but they trusted us. We betrayed them.

*George Ball, Former US Under-Secretary of State Source: Error and Betrayal in Lebanon, Foundation for Middle East Peace, Washington DC, 1984*

which political reform and the creation of stable government could be achieved.

This brief account of politics and the civil war in Lebanon from 1975 to 1989 should be sufficient to convey to the reader the scale of the task which the Tripartite Arab Committee was undertaking. Throughout the years of strife, Saudi Arabia had used its good offices to try to resolve the anarchy into which Lebanon had declined. Saudi Arabia had always been ready to mediate between various interested parties but the driving force for the various conflicts resided with the troops and militiamen on the ground and all diplomatic efforts, including those by the United States, had failed.

The Committee members began by sending their Ministers of Foreign Affairs to Damascus in June 1989, with a letter to President Assad of Syria, enlisting Syria's cooperation in this new search for a solution to the Lebanon problem. In the same month, the Committee announced its peace plan which entailed a general ceasefire, the removal of blockades from both Muslim and Christian ports and the reopening of the roads between west and east Beirut. These moves to normalize the situation were to be followed by a meeting of the Lebanese National Assembly in a foreign country.

*King Fahd receives Syrian President Hafez Al Assad*

*King Fahd receives Lebanese parliamentarians during the Taif Conference*

On 11th April 1996, Israel launched "Operation Grapes of Wrath". What prompted the operation is unclear. Israel claimed Hezbollah rockets had injured 13 Israeli citizens; Hezbollah claimed the rocket attacks were in retaliation for Israeli-inspired attacks on Lebanese civilians. Whatever the facts, 400,000 Lebanese were displaced by the massive assault which was directed at Christian as well as Muslim targets. On 18th April, Israel attacked the UN base at Qana, killing 100 Lebanese refugees who had fled there for protection, and four UNIFIL soldiers.

On 18th September 1989, the Tripartite Arab Committee reactivated its efforts to resolve the crisis in Lebanon. Once again the Committee stipulated a ceasefire and the removal of blockades but this time they proposed that the Lebanese National Assembly should convene on 30th September and discuss a charter of national reconciliation drafted by the Tripartite Arab Committee itself. The charter attracted the support of almost every Arab country and was endorsed by the United States, the Soviet Union, the United Kingdom and France. The location for what proved to be a historic meeting was the mountain town of Taif in the Kingdom of Saudi Arabia.

The first meeting in Taif was attended by 31 Muslim deputies and 31 Christian deputies. At a second meeting, held on 22nd October, a charter of national reconciliation was endorsed by 58 of the 62 deputies. Probably the most important provision in the agreement was the transfer of power from the President to the Cabinet which allowed for power to be evenly distributed between the Muslim and Christian cabinet members. Following the formation of a new Government all militias in the country were to be disbanded within six months and the Lebanese army was to be strengthened. The Syrian army was to assist in this process.

The Taif Agreement did not immediately solve all Lebanon's problems. But it is nevertheless the case that, with an extraordinary degree of diplomatic skill, the Tripartite Arab Committee somehow managed to bring together the diverse political interests of almost all the Arab countries and the world's leading industrial powers in support of a negotiating position that brought the Lebanese civil war which had dragged on for fifteen years to an end.

Lebanon's troubles were far from over. But at least the foundations of stable Government had been laid and the start of social and economic reconstruction could begin.

## THE IRAQ–IRAN WAR

In terms of land mass, the Kingdom of Saudi Arabia is easily the largest country in the Middle East. In terms of population, Iran and Egypt vie for top position, with some 66 million people each. Iraq, with some 22 million people is in third place, with the Kingdom of Saudi Arabia very close behind.

In terms of oil reserves, the Kingdom of Saudi Arabia dominates the picture, with Iraq in second place, with less than half the oil reserves of the Kingdom.

In formulating foreign policy, the Kingdom of Saudi Arabia has had to take into account the balance of power in the region and it is helpful to summarize some of the main political considerations which confronted King Fahd at the start of his reign.

Iraq had long nurtured territorial ambitions in the region, in particular a desire to assert sovereignty over Kuwait. (Shortly after Kuwait attained independence in 1961, Iraq laid claim to Kuwait. In March 1973, Iraqi troops occupied a Kuwaiti outpost on the Kuwait–Iraq border and asserted a claim to two islands belonging to Kuwait. Although the Iraqi forces abandoned the border post, the dispute remained unresolved.)

After the fall of the Shah, Iran, under Ayatollah Khomeini, showed an eagerness to export its own brand of revolutionary fervor, and was only too happy to interfere or encourage interference in the affairs of other countries in the region.

| COUNTRY | SIZE | | POPULATION | PROVEN OIL RESERVES BILLIONS OF BARRELS 1999 |
|---|---|---|---|---|
| | SQ MILES | [SQ KM] | | |
| Saudi Arabia | 865,000 | [2,240,000] | 21,400,000 | 263.5 |
| Egypt | 387,000 | [1,002,000] | 66,000,000 | 2.9 |
| Iran | 636,000 | [1,648,000] | 65,800,000 | 89.7 |
| Iraq | 169,000 | [438,000] | 22,018,000 | 112.5 |
| Syria | 71,000 | [185,000] | 14,951,000 | 2.5 |

The third major player in the political complexities of the region, Egypt, had made a bilateral peace with Israel in 1979 and, as a result, was effectively excluded from the Arab world.

It was against such a background that King Fahd had to devise and sustain the Kingdom's foreign policy in the 1980s. Once the preconditions are understood, the consummate skill with which King Fahd maneuvered in this period in extraordinarily difficult and dangerous circumstances becomes apparent. At a time when two of the major powers of the region seemed determined to destroy each other, with scant regard for the well-being or stability of their neighbors, King Fahd somehow managed to combine political practicality with an unshakable belief in the need for and the possibility of Arab unity.

On 22nd September 1980 (little more than a year after Saddam Hussein had become President) war between Iraq and Iran began in earnest. It was to be a particularly unpleasant war. Saddam Hussein had proved his ruthlessness in the internal politics of Iraq and he was now eager to prove himself as a conqueror and the dominant power in the region. Iraqi troops quickly occupied Iranian territory along a 300-mile [480 km] front and it was clearly Saddam Hussein's expectation that the seemingly disorganized Khomeini regime in Iran would collapse. While Iran had been too powerful to challenge under the Shah, Iran governed by the Ayatollah, with the Iranian military seemingly in total disarray, looked temptingly vulnerable. As it turned out, the Iranians proved surprisingly resilient and a war of attrition ensued in which young Iranians in particular became cannon fodder and civilians on both sides suffered as much as the combatants. In 1982, the Iranians launched the first of a number of counter-offensives and in May they retook Khorramshahr, a strategically important seaport in southwest Iran. By June, 1982, Iranian troops had invaded Iraqi territory.

For the Kingdom of Saudi Arabia, the Iraq–Iran war meant that the stability of the entire region was threatened; vast resources which could have been put to far better use were being squandered on death and destruction; the root cause of so many of the problems in the region (the Palestinian–Israeli conflict) was being sidelined; and the cause closest to King Fahd's heart, the cause of Arab unity, was facing serious setbacks, with Syria, an Arab country, siding with Iran against Iraq.

Iran at that time was attempting to export its extremist revolutionary zeal to the Muslim world in general and the Arabian Peninsula in particular. Such a policy could only be a destabilizing factor in a region already threatened by the turmoil of a war which set Muslim against Muslim.

Meanwhile King Fahd pursued his own vision of Arab unity by promoting the idea of closer cooperation between the States of the Arabian Gulf. He worked assiduously for the formation of the Gulf Cooperation Council (GCC) and saw his efforts rewarded with the formation of the organization in May 1981. The Arab world needed a model of how Arab States could work together, benefit from such cooperation and resolve their differences by dialogue rather than force and King Fahd aimed to make the GCC such an example. The GCC could also serve to strengthen the security of the resource-rich but sparsely populated peninsula by coordinating defense policies and, if appropriate, pooling resources.

The Iraq–Iran war dragged on for years. By 1987, the United States had become involved in the politics of the conflict. Iran had been targeting Kuwaiti oil tankers and installations as a punishment for Kuwait's support for Iraq and the United States had agreed to protect Kuwaiti oil tankers, reflagged as American vessels. Moscow too had been eager to exploit the conflict as an opportunity to strengthen its influence in the region.

In July 1987, the Security Council of the United Nations passed Resolution 598 which called on both parties in the war to implement an immediate cease-fire. A ceasefire came into effect on 20th August 1988. Negotiations finally to end the state of war between the two countries continued for almost two years, while each side blamed the other for starting the war and Iran sought war reparations which Iraq refused to consider. Eventually, on 16th August 1990, for reasons which soon became apparent to the rest of the world, Saddam Hussein sought and achieved an immediate and comprehensive settlement of all outstanding issues by accepting almost all the Iranian demands.

In the end, to resolve the conflict, it had been necessary to internationalize the war and Saudi Arabia played a major role in formulating and promoting United Nations Resolution 598. The loss of life and property in almost a decade of war had been appalling and, throughout the years of war, the Kingdom of Saudi Arabia had, by constant diplomatic effort, done its best to bring the conflict to an end. Nevertheless, the damage done to the stability of the region, to relations between Muslim States in the region and to the cause of Arab and Islamic unity cannot be overestimated. Finally, although both of the combatants in the war had claimed to have the cause of the Palestinians and the liberation of Israeli-occupied Arab lands as a core objective, together they succeeded in diverting attention and resources away from the Arab–Israeli conflict and the plight of the Palestinians for almost a decade.

> It was widely estimated that one million people had been killed or injured in the Iraq–Iran war.

## The Gulf War

Despite the outcome of the conflict with Iran, Saddam Hussein declared himself the victor and, flushed with the success of his victory, he decided to embark on his next military adventure. He was also determined that, if the States of the Arabian Peninsula had supported and helped to finance his regime during his

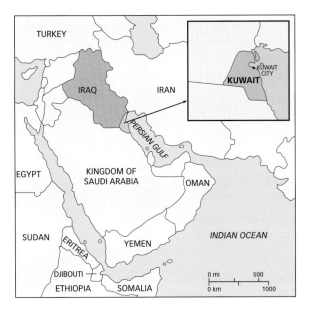

In area, Kuwait is a little over 100th the size of Iran. Kuwait's total armed forces were no more than 20,000 men. Iraq had a million men under arms and, to make sure of success, deployed 100,000 troops in Kuwait.

conflict with Iran, then they should be prepared to continue their subventions after it had ended. After all, as a result of the war which he himself had initiated and which he had prolonged as long as possible, the Iraqi economy was severely debilitated and his exchequer sorely depleted. Saddam needed money to rebuild the economy.

In the course of the first few months of 1990, Saddam Hussein became increasingly aggressive in his relations with Kuwait. Both Kuwait and the United Arab Emirates were persistently exceeding their OPEC quotas. In May, at the Arab League Summit in Baghdad, Saddam Hussein strongly criticized unnamed States for exceeding their OPEC oil production quotas, thus depressing the oil price which Iraq in particular wished to see rise. He then accused Kuwait of stealing oil worth $2.4 billion from an Iraqi oil field. By July, Kuwait was being told that it must not only cancel all war debts but also "refund" the $2.4 billion of the "stolen" oil and compensate Iraq for the loss of oil revenue resulting from the low oil price caused by Kuwait's over-production. Although an attempt was made to resolve the dispute on 31st July 1990, when a meeting took place between Kuwaiti and Iraqi negotiators in Jeddah, it was clear from the nature of Iraq's demands that agreement was impossible. Nevertheless, since Saddam Hussein had given his word to King Fahd, President Mubarak and the late King Hussein of Jordan that he would not invade Kuwait, the invasion when it came, came as a shock.

On 2nd August 1990, Saddam Hussein executed the type of *blitzkrieg* attack he had used against Iran, on that occasion with such disastrous consequences. This time, however, the victim was of a more appropriate size.

Within a few hours, Saddam's forces were in control of Kuwait. The United Nations Security Council immediately passed Resolution 660, which condemned the Iraqi action and called on the Iraqi forces to withdraw forthwith, threatening sanctions and possible military action if Iraq failed to comply. Following the collapse of communism in the Soviet Union, the United Nations Security Council was able to act quickly and decisively on this occasion, with the United States and the Soviet Union in agreement.

Saudi Arabia immediately sent troops to its border with Kuwait and endorsed, in Cairo, the Arab League resolution condemning Iraq. The resolution was approved by the majority of members but was opposed by Jordan, Mauritania, Sudan, Yemen, the Palestine Liberation Organization and, of course, Iraq. When the Arab League Heads of State met in Cairo on 10th August, twelve of the twenty member countries present voted to contribute to the multinational force that was assembling to protect the Kingdom of Saudi Arabia; 8 demurred.

It was already clear that a majority of Arab States condemned Iraq's blatant act of aggression. Just as Saddam Hussein's initiation of the Iraq–Iran war had diverted attention away from the problem of Israel, so his action now drew Western powers into Arab affairs.

In what may have been an attempt to reconcile this paradox (that the outcome of his actions always seemed to be the opposite of his stated objectives) Saddam Hussein announced on 12th August that, if Israel would withdraw from the occupied territories, he would withdraw from Kuwait. While the United States undoubtedly applies a double standard in the Middle East where Israel is concerned, Saddam Hussein's attempt at "linkage" (linking the question of his occupation of Kuwait with Israel's occupation of Arab lands), in the circumstances, was nothing more than rhetoric aimed at Arab popular sentiment.

As the multinational forces assembled, the United States was meticulous in ensuring that it was acting in conformity with the provisions of the United

*King Fahd and the Emir of Kuwait, Sheikh Jaber Al Sabah (1991)*

Nations charter. In parallel, the United Nations, other organizations and individual countries launched a number of diplomatic initiatives to resolve the problem without the use of force. Reports of atrocities perpetrated by Iraqi troops in Kuwait served to stiffen the resolve of all members of the alliance to expel Saddam's forces and confirmed the wisdom of King Fahd's decision to enlist international help to liberate Kuwait.

In order to ensure that the alliance was acting with United Nations authority, on 29th November the United States drafted a resolution which, in essence, declared that if Iraq had not fully complied with earlier United Nations resolutions demanding its withdrawal from Kuwait by 15th January 1991, the alliance could use "all necessary means" to compel compliance. This resolution (No 678) was adopted.

In the middle of January 1991, after President Bush had gone the "extra mile for peace" to no avail, Operation Desert Storm began. Saddam Hussein had promised "the mother of all battles" but, as it turned out, the contest was entirely one-sided. Desert Storm began with a massive aerial assault which effectively neutralized the Iraqi air force. In the following weeks, alliance forces systematically degraded Iraq's military command and control system and a considerable proportion of Iraq's infrastructure. In response, at the end of January, Iraq emptied oil from some Kuwaiti storage tanks (the equivalent of some four million barrels) into the Gulf in an act of mindless ecological irresponsibility. The oil spill, probably the worst ever, caused considerable environmental damage but clearly had no military purpose or effect.

Also in late January, Iraqi forces crossed into Saudi Arabia, briefly occupying the deserted northern town of al-Khafji. The Iraqi invaders were speedily repelled by alliance forces with Saudi units in the van.

While the alliance was deconstructing Iraq, Saddam Hussein retaliated with Scud missiles (armed with conventional explosive warheads) launched against Riyadh and other targets in the Kingdom. Most of the missiles were inaccurate.

When the land war to liberate Kuwait was launched, it was over almost before it began. What was left of Iraq's occupying forces was incapable of serious resistance.

Saudi Arabia had committed its entire armed forces to the operation of liberating Kuwait.


## BOSNIA

In the spring of 1992, the Government of Bosnia and Herzegovina held a referendum on independence. The result of the referendum (which the Bosnian Serbs decided to boycott) was a majority in favor of independence. Alarmed at the prospect of formal separation from Serbia and hostile to an independent State headed by Bosnian Muslims, Bosnian Serbs, supported and encouraged by Serbia itself, embarked on a civil war aimed at fragmenting the country and joining the regions of Bosnia where Serbs were in control to Serbia. Despite international recognition of the independence of Bosnia-Herzegovina in April 1992, the Bosnian Serbs seized control of 70% of the country and embarked on a program of murder, terror and expulsion of Bosnian Muslims.

As the civil strife gathered momentum King Fahd recognized sooner than most the plight of the Bosnian Muslims and the dreadful seriousness with which the Serbs intended to pursue their program of ethnic cleansing. He immediately condemned Serbian aggression, alerting the international community to the scale of Serbian atrocities and called for international action to end the suffering of the Bosnian Muslims. He met with the Bosnian President Alija Izetbegovic and, in December 1992, hosted an extraordinary meeting of the Organization of Islamic Conference (OIC) to focus on the plight of the Muslims in Bosnia. At an OIC meeting in July 1993, seven OIC Member States committed themselves to provide 17,000 troops to serve in the United Nations Protection Force in the former Yugoslavia. These meetings marked the start of a concerted effort by the Kingdom of Saudi Arabia to use every diplomatic channel available to resolve the conflict in Bosnia. As part of this process, King Fahd held regular meetings with President Izetbegovic to coordinate both diplomatic and aid efforts.

To provide direct relief for the Bosnian Muslims, the Government of Saudi Arabia immediately launched a sustained aid effort, supplemented by private donations from the Saudi population. (In May 1992 the Supreme Committee for the Collection of Donations for the Muslims of Bosnia, headed by Prince Salman, the Governor of Riyadh, was set up in the Kingdom as the channel for private donations.) This aid effort demanded a major distribution system which the Kingdom provided by establishing fourteen offices in Bosnian cities and towns and supplying aid, through these offices, by air and sea.

While the crisis in Bosnia and Herzegovina was at its height and while the attention of the world's media was focused on the plight of the Bosnian Muslims, many countries provided aid. Saudi Arabia's aid continued long after the camera crews had left. At King Fahd's direction, refugee camps were set up to cater for those made homeless by the Serbs; medical services were provided through Saudi-financed clinics; water supplies were restored; schools established;

Mosques restored; houses built. The Kingdom financed the care of some 7,000 orphans. The list of aid activities is long. Simply to relieve the suffering of the Bosnian Muslims in the period of "ethnic cleansing" (i.e. excluding aid for reconstruction after the violence ended), Saudi Arabia provided approximately $450 million in aid. King Fahd himself gave more than $100 million.

*(Source: Saudi Press Agency news release)*

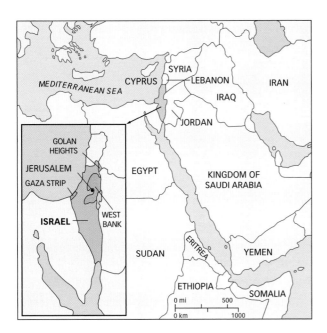

## THE PALESTINE–ISRAEL ISSUE

All readers of this book will be familiar with how the State of Israel was formed. Zionist agitation throughout the early decades of the twentieth century, given renewed impetus by the Nazi persecution of the Jews in Europe in the 1930s and throughout the Second World War, eventually led in 1948 to Ben Gurion's declaration of a new State – the State of Israel – thus fulfilling Jewish aspirations for their own homeland.

But what is seen in the West as a truly epic story, as the legitimate aspiration of a people to find a home, was and is seen in the Arab world as the ruthless and systematic persecution and dispossession of the Palestinians by an immigrant, if not a colonial, power. The land where Israel was founded was not a vacuum, waiting to be filled; it was Palestine, a land peopled by Palestinians for centuries. Thus, as one people found, or perhaps more accurately occupied, a home, another lost theirs.

Throughout the history of Saudi Arabia, from the time of King Abdul Aziz, the Kingdom has resolutely supported the Palestinian cause and has condemned Israel's conduct in the harshest possible terms. King Fahd has continued this policy and has done everything in his power, politically, diplomatically and financially to fight for the legitimate rights of the Palestinians. It is therefore essential to set out here the Arab perspective on the Palestine–Israel problem, partly to explain why King Fahd has expended so much energy on trying to find a just solution to the problem and partly to attempt to counter one of the most pervasive distortions of historical truth, and indeed to expose one of the most serious political crimes, of the last century.

The Zionist movement (the movement to establish a Jewish State in Palestine) was officially launched in 1897 by a Hungarian Jew, Theodor Herzl. The objectives of the movement, as set out by the First Congress held in Basle, Switzerland, were clear enough:

Zionism strives to create for the Jewish people a home in Palestine secured by public law. The Congress contemplates the following means of attaining this end:

1. The promotion on suitable lines of the settlement of Palestine by Jewish agricultural and industrial workers.
2. The organization and binding together of the whole of Jewry by means of appropriate institutions, local and general, in accordance with the laws of each country.
3. The strengthening and fostering of Jewish national sentiment and consciousness.
4. Preparatory steps towards obtaining Government consent where necessary to the attainment of the aims of Zionism.

It might have seemed to the casual observer that "settlement" on a foreign land (i.e. colonization) was a rather discreditable aim and expressions such as "suitable lines" and "appropriate institutions" to assist the Zionists in fulfilling their aims had a rather sinister ring to them. It therefore has to be understood that the Zionists believed that Palestine was "the Promised Land": i.e. the land promised to them by God as the descendants of Abraham, and that, in their view, their claim to Palestine transcended all other considerations.

It is difficult and generally pointless to argue with a zealot but it is worth pointing out that, even in their own terms, the Zionists' position was riddled with contradictions. The Arabs, descendants of Ishmael, the elder son of Abraham, are as much the seed of Abraham as the Jews, descendants of Isaac, and, in any case, according to Scripture, possession of the Promised Land was conditional on the righteousness of the people. In the event of failure, Moses warned: "The Lord shall scatter thee among the peoples, from one end of the earth even unto the other end of the earth."

By any reasonable criterion, in the context of the history of Palestine over the last 1,800 years, Jewish aspirations for a national home in Palestine in the twentieth century were without legal or moral justification.

Throughout the Jewish agitation for a State in Palestine, the Zionists' plans were opposed by the Palestinians in particular and the Arab world in general. The ultimate objectives of the Zionists were clear. In order to achieve their objectives, they would have to effect an extraordinary piece of population engineering. Jews would have to be gathered in from around the world and, as far as possible, the existing Arab population must be driven out. According to the best available estimates (the first Census under the British Mandate), the population of Palestine in 1922 stood at 752,000, of which only 83,790 (12%) were Jews. The injustice of the Zionists' intention became apparent to the British who were administering the Mandate in Palestine but British attempts to limit immigration prompted a campaign of terrorism against the

On 6th November 1944 in Cairo, two assassins, members of the Stern gang, murdered British Minister of State Lord Moyne for his outspoken opposition to Zionist ambitions.

On 30th July 1947, two British sergeants were abducted in the town of Natanya, and dragged away to the outskirts of the town where they were hanged in a eucalyptus grove and their bodies booby-trapped.

On 9th April 1948, Menachim Begin led an attack on the Arab village of Deir Yassin. After a short battle, the Zionists took control of the village and shot or blew up all those who still remained in the village houses. Reports agree that some 250 men, women and children were massacred. Both Arab and Israeli sources agree that the fear this incident induced in the Arab population was a significant factor in the flight of many Palestinians.

British authorities in Palestine which eventually persuaded the British Government that their position was untenable.

This is not the place to recount in detail the methods used by the Zionists, in effect, to invade and occupy Palestine. It is a story which, in the West at least, is seldom if ever told but, for the record, it is a story of ruthless determination in which deceit, terrorism, murder and ethnic cleansing played pivotal roles; in which hundreds of thousands of people were driven from their homes and their land to remain in refugee camps for decades; in which the rights of the indigenous Arabs were treated with the contempt sadly typical of racist ideologies which teach that one people is inherently superior to another by virtue of their racial origin. Even when Israel was preparing to declare itself a State, Arabs outnumbered Jews in Palestine by two to one (there were 1,380,000 Arabs; 700,000 Jews in 1947–8). After decades of the Zionist ingathering, the Jewish proportion of the population of Palestine was still only one third. Even within the proposed Jewish State, half the population was Arab. A speedier way to improve the ratio of Jews to Arabs and to acquire more land for further expansion of the Jewish population was obvious. The Arab Palestinians had to be encouraged to leave. A policy of ethnic cleansing was adopted.

The twentieth century saw many acts of terrorism perpetrated by people who sought freedom from colonial rule. The Zionist atrocities were different. They were enacted in order to impose alien rule on an indigenous people, in effect to impose the colonial rule of predominantly Western Jews on the Palestinians.

When the founder of the Kingdom of Saudi Arabia, King Abdul Aziz met President Roosevelt on the cruiser *USS Quincy* in February 1945, they discussed the issue of Palestine. President Roosevelt gave a promise – or rather two promises – to the Saudi King:

– he would never do anything which might prove hostile to the Arabs;

– the US Government would make no change in its basic policy on Palestine without full and prior consultation with both Jews and Arabs.

Immediately after Roosevelt's death, President Truman ignored these promises and, perhaps more concerned with popularity at home than justice abroad, worked tirelessly for the formation and recognition of the State of Israel – and thus for the dispossession of the Palestinians.

Whatever the reasons for President Truman's decision to ignore the undertakings of his predecessor, this much is certain. When the State of Israel was declared, the worst fears of the Palestinians were fulfilled.

And the seeds of several wars, the sufferings of millions of refugees and the grim situation we still face today were sown.

Well, some said, that is all history. Israel and those who support her hoped that, with time, the Palestinian problem would fade away; that the Palestinians would be absorbed by other countries; and that their aspirations for nationhood and for the land of their fathers would somehow disappear. This has proved an irrational and extremely dangerous notion. The Palestinians can scarcely forget that they have been dispossessed. Those who remain under Israeli rule are deeply resentful. The *Intifadas*, the Palestinian uprisings in the occupied territories, in 1988–9 and in 2000–2001, in which hundreds of Palestinians, armed only with sticks or stones, were shot dead by Israeli troops, gives some indication of how deep that resentment runs. And the Palestinian refugees living in camps in other Arab countries have not forgotten the homes and the land which belonged to them.

To the Saudi Government it has always seemed (as indeed King Abdul Aziz explained to President Roosevelt) that with a twisted logic, in some way, the Palestinians are being made to expiate the crimes of the Nazis. And that, because of those Nazi crimes, the Israelis are somehow excused for whatever action they take against those whom they have dispossessed. If this is the case, it is time the West acknowledged that the crimes of one society cannot be expiated by allowing the victims of those crimes to perpetrate crimes against another.

For obvious historical reasons, the West has great sympathy for Israel. The persecution of the Jews by the Nazis led, understandably, to feelings of guilt both in the country of the erstwhile persecutors and amongst other Western countries who could have done more to save the Jews from that persecution. (An indication of how deep that guilt runs and how assiduously it is exploited is to be found in the frequency with which television programs and films in Britain and the United States still feature the Nazi persecution of the Jews.) But Arabs have never understood how justifiable sympathy for one persecuted people can somehow excuse the persecution of another. If it was wrong for the Nazis to deny the rights of citizenship to the Jews, it must surely be wrong for Israel to deny the rights of citizenship to the Palestinians; if it was wrong for the Nazis to use the military power of the State to oppress a people, it must be wrong for the Israelis to oppress the Palestinians. If it was wrong for the Nazis to arrest Jews without due process of law, it must be wrong for the Israelis to carry out mass arrests of Palestinians without due legal process.

Of course the parallel is not exact. But it is sufficiently close for any reasonable person to realize that similar issues of moral principle are involved.

The purpose of this brief historical résumé is to try to explain why the Arab world in general and the Kingdom of Saudi Arabia as guardian of Islam's Holy Sites in particular have found it so difficult to accommodate what has been essentially a twentieth century act of colonization. It also helps to explain why

King Fahd, following in the tradition of his predecessors, has given special attention to the plight of the Palestinians and has used every means at his disposal to find a way to a just peace.

## Fahd Plan

In August 1981 Crown Prince Fahd put forward an eight-point peace plan. The plan became known as the Fahd Plan. The Plan consisted of the following provisions:

1. Israel to withdraw from all Arab territory occupied in 1967, including Arab Jerusalem.
2. Israeli settlements built on Arab land after 1967 to be dismantled, including those in Arab Jerusalem.
3. A guarantee of freedom of worship for all religions in the Holy Places.
4. An affirmation of the right of the Palestinian Arab people to return to their homes and compensation for those who do not wish to return.
5. The West Bank and the Gaza Strip to have a transitional period under the auspices of the United Nations for a period not exceeding several months.
6. An independent Palestinian State should be set up with Jerusalem as its capital.
7. All States in the region should be able to live in peace in the region.
8. The United Nations or Member States of the United Nations to guarantee the carrying out of these provisions.

The Fahd Plan was significant in several ways.

First, it showed that the Kingdom of Saudi Arabia was prepared to take the initiative in trying to solve the intractable problems posed by Israel.

Secondly, it indicated the type of approach King Fahd would take to international diplomacy. From an Arab point of view, the proposal was bold in that, implicitly, it accepted the existence of Israel and its right to live in peace in the region, subject to the other provisions of the Plan. (It has to be remembered, as noted above, that Israel was founded by displacing and dispossessing hundreds of thousands of Arab Palestinians who were and are still living in refugee camps around the Middle East, hoping for justice under international law.) The Fahd Plan recognized the reality of the situation. The provisions of the Plan gave Israel a guarantee of security within agreed borders, a guarantee that would of course be enforced by the United States if the United Nations were to prove ineffectual. At the same time, the Plan sought justice for the Palestinian Arabs or as much justice as was pragmatically possible. This combination of boldness in taking initiatives, combined with pragmatism, all undertaken through quiet diplomacy, has been the hallmark of King Fahd's approach to international affairs.

Third it showed King Fahd's commitment to the Holy Places of Islam (in

this instance, Jerusalem) and his respect for the Holy Places of the other People of the Book (Christians and Jews) and their right to worship.

*King Fahd receives the Palestinian leader Yasser Arafat*

The Fahd Plan was formally presented at the Arab Summit in Fez in November 1981. Between August and November, the Plan had caused considerable debate in the Arab world. It was contentious in that it recognized the right of Israel to exist; it was also contentious because it aimed to solve the Palestinian/Israel problem once and for all, thus providing the Palestinians with the independence they sought. The PLO and many other Arab countries voiced support for the Plan.

The Fahd Plan was adopted with minor changes and became known as the Fez Plan. It remains true that any settlement of the Palestine–Israel problem will have to be based on its provisions. The collapse of Israeli Prime Minister Ehud Barak's attempts to negotiate a peace settlement in 2000–2001 stemmed from his failure to grasp that the provisions of the Fahd Plan are the only basis on which a peaceful resolution is possible.

The years both before and after the Fahd Plan have not been happy ones for the Palestinians. Throughout these years, in addition to diplomatic efforts to encourage the peace process, the Kingdom of Saudi Arabia has been unstinting in its generosity to the Palestinian people. It is clear that the plight of the Palestinians has been in the forefront of King Fahd's mind throughout. A scrutiny of the minutes of almost any of the weekly meetings of the Saudi

Council of Ministers will reveal mentions of the Palestinians and the aid that King Fahd personally, or the Saudi Government, or the Saudi people as a whole, are sending to them.

For a selection of key documents relating to the Arab–Israeli conflict, see Appendix 2.

For thoughts on why the Western media, in general, portray such a distorted version of the Arab–Israeli conflict, see Appendix 3.

## The Gulf Cooperation Council (GCC)

The Cooperation Council for the Arab States of the Gulf, more commonly known as the Gulf Cooperation Council (GCC), was founded on 25th May 1981, when the Heads of State of the Kingdom of Saudi Arabia, Bahrain, Kuwait, Qatar, the Sultanate of Oman and the United Arab Emirates signed the new organization's constitution.

The structure of the GCC consists of the Supreme Council, the Ministerial Council and the Secretariat General:

– the Supreme Council (the highest authority of the GCC) comprises the Heads of State of the six member countries. The Supreme Council meets once a year in ordinary session. Emergency sessions can be convened at any time by the heads of any two Member States. The chairmanship of the Supreme Council is held by each Member State in turn. Resolutions are carried by majority vote. The Supreme Council is responsible for determining the overall policy of the GCC and for ratifying recommendations presented to it by the Ministerial Council or the Secretariat General.

| Country | Size | | Population |
|---|---|---|---|
| | Sq Mls | [Sq Km] | |
| Saudi Arabia | 865,000 | [2,240,000] | 21,400,000 |
| Bahrain | 267 | [691] | 607,000 |
| Kuwait | 6,880 | [17,818] | 1,897,000 |
| Oman | 116,000 | [300,000] | 2,460,000 |
| Qatar | 4,416 | [11,437] | 589,000 |
| United Arab Emirates | 30,000 | [77,700] | 2,397,000 |
| **TOTAL** | **1,022,563** | **[2,647,646]** | **29,350,000** |

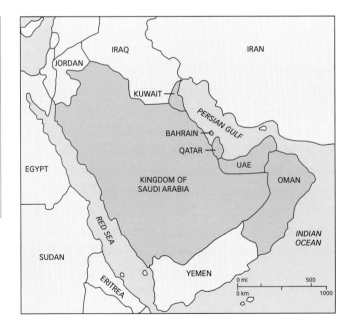

- The Ministerial Council comprises the Foreign Ministers of the six member countries. The Ministerial Council meets once every three months in ordinary session. Emergency sessions can be convened at any time by the Foreign Ministers of any two Member States. The Ministerial Council draws up policies and makes recommendations on means of developing cooperation and coordination amongst Member States in the economic, social and cultural spheres.
- The Secretariat General prepares reports, studies, accounts and budgets for the GCC. It drafts rules and regulations and is charged with the responsibility of assisting Member States in the implementation of decisions taken by the Supreme and Ministerial Councils. The Secretary General is appointed for a three-year period (renewable) by the Supreme Council on the recommendation of the Ministerial Council.
- The Secretariat is based in the city of Riyadh. The GCC headquarters are located in the Diplomatic Quarter, where a substantial complex, financed by a gift from King Fahd, has been built to meet the Secretariat's present and future needs.

The constitution of the GCC precisely reflected King Fahd's own view of the importance of seeking ways to make the unity of Arab States a reality. The constitution required the organization to provide "the means for realizing coordination, integration and cooperation" in economic, social and cultural affairs. Specifically, the GCC aimed:

- to achieve coordination, integration and close ties leading to unity between the Member States;
- to deepen the ties, relations and all aspects of cooperation between the peoples of the region;
- to adopt similar systems and laws in: economics and financial affairs; commercial, customs and transportation affairs; education and cultural affairs; social and health affairs; communication, informational, political, legislative and administrative affairs;
- to encourage progress in the sciences and technologies involved in industry, mining, agriculture, water and animal resources, and to establish scientific research centers and to undertake joint projects.

Inevitably, when independent sovereign States come together to seek a degree of integration, progress depends on consensus. In this context, the GCC has achieved much in its twenty years.

AGRICULTURE: The directive to harmonize agricultural policy was officially promulgated in 1985 and measures to harmonize many aspects of agriculture (including water conservation, the use of fertilizers and insecticides and various veterinary matters) have since been taken.

TRADE: A process of complete tariff unification was set in motion in 1994.

In June 1998, by which time Member States had agreed on the classification of most goods for external tariff purposes, a technical committee was set up to explore the possibility of a customs union. At the 20th Session of the GCC Supreme Council in November 1999, it was agreed that customs union should be achieved by 2005. In December 2000, the 21st Summit Meeting aimed to bring that date forward to 2002.

In 1998 a GCC Patent Office was established to protect intellectual property rights in the area.

Measures, including foreign investment guidelines published in 1997, have been taken at various times to encourage foreign investment.

Trade amongst the GCC Member States has flourished. In 1999, the Kingdom of Saudi Arabia imported more than SR 4 billion worth of goods from other GCC Member States, an increase of 8% on the preceding year.

EASE OF MOVEMENT WITHIN THE GCC: In 1997, a simplified passport system was approved by the Ministers of the Interior of the GGC Member States.

COORDINATION OF INFORMATION POLICY: From the mid-1990s, Ministers of Information from the GCC Member States met regularly to coordinate their work. At their meeting in the United Arab Emirates in 1999, the GCC Information Ministers affirmed the importance of strengthening the external information flow in the GCC States. They expressed their satisfaction with the success already achieved in bringing about the existing cooperation between the GCC information bodies and reaffirmed their commitment to the activation of the joint information projects between Member States in print, audio and video spheres.

OIL POLICY: Efforts to coordinate oil production and pricing policy have been maintained throughout the life of the GCC, with special emphasis on ensuring adequate supplies and the ability of each Member State to fulfill its quota in the event of any production problems.

DEFENSE: The Summit Meeting of the GCC in November 1981 decided to include cooperation in matters of defense in its remit. GCC defense ministers met early in 1982 to discuss a joint air defense system and the possibility of standardizing weaponry. In November 1984, it was agreed that a GCC rapid deployment force should be formed, made up of troops from all GCC Member States, to confront and repulse any aggressor. The force was named the "Peninsula Shield".

In October 1987, the GCC agreed on a mutual defense pact whereby an attack on any Member State would be construed as an attack on all Member States.

Iraq invaded Kuwait on 2nd August 1990. The GCC immediately condemned the invasion. As the coalition against Saddam Hussein was put in place, the

*King Fahd with other GCC leaders*

complex relations between the different Arab countries of the region shifted significantly. The GCC moved closer to Egypt and Syria, as it became clear that the Kingdom of Saudi Arabia, Egypt and Syria would spearhead the Arab component of the multinational alliance ranged against Saddam Hussein.

There have, of course, been disagreements between the Member States of the GCC. Border disputes have flared up from time to time (e.g. between the Kingdom of Saudi Arabia and Qatar in 1992 and between Bahrain and Qatar in 1996) but the commitment of the GCC leaders, and King Fahd's determination to show that Arab unity can be a reality, have ensured cohesion and progress, even on such sensitive issues.

*** 

As the sections of this chapter show, the diplomatic role played by the Kingdom of Saudi Arabia under King Fahd has been extensive and derives from the unique place that Saudi Arabia occupies in the Arab and Islamic world. Five times each day, Muslims turn towards the Holy City of Makkah to pray. This act symbolizes the unity of faith and purpose that Islam calls for and which King Fahd has always promoted. The Kingdom provides a focal point for the view that we all live in an interdependent world. In such a world, it is in the interests of the developed nations to help the developing world with technology and freedom to trade, so that they may prosper; it is in the interests of both oil producers and oil consumers that the finite oil reserves should be managed in a way which is fair to both parties; and it is in the interests of world peace that the international community applies fair and consistent criteria in judging and acting in instances of conflict between nations. These have been the guiding principles underpinning King Fahd's redoubtable diplomatic efforts over the years.

*Right: King Fahd during his visit
to the United States in 1985*

*King Fahd, durimg his visit to
Morocco, with King Hassan II
of Morocco (1982)*

*Above: King Fahd with President Mitterand of France in 1984*

*Left: King Fahd with President Reagan*

*Top: King Fahd with Margaret Thatcher during his visit to the United Kingdom in 1986*

*Above: King Fahd with Queen Elizabeth II, the Queen Mother and Prince Philip during his visit to the United Kingdom in 1986*

Top center: King Fahd with President Ben
Ali of Tunisia (1988)

Top: King Fahd with Sultan Qaboos of
Oman (1988)

Left: King Fahd with Sheikh Zayid Al
Nahayan, President of the UAE (1986)

Above: King Fahd with President Ali
Abdullah Saleh of Yemen (1990)

*Above: King Fahd and Crown Prince Abdullah with President Hosni Mubarak of Egypt (1991)*

*Right: King Fahd with former President George Bush in Riyadh (1996)*

*Above: King Fahd with British Prime Minister John Major (1996)*

*Left: King Fahd receiving Chinese President Jiang Zemin (1999)*

*Right:King Fahd with Syrian
President Bashar Hafez Al-
Assad (2000)*

*Below: King Fahd receiving
King Abdullah of Jordan
(2000)*

# KING FAHD AND SUPPORT FOR ISLAM AND ISLAMIC INSTITUTIONS AROUND THE WORLD

THE DETERMINATION OF the Kingdom to support Islam and Islamic institutions to the best of its ability was evident from the formation of the Kingdom by King Abdul Aziz but it was only when oil revenues began to generate real wealth that the Kingdom could fulfill its ambitions of spreading the word of Islam to every corner of the world, of assisting Muslim countries less well endowed economically and of alleviating the suffering of Muslim minorities wherever they might live.

When King Fahd gave his support, either personally or through his Government, to these institutions, it was also part of his purpose to challenge and expose the caricature of Islam which is widely promoted by sections of the Western media. Islam is a religion of compassion which has exercised a profoundly civilizing influence on mankind. By ensuring that there should be, where most needed, voices to promote the true teachings of Islam and the contribution of Arab culture and Islam to the history of mankind, King Fahd hoped to counteract and challenge negative stereotyping. In this enterprise, King Fahd has enjoyed only partial success. The voice of Islam and Arab culture is stronger now than it has been for many decades and certainly far stronger than it would have been without King Fahd's contribution, but the bias against Islam, the tendency, in some quarters, to identify Islam with fanaticism or even terrorism persists and has not been completely erased from the popular mind in the West.

The cost of King Fahd's efforts in this field has been astronomical, amounting to many billions of Saudi Riyals. In terms of Islamic institutions, the result is some 210 Islamic Centers wholly or partly financed by Saudi Arabia, more than 1,500 Mosques and 202 colleges and almost 2,000 schools for educating Muslim children. (*Source:* Kingdom of Saudi Arabia, 100 Years in the Service of Islam and Muslims, *The Islamic Center for Information and Development and* King Fahd bin Abdul Aziz, *Saudi Desert House Agency, 2000*)

> **NEWS RELEASE**
> Dateline 12th April 2000
>
> The Kingdom of Saudi Arabia has provided financial assistance to two Islamic institutions in Pakistan – the Holy Quran Teaching University for Girls and the Grand Khadija School for Girls in Karachi.
> *Source: SPA*

Here we list some of the major projects, with many of which King Fahd has been directly and personally involved.

## ACADEMIES

**NEWS RELEASE**

Dateline 13th July 2000

The Government of the Custodian of the Two Holy Mosques, King Fahd, has decided to set up a school in Italy and study classrooms in China to provide Arab and Muslim residents abroad with quality Islamic and Arabic education.

*Source: SPA*

With his lifelong commitment to education as the key to unlocking the potential of the individual, it is not surprising that King Fahd initiated a program to establish Islamic academies in some of the major capitals of the world. These academies were conceived in order to provide Muslim children abroad with the opportunity to attend an institution of academic excellence which could reinforce their commitment to their culture, religion and language while at the same time opening constructive dialogue with the societies in which they lived.

*Islamic Academy in Washington*

Established in 1984–5, the Islamic Academy in Washington teaches Arabic and Islamic studies. The academy has 1,200 students, both male and female. Of these, a little under half are from the Kingdom of Saudi Arabia; the others come from many other countries. In the ten-year period 1984 to 1994, the costs of establishing and running the academy were in excess of SR 100 million. (*Source:* Ibid)

*King Fahd Academy in London, England*

The King Fahd Academy in London caters for 1,000 students, amongst them the children of Arab diplomats serving in London, as well as other Arab and Muslim children living in London. The syllabus of the Academy covers not only Islamic studies and the Arabic language but also the British GCSE and "A" Level subjects in both science and arts. The Academy has established a high reputation for academic excellence.

*King Fahd Academy in Moscow, Russia*

The King Fahd Academy in Moscow is not only a major educational institution; it is a resolute attempt to undo the harm done to Islam and Islamic culture by the totalitarian communist regime of the erstwhile Soviet Union. Under communism, Muslims were persecuted, Mosques were desecrated and an alien ideology of materialism was imposed on the individual by the State. The King Fahd Academy in Moscow is one step towards reasserting Arab and Islamic culture and values.

The Academy is well equipped for language tuition in Arabic, Russian and English. Apart from educating its pupils in Islamic studies and Arab culture, the Academy aims to increase awareness, understanding and appreciation of Arab and Islamic culture amongst the Russian people.

*King Fahd Academy in Bonn*

The King Fahd Academy, opened in Bonn in 1995, comprises a school catering for 500 students and a Mosque which can accommodate 700 worshippers. It combines education in Arabic and Islam with a concerted effort to build bridges with German society by increasing understanding of Arab and Islamic culture. The total cost of the Academy was DM 30 million (equivalent to SR 76.5 million). (*Source:* Ibid)

*Bihac Islamic Academy*

The Kingdom of Saudi Arabia allocated SR 5 million for the establishment of this important educational institution, as part of its extensive aid program for the Republic of Bosnia-Herzegovina.

## ACADEMIC CHAIRS

In addition to setting up schools, King Fahd, in the course of his reign, has overseen the establishment of a number of academic chairs in some of the most respected universities in the developed world. In setting up these prestigious chairs, the Kingdom has pursued a number of objectives. They are further evidence of King Fahd's determination to encourage and enhance communications between Islamic culture and other cultures; to encourage understanding of the true nature of Islam by explaining clearly Muslim beliefs and by correcting common misconceptions and misrepresentations; and to show that Islam embraces knowledge with enthusiasm.

*King Abdul Aziz Chair at the University of California, Santa Barbara*
The King Abdul Aziz Chair in Islamic Studies was set up by the Saudi Royal Family in 1984.

*King Fahd Chair at Harvard University*
The King Fahd Chair in Islamic Studies was set up in 1993, with a donation of US$ 5 million from King Fahd himself.

*King Fahd Chair at the School of Oriental and African Studies, University of London*
The King Fahd Chair in Islamic Studies was set up in 1995, with a grant from King Fahd of £1 million.

*Prince Naif Chair at the University of Moscow*
The Prince Naif Chair of Islamic Studies was set up in 1996.

*Custodian of the Two Holy Mosques Chair at the Gulf University in Bahrain*
The Custodian of the Two Holy Mosques Chair at the Gulf University was set up to provide a resident professor in the Faculty of Medicine and Science.

## INSTITUTES TO PROMOTE ARAB AND ISLAMIC STUDIES

### Institutes Supported by the Kingdom

- Arab Islamic Institute, Tokyo
- Islamic Institute, Louga, Senegal
- Islamic Institute, Tivaouane, Senegal
- King Faisal Institute, Dhaka, Bangladesh
- Teacher Training Institute, Kibouli, Uganda
- Teacher Training Institute, Timbuktu, Mali

### Islamic Research & Study Institutes Supported by the Kingdom

*Within the Arab and Islamic World*

- Islamic Studies and Development Center, Shiany, Indonesia
- Islamic University of Malaysia
- Center of International Islamic Studies, Malaysia
- Islamic University of Pakistan
- Islamic University of Um Durman in Sudan
- Islamic University of Uganda

*Outside the Arab and Islamic World*

- American University of Colorado
- American University in Washington
- Arab World Institute, Paris, France
- Duke University, North Carolina
- Howard University, Washington
- Institute of the History of Arab and Islamic Science, Frankfurt, Germany
- Johns Hopkins University, Maryland
- Middle East Institute, Washington
- Shaw University, North Carolina
- Syracuse University, New York

Saudi Arabia has lent its support to all the following institutions:

- Al-Azhar University in Egypt
- Al-Zahira College in Sri Lanka
- Arabic Language Institute in Indonesia *(teaches Arabic and religious science, with annual running costs of SR 3.5 million)*
- Darul Hadith Al-Hasaniyah in Morocco
- Djibouti Institute

*Islamic Institute in Djibouti*

- Institute for Teaching Arabic in Japan
- Islamic University of Constantine in Algeria
- Islamic University in Dhaka, Bangladesh
- Mauritania Institute of Religious Sciences
- Palestine University in Algeria
- Ras al-Khaymah Institute *(SR 29 million to establish and SR 3 million annual running costs)*
- University Institutions in Palestine
- Zeitounia College in Tunisia (*Source:* Ibid)

## MOSQUES AND ISLAMIC CENTERS

### Canada

- Calgary Mosque
- The Islamic Center in Quebec
- The Islamic Center in Toronto
- Ottawa Mosque

### United States

- Dar al-Salam Institute
- Fresno Mosque in California
- The Islamic Center in Colombia, Missouri
- The Islamic Center in East Lansing, Michigan
- The Islamic Center in Los Angeles, California
- The Islamic Center in New Brunswick, New Jersey
- The Islamic Center in New York
- The Islamic Center in Tida, Maryland
- The Islamic Center in Toledo, Ohio
- The Islamic Center in Virginia
- The Islamic Center in Washington
- The Islamic Cultural Center in Chicago
- King Fahd Mosque in Los Angeles
- The Mosque of the Albanian Community in Chicago
- South-West Big Mosque of Chicago
- Umar bin Al-Khattab Mosque in Los Angeles

### Australasia

- The Australian Union of Islamic Councils
- The Islamic Center in Christchurch (New Zealand)
- The Islamic Center in the State of Victoria
- The Islamic Center in Townsville, Queensland
- Muslim Association in the Isles of Fiji

### South America & Elsewhere

- Guyana Mosque
- The Islamic Center in Brasilia
- The Islamic Center in Buenos Aires
- The Islamic Center in Campinas
- The Islamic Center in Forzwa Waikuwaso

- Lagos Society Mosque
- Mandusaba Mosque
- The Mosque and School of the Muslim Charity in Korea
- Paranajobsa Mosque
- São Paolo Charity Mosque
- Santo Amaro Mosque
- Santos Mosque (*Source:* Ibid)

## Europe

### Cultural Information Center in Brussels, Belgium
The Center has received total support of SR 19 million.

### Islamic Center in Geneva, Switzerland
The Center, which receives annual support of SR 19 million, contains a large Mosque, a cultural center, a school and a lecture hall.

### Islamic Center in Madrid, Spain
The Islamic Center in Madrid, which has had total support of SR 27 million, is one of the largest in Europe. It comprises a very capacious Mosque, a prayer hall for women, a library, a lecture hall and a medical clinic.

*Islamic Cultural Center in Spain*

*HRH Prince Abdul Aziz bin Fahd inaugurating King Fahd Mosque in Edinburgh*

*Islamic Center in London, England*

The Kingdom has contributed some SR 25 million to the cost of the London Islamic Center.

*Islamic Center in Edinburgh, Scotland*

The Islamic Center in Edinbugh, located in the city center, contains a Mosque which can accommodate 1,000 worshippers, and includes a library, a lecture hall and classrooms. It cost around SR 15 million.

*Islamic Center in Rome, Italy*

The Islamic Center in Rome comprises a Mosque, a library and a lecture hall. King Fahd donated US$ 50 million (some 70% of the total) to cover the cost of construction. The Center also receives an annual donation of US$ 1.5 million.

*Mosque of the Custodian of the Two Holy Mosques in Gibraltar*

The complex, which cost in excess of SR 30 million, comprises a Mosque for men, a prayer hall for women, a school, a library and a lecture hall.

## Africa

*Bamaco Mosque in Mali*

The Bamaco Mosque incorporates a residence for the imam and muezzin, a library and a lecture hall, and cost approximately SR 25 million.

*Islamic Center in Abouja, Nigeria*

This Center, constructed in the new capital, comprises a large Mosque, a library, a school, a lecture hall and housing. The Kingdom's contribution to the cost of the Center was SR 100 million.

*King Abdul Aziz Mosque in Tunisia*

One of the largest and surely one of the most beautiful Mosques in Tunisia, the King Abdul Aziz Mosque was built at a cost of 610,000 Tunisian dinars. The Mosque can accommodate more than 2,000 worshippers and includes a prayer hall for women with a separate entrance.

*King Faisal Mosque and Center in Conakry, Guinea*

The Mosque, the biggest in West Africa, is one of the main features of Conakry (the capital of Guinea). The Mosque itself cost SR 60 million to build, while the Center cost a further SR 20 million.

*King Faisal Mosque in N'djamena, Chad*

The complex includes two schools, a lecture hall and a library. The Mosque enjoys financial support from the revenues of a group of commercial shops, established by endowment. The total cost of construction was in excess of SR 60 million.

*Ten Mosques in the Arab Republic of Egypt*

These Mosques which, taken together, can accommodate approximately one million Muslims were built by the Kingdom of Saudi Arabia for the victims of earthquakes in Egypt, at a cost of almost SR 7 million:

- Mosque of the Custodian of the Two Holy Mosques King Fahd bin Abdul Aziz in Halwan
- Riyadh Mosque in Kafr al-Shaikh
- Makkah al-Mukarramah Mosque in Hahya in al-Sharqiya Governorate
- Al-Madinah al-Munawwarah Mosque in the village of al-Ibraheemiya in the al-Shariqiya Governorate
- Prince Abdullah Mosque in the city of Toukh in al-Qaliobiya
- Prince Sultan Mosque in al-Khanka city
- Prince Sattam Mosque in the village of Qareen
- Prince Salman Mosque in the city of al-Qanatir in al-Khayriya
- Al-Shinnawi Mosque in the village of Dijoy in al-Qaliobiya
- Al-Arabaeen Mosque in the village of al-Marj

*Yaondi Mosque in Cameroon*

This is a grand Islamic monument in the heart of Africa and an important center for the promotion of Islam. It accommodates 5,000 worshippers and includes a school and a library. It cost almost SR 19 million.

## Asia

*King Faisal Mosque in Islamabad*

Building work started in 1976. Costing an estimated SR 130 million, it covers an area of 53,821 square feet [5,000 sq m] and can accommodate 10,000 worshippers and a further 40,000 in the adjacent squares.

*King Faisal Center in the Maldives*

Built at a cost of SR 7 million to accommodate 4,000 worshipers, it also contains an Islamic library and classrooms for the study of the Holy Quran.

*Islamic Center in Tokyo, Japan*

The Kingdom of Saudi Arabia contributed SR 1.8 million to the cost.

*Indonesian Islamic Center*

The Kingdom contributed SR 7 million to the Center, which comprises a Mosque, a nursery school, a dispensary, a library and an information center.

*Mosques in the People's Republic of China*

The Kingdom contributed some SR 4 million to the building of three Mosques, one in Taipei, one in Tiegan and one in Kao-hsiung.

# KING FAHD'S SUPPORT FOR INTERNATIONAL ISLAMIC ORGANIZATIONS

In addition to financing Islamic academic institutions and Islamic centers and Mosques around the world, the Kingdom of Saudi Arabia has always been a leading member of international Islamic organizations. Throughout King Fahd's reign, the Kingdom of Saudi Arabia has played an active role in all these organizations, using its influence to nurture and encourage unity in the Islamic world.

## Organization of the Islamic Conference

The Organization of the Islamic Conference (OIC) was founded in May 1971, following agreement of Muslim leaders at their summit meeting in Morocco in September 1969 that such an organization should be formed.

The OIC objectives were defined as the following:

- promoting Islamic solidarity
- consolidating cooperation between Member States in the economic, social, cultural and scientific fields and arranging consultations among Member States belonging to international organizations
- endeavoring to eliminate racial discrimination and segregation and to eradicate colonialism in all its forms
- taking necessary measures to support international peace and security, founded upon justice
- coordinating all efforts to protect the Holy Places and supporting the struggle of the Palestinians to regain their rights and liberate their land
- strengthening the struggle of all Muslims in order to safeguard their dignity, independence and national rights
- creating an atmosphere conducive to the promotion of cooperation and understanding among Member States and other countries

There are currently fifty-six countries belonging to the OIC, with a number of other countries accorded observer status.

In fostering cooperation the OIC, like the entire Muslim world, has faced many challenges. In the course of King Fahd's reign, the OIC has had to contend with the Iraq–Iran War, the Gulf War and Israel's persistent abuse of the Palestinians and periodic assaults on Arab nations. It has not always been possible to achieve the unity which the OIC charter calls for but, throughout, the Kingdom of Saudi Arabia has followed King Fahd's principle of seeking peace with justice whenever possible by diplomacy.

The OIC has its head office in Jeddah and Saudi Arabia is the home of several of the OIC's subsidiary/affiliated organizations:
- Islamic Jurisprudence Academy, Jeddah
- Islamic Solidarity Fund, Jeddah
- International Islamic News Agency, Jeddah
- Islamic States Broadcasting Organization, Jeddah
- International Association of Islamic Banks, Jeddah
- Islamic Committee for the International Red Crescent, Jeddah
- Islamic Solidarity Sports Federation, Riyadh
- Organization of Islamic Capitals and Cities, Jeddah
- Organization of the Islamic Shipowners' Association, Jeddah

## World Assembly of Muslim Youth

Founded in 1972, the World Assembly of Muslim Youth, which has its head-quarters in Riyadh, aims to assist young Muslims around the world in leading fulfilled lives through Islam. Amongst its many and diverse activities, the Assembly encourages young people to make a very real contribution to Islamic society, supports organizations around the world which cater for young Muslims, holds international meetings at which young Muslims can meet and discuss issues of importance to them and publishes a vast array of material ranging from leaflets to encyclopedias in various languages.

A distinguishing feature of King Fahd's public life has been his evidently clear concern for children and young people. He has often referred to the people of the Kingdom as its true wealth. Its young people are its future wealth and King Fahd has shown through his actions a genuine conviction that it is the duty of the Government and society to do all in their power to ensure that young people are brought up in a decent society which clearly distinguishes between right and wrong.

In addition the Kingdom of Saudi Arabia has played a role in nurturing Islamic unity through the Muslim World League, based in the Holy City of Makkah.

## PROVISION OF COPIES OF THE HOLY QURAN

In Madinah stands the King Fahd Complex for Printing the Holy Quran. The Complex is a unique publishing venture. It was opened by King Fahd in 1984 with the aim of printing and distributing copies of the Holy Quran to as wide an audience as possible. It produces the Holy Quran in Arabic and, in translation, in many other languages. It produces the Holy Book as a whole and in sections. When operating a single-shift system, the Complex is able to produce 10 million copies of the Holy Quran each year. On a three-shift operation, the Complex is able to produce 30 million copies.

Since its inauguration, the Complex has produced more than 60 editions, amongst them copies of the Holy Quran in full, sections of the Holy Quran, translations of the Holy Quran, recordings of verses of the Holy Quran, books on the prophetic tradition and biographies of the Prophet Muhammad, peace be upon him. The Complex has translated the Meanings of the Holy Quran into more than twenty languages, including Bengali, Bosnian, Chinese, English, French, Korean, Somali, Thai, Turkish and Urdu. Translations of the Meanings of the Holy Quran into many other languages are under way.

By the year 2000, the Complex had printed 138 million copies of the Holy Quran which had been widely distributed inside the Kingdom (through the Two Holy Mosques, other Mosques and Government and religious institutions) and abroad (through embassies, overseas information offices and Islamic organizations). The Complex also produces recordings of the Holy Quran, read by the most respected readers within and outside the Kingdom, in video and audio form.

In a further and much needed initiative designed to make the teaching of Islam as widely and easily accessible as possible, the Complex produced a Braille version of the Holy Quran so that every blind Muslim, anywhere in the world, can have ready access to the Word of God.

In fulfilling the wishes of King Fahd, the Complex has become much more than a printing and distribution operation. It is a preeminent study and research facility for all aspects of the Holy Quran and stands as an authority on the Book of God and the Sunnah of the Prophet Muhammad, peace be upon him.

*King Fahd Complex for Printing the Holy Quran, Madinah*

# KING FAHD AND FOREIGN AID

THROUGHOUT ITS OWN development, the Kingdom of Saudi Arabia has been mindful of the Muslim obligation to cooperate with those less fortunate and of its responsibilities in the community of nations, especially in the Arab world and amongst the less developed countries. King Fahd, throughout his time as Crown Prince and King, has accepted this responsibility unequivocally.

Although a relatively young country, Saudi Arabia has quickly understood the reality of interdependence, which exists between one nation and another. The Kingdom is, of course, particularly involved with the industrialized nations of the West, supplying much of these countries' energy requirements and importing much of the West's technology. But there is also an interdependence, both moral and economic, between rich nations and poor. This belief in a global community in which the interests of all peoples (rich and poor, developed and developing, producer and consumer) should be taken into account, underpins King Fahd's views in many areas, including the provision of aid.

The catalog of grants and loans provided by the Kingdom of Saudi Arabia would fill a book. Here the aim is simply to give some indication of the magnitude of the Kingdom's aid program under King Fahd and some insight into the thinking that has led him to sustain and extend it.

In the twenty years from 1973 to 1993, despite considerable variations in national revenues and many competing demands, the Kingdom of Saudi Arabia provided 5.5% of its Gross National Product in overseas aid. Given that the United Nations has suggested 0.7% as the lower limit for donor countries, the Kingdom's contribution has been outstanding.

The most important channel for Saudi Arabian aid is the Saudi Fund for Development which was established by Royal Decree in 1974 and began operations in 1975. At the time of its inception, the Fund's capital amounted to SR 10 billion; however, because of the developing countries' increasing need for assistance in order to implement development projects, the Fund's capital has been augmented twice, and now totals SR 25 billion.

Underlying the Fund and its objectives is the conviction that, by assisting less fortunate countries to develop with grants and soft loans, the Kingdom is helping to realize the ideal of a global community in which self-interest coincides, and is seen to coincide, with the interests of the planet as a whole.

| COUNTRY | % SHARE OF SFD LOANS |
|---------|---------|
| Tunisia | 13.6% |
| Sudan | 10.5% |
| Jordan | 10.3% |
| Syria | 9.6% |
| Morocco | 8.8% |
| Egypt | 8.0% |
| Mauritania | 7.0% |

The terms under which the Saudi Fund for Development provides loans were formulated to provide recipients with the greatest possible help:

- the loans are without conditions
- funds are made available quickly and easily
- repayment terms are generous (up to 50 years with a 10-year grace period)
- the outright grant component of such loans can amount to 60% of the total
- the cost of loans is generally 1%

By 1995, the Fund had loaned more than SR 21 billion. By 1998, 62 countries had benefited from Saudi Development Fund help which had financed 298 projects. Asia accounted for 52% of Fund loans and Africa for 46%.

Arab countries have been major beneficiaries of Saudi Fund for Development loans but other countries in need of developmental aid have not been neglected.

In addition to the moneys which the Saudi Fund for Development has been able to make available, the Kingdom is a major contributor to a number of other regional and international financial institutions established to provide aid to the developing world.(See table at right)

King Fahd's approach to foreign aid has always been to provide as much as possible whenever it is needed. Even when oil revenues have plummeted and subjected the Kingdom to economic difficulties which would have entirely disrupted a less coherent society, King Fahd has overseen a continuous program of substantial overseas aid:

*Under pressure of sharply falling oil revenues, uncertainties regarding the future of the oil market and the regional security situation, Saudi Arabian ODA volume declined from a peak of US$ 5.5 billion in 1981 to US$ 2.6 billion in 1985, but recovered to US$ 3.5 billion in 1986. In 1987, it was about US$ 2.9 billion. As a proportion of the Kingdom's oil revenues, ODA rose from 10% in 1983–5 to 15% in 1986–7, and Saudi Arabia's ratio of ODA to GNP has remained by far the highest among all donors. Saudi aid is untied, quick-disbursing, and highly concessional, with a grant element of 96% (1986). (Source: The World Bank, August 1988)*

| ORGANIZATION | SAUDI CONTRIBUTION IN US$ | SAUDI CONTRIBUTION AS % OF TOTAL CAPITAL |
|---|---|---|
| International Monetary Bank | 6,534,200,955 | 3.42% |
| International Bank | 3,032,764,000 | 3.32% |
| International Development Institute | 1,665,700,000 | 3.5% |
| OPEC International Development Bank | 1,033,279,607 | 30.1% |
| Arab Bank for Economic & Social Development | 553,100,000 | 22.9% |
| Islamic Development Bank | 536,440,000 | 25.5% |
| International Fund for Agriculture | 333,778,000 | 14.26% |
| Arab Bank for Economic Development in Africa | 255,584,153 | 24.4% |
| Funding within the Islamic Conference Organization | 214,662,000 | – |
| Arab Monetary Fund | 187,300,000 | 14.5% |
| Arabian Gulf Program for Support of the UNDF | 150,000,000 | 76% |
| Programs for Fighting Drought | 130,000,000 | 54% |
| African Development Fund | 116,524,973 | 3.4% |
| International Agency for Insurance of Investment | 31,370,000 | 3.14% |
| Programs for Treating River Blindness | 25,000,000 | 8.36% |
| International Financing Institute | 17,911,000 | 1.37% |
| African Bank for Development | 14,279,460 | 0.25% |
| Arab Bank for Technical Support of Arab & African Countries | 13,563,000 | 22.6% |
| Arab Institute for the Insurance of Investment | 3,750,000 | 15% |

*Source:* Kingdom of Saudi Arabia – One Hundred Years in the Service of Arabs and Muslims, *Alwaa Publishing House*

*Saudi assistance to Somalia*

*Saudi assistance to Somalia*

In a world where aid is so often in the form of interest-bearing loans which have to be spent by the recipient on purchasing goods or services from the donor country, it is not only the scale but the nature of Saudi aid which is noteworthy.

A very considerable amount of Saudi aid is channeled through the OPEC Development Fund. The table above right sets the Saudi contribution into context. Under King Fahd, Saudi Arabia is distinguished not only by the size of its contributions but also by the promptness with which it honors its obligations.

There is a danger that a presentation of the figures for Saudi Arabian aid may appear rather dry. That is a pity because these figures represent jobs for people in the developing world – in agriculture and industry, in construction and transport, in healthcare and tourism. Around the developing world, men and women work and, as a result, their families are housed and fed, because of this money.

| CONTRIBUTIONS TO THE OPEC DEVELOPMENT FUND (PLEDGED AND PAID IN, BY COUNTRY) IN US$ | | |
|---|---|---|
| COUNTRY | PLEDGED | PAID IN |
| Algeria | 100,720,000 | 96,799,075 |
| Ecuador* | 5,120,000 | 4,115,684 |
| Gabon | 5,120,000 | 4,804,486 |
| Indonesia | 12,440,000 | 11,983,362 |
| Iran, Islamic Republic of | 516,185,808 | 167,869,526 |
| Iraq | 178,508,831 | 87,013,238 |
| Kuwait | 372,748,175 | 358,525,916 |
| Libya, S.P.L.A.J. | 205,005,159 | 157,000,459 |
| Nigeria | 244,161,797 | 236,841,831 |
| Qatar | 93,635,497 | 89,899,937 |
| Saudi Arabia, Kingdom of | 1,033,279,607 | 995,038,196 |
| United Arab Emirates | 168,446,623 | 161,939,683 |
| Venezuela | 499,636,941 | 488,360,532 |
| **TOTAL** | **3,435,008,438** | **2,860,191,925** |

* Ecuador withdrew from the Fund in December 1993.

*Source:* Annual Report of the OPEC Fund for International Development, 1997

*Saudi assistance to Turkey*

Dateline: Makkah, 12th February 2001

**MUSLIM WORLD LEAGUE SECRETARY GENERAL PRAISES SAUDI RELIEF AID**

Dr. Abdullah bin Abulmohsin Al-Turki, Secretary General of the Muslim World League (MWL), highlighted here today the charitable and relief work being extended by the Kingdom of Saudi Arabia...MWL's Secretary General pointed to the raising of funds, collection of material donations, and their distribution to support the Palestinian people and the uprising over the last four months. These charitable schemes have cost more than SR 120 million since last Rajab.

*Source: SPA*

Before we leave this subject, there is another aspect of King Fahd's approach to aid that is distinctive and worthy of note. Whenever natural or manmade disasters afflict a population, whether in the Arab, the Islamic or the wider world, King Fahd's response has been immediate. By the time the world has heard of the latest incident, the relief planes are on the tarmac at one of the Kingdom's international airports. Whether it is an earthquake in Algeria, Egypt or India, or drought in Africa, or ethnic cleansing in Bosnia, or the suffering of the Palestinians in their occupied homeland, King Fahd issues instructions for the aid to be assembled and dispatched.

Indeed the Council Meetings of the Kingdom provide not only a record of the frequency and generosity of the Kingdom's donations but also an extraordinary insight into the Kingdom's priorities. There must be few governments where the Head of State and his cabinet spend so much time discussing the needs of peoples in foreign countries and allocating financial and material aid to meet them.

It is also the case that while the Saudi Government itself is organizing State relief, King Fahd and many others in the Kingdom add generously to the aid effort from their own resources.

# KING FAHD, THE MAN

PRINCE FAHD WAS BORN in Riyadh in 1923, at a propitious time when his father, Abdul Aziz, was completing his unification of the land that was to be the Kingdom of Saudi Arabia, the land which sixty years later would be ruled by King Fahd.

By all accounts, the relationship between Prince Fahd and his father was a close one. Clearly, as Prince Fahd observed in his father the qualities that had enabled him to unite the fractious tribes of the Arabian Peninsula into a united country (the Kingdom was formally founded in 1932 when Prince Fahd was 9 years old), so King Abdul Aziz evidently discerned in his son the potential for leadership. The young Prince Fahd must therefore be given the best education the new Kingdom could at that time offer. King Abdul Aziz was determined to ensure that Prince Fahd should be fully versed in the Holy Scriptures of Islam, and in Arab history and culture.

Prince Fahd's first formal schooling was at the "Princes' School" in Riyadh, a school established by his father to ensure that his own sons and the children of other leading citizens were well equipped for the challenges that lay ahead. At the Princes' School, Prince Fahd was tutored by men such as Ahmed Al Arabi and Sheikh Abdul-Ghani Khayat. After completing his time at the Princes' School, Prince Fahd then attended the Religious Knowledge Institute in the Holy City of Makkah where he received further instruction from the most eminent Islamic scholars in the Kingdom.

In short, by the time Prince Fahd's schooling was completed, he was steeped in the traditions of his society, the teachings of Islam and, through his regular contact with his father, the mechanisms of power and the qualities required to operate those mechanisms judiciously.

Prince Fahd's first official visit outside the Kingdom was to attend the inauguration of the United Nations in New York in 1945, as part of the Saudi delegation led by the then Foreign Minister, later King, Faisal.

| YEAR | DAY/ MONTH | EXPERIENCE BEFORE BECOMING KING |
|------|-----------|----------------------------------|
| 1945 | 24th October | Prince Fahd member of Saudi delegation at signing of UN charter |
| 1953 | | Prince Fahd appointed first Minister of Education and charged with establishing a nationwide educational system |
| 1953 | | Prince Fahd leads Saudi delegation to coronation of Queen Elizabeth II |
| 1959 | | Prince Fahd heads Saudi delegation to 33rd session of League of Arab States in Casablanca, Morocco |
| 1962 | | Prince Fahd appointed Minister of the Interior |
| 1965 | | Prince Fahd represents Saudi Arabia at meeting of Arab Heads of State in Cairo, Egypt |
| 1967 | | Prince Fahd appointed Second Deputy Prime Minister |
| 1967 | | Prince Fahd visits France and meets with former President de Gaulle |
| 1970 | | Kingdom's first Five-Year Plan launched |
| 1970 | | Prince Fahd leads Saudi delegation in talks with Britain on future of Arabian Gulf |
| 1974 | | Prince Fahd makes first official visit to Washington. Saudi–US joint Commission on Economic Cooperation set up |
| 1975 | | Prince Fahd attends OPEC Summit in Algeria |
| 1975 | | Prince Fahd makes second visit to France |
| 1975 | 25th March | Khalid becomes King on the assassination of King Faisal |
| 1975 | | Prince Fahd becomes Crown Prince and Deputy Prime Minister |
| 1975 | | Kingdom's second Five-Year Plan launched |
| 1977 | 19th May | Crown Prince Fahd hosts talks with President Assad of Syria and President Sadat of Egypt in Riyadh |
| 1977 | 23rd May | Crown Prince Fahd visits US to discuss Middle East peace plan with President Jimmy Carter |
| 1979 | March | Crown Prince Fahd leads Saudi delegation to Arab Summit in Baghdad |
| 1980 | | Kingdom's third Five-Year Plan launched |
| 1981 | August | Fahd Plan for resolution of Arab–Israeli conflict published |
| 1981 | November | Fahd Plan is formally presented at the Arab Summit in Fez |
| 1981 | | Crown Prince Fahd leads Saudi delegation to North–South Conference in Cancun, Mexico |

At the age of 30, in 1953, Prince Fahd was appointed as the Kingdom's first Education Minister which is where the story told in this book begins. It was to be another thirty years before Prince Fahd became King but a summary of some of his duties in the intervening period shows that, by the time his reign began, he had a rich and varied experience of government, politics and diplomacy both at national and international level.

As ruler, King Fahd's first concern has had to be the security and stability of the country. This is the primary responsibility of any Head of Government but, in the case of Saudi Arabia, the responsibility is of paramount importance since the Kingdom is home to the Holy Cities of Makkah and Madinah and their guardianship is an integral part of the monarch's responsibility.

Achieving security and stability has not always been entirely straightforward. The demands of modernization have inevitably created tensions from time to time in a deeply conservative society. Striking the balance between those who wish to modernize as quickly as possible and those who are concerned that modernization could threaten the unique character of the Kingdom has demanded a high degree of skill. In exercising this skill, King Fahd has been helped by the tradition of consultation which permeates Saudi society. There have always been channels for every party to express their views. That has not necessarily helped King Fahd to find solutions but it has made him and his Government aware of any problems and sensitive to the balance of opinion on any issue.

The need to ensure the Kingdom's security and stability has also created complex challenges for King Fahd at the level of international relations. Saudi Arabia and the United States have had a close and reciprocally beneficial relationship from the time when American oil companies initiated the exploitation of the Kingdom's oil. The Kingdom has enjoyed the benefits of technology transfer from the United States and the United States has enjoyed not only guaranteed supplies of oil but oil at a price which, as far as the Kingdom is able to influence it, is fair to both producer and consumer. Saudi Arabia has invested large sums in the American economy and American companies, through joint ventures and other forms of commercial enterprise, have invested in the Kingdom. When Iraq invaded Kuwait, the United States led the international alliance which expelled the Iraqis from Kuwaiti territory. All this is illustrative of a mutually beneficial relationship.

At the same time, the bias of the United States in favor of Israel, its readiness to excuse the most atrocious acts by Israel against an occupied and dispossessed people, its apparent inability to see through Zionist propaganda, have alienated the Arab world. We have dealt with the Palestine–Israel issue elsewhere in this book at some length. Here it is sufficient to say that the relationship between Saudi Arabia and the United States will become one of full reciprocity only when Israel gives some measure of justice to the Palestinians and the third most Holy Site in Islam is returned to Arab sovereignty. That day is most likely to come when the United States realizes that 200 million Arabs and 1,000 million Muslims who simply seek justice are rather more important

*Crown Prince Fahd*

than Israel and its Zionist supporters who are determined to perpetuate a crime against a people whose only offense was to have lived for centuries on land the Zionists coveted.

We have shown, in the pages of this book that, in every act of diplomacy, King Fahd has sought to negotiate peace with justice. Even in the most vexed of issues, border disputes, the Kingdom, under King Fahd, has tried to resolve argument by international arbitration rather than force. The agreement with Yemen on the delineation of the Saudi/Yemen border is a model of the civilized way to resolve such matters.

At the same time, King Fahd has never been an advocate of peace at any price. When circumstances have necessitated it, King Fahd has always been prepared to place his authority behind a just cause and devote whatever resources, in men or money, are required to support it. Saudi troops led the way into Kuwait against the Iraqi invasion force and, whenever the Palestinians have needed help, the Kingdom has been unstinting in the humanitarian aid it has supplied.

It is difficult to find a corner of the world where Saudi Arabia, under King Fahd, has not made a contribution, either in humanitarian aid (which flows forth as soon as a need is recognized) or in promulgating Islam by building Mosques and Islamic centers and by distributing copies of the Holy Quran.

At home, King Fahd's achievements speak for themselves. Those visitors to the Kingdom who have known the country throughout King Fahd's reign will attest to the extraordinary development of the Kingdom's infrastructure, education, health services, agriculture and industry over the last twenty-five years. But King Fahd's legacy at home is not the buildings, the roads, the ports and airports; it is the people who, through education and social services, have been transformed from simple, generally illiterate, tribesmen or traders into literate individuals capable of holding their own and competing in the modern world.

Of course the foundations for much of this achievement were laid down by King Fahd's predecessors but the drive and determination to make what seemed impossible happen over the last twenty-five years belonged to King Fahd.

Some cynics will say that a survey of the Kingdom today simply shows what you can achieve with money. And it is true that without the resources provided by oil revenues, the achievements would not have been possible. But the money was a necessary but not a sufficient condition. The factor which determined how best to exploit the Kingdom's resources in order to produce the Saudi Arabia of today was the vision of King Fahd.

There is another side to King Fahd which we have scarcely touched upon. It is his humanity, not as a King able to dispense vast sums to relieve the suffering caused by the latest natural or manmade disaster, but as one individual touched by the needs of another. The stories of his personal generosity are legion. Whether it is a small child in England in need of a liver and bowel transplant or children in Egypt needing an expensive eye operation beyond their parents' means, or a young man in Tunisia with a skin disease requiring specialist treatment, King Fahd has acted.

There are still many challenges ahead for King Fahd and his successors. How to manage the Kingdom's fluctuating oil revenues, how to find sufficient work for a young and fast-growing population, how to foster the elusive Arab unity without which the Arab nation will never reach its full potential, how to counter disinformation about Islam and about the Kingdom – these are just some of the challenges which are easy to identify – and, with the passage of time, no doubt new challenges will arise. But, in terms of what a man can achieve in his allotted life span, King Fahd has proved to be the right man at the right time and, with the help of God, has taken the opportunity to achieve far more than most.

There have been monuments built to mark the passing on earth of great men. Across the Red Sea, the pyramids still stand as giant tombs to long-dead pharaohs. King Fahd has a finer monument – a nation and a country that he has left far better than he found it.

# UNIVERSITIES OF THE KINGDOM OF SAUDI ARABIA

SAUDI ARABIA NOW has eight major universities:

- King Saud University in Riyadh
- Islamic University in the Holy City of Madinah
- King Abdul Aziz University in Jeddah
- Imam Muhammad bin Saud Islamic University in Riyadh
- King Faisal University in Dammam and Hofuf
- King Fahd University of Petroleum and Minerals in Dhahran
- Umm Al-Qura University in the Holy City of Makkah
- King Khalid bin Abdul Aziz University in Abha

All but two of these universities (the King Fahd University of Petroleum and Minerals and the Islamic University) admit women as well as men, and all universities admit foreign as well as Saudi Arabian students.

Below we look at these universities in more detail.

### King Saud University

The King Saud University (PO Box 2454, Riyadh 11451), founded in 1957 as the Riyadh University and renamed in 1982, has 2,000 teachers, more than 30,000 undergraduate students and more than 600 postgraduate students (almost 40% of whom are female). As one of the first institutions of higher education in Saudi Arabia, it has on its register more than a quarter of all the Kingdom's university level students (male and female) and more than one third of all the Kingdom's university and administrative staff.

The University has the following colleges:

- Administrative Sciences
- Agriculture, Agriculture and Veterinary Sciences (in Al-Qassim)
- Arts
- Computer Sciences

- Dentistry
- Economics and Administration (in Al-Qassim)
- Education (in Abha)
- Engineering, Medicine (in Abha and Al-Qassim)
- Allied Medical Sciences
- Pharmacy
- Science

There is also a College for Graduate Studies, a Center for Women's University Studies and an Arabic Language Institute.

The faculties authorized to confer higher degrees are as follows:

1. The Faculty of Arts has conferred Master of Arts degrees in Geography and History since 1973–4 and in Arabic Language since 1975–6. Since 1975, the Faculty of Arts has also offered a one-year program leading to a Diploma in Information and now confers a Bachelor of Arts degree in that subject.

2. The Faculty of Education offers:
   (a) a one-year diploma program in Educational Administration, usually offered to the directors (principals) of the general high schools;
   (b) a diploma in Education.

There are several other higher education programs offered by this faculty.

The King Saud University admits women. As early as 1961–2 women were allowed to enrol as external students in the colleges of Arts and Administrative Sciences. In 1975–6, they were accepted as full-time students. The Center for Women's University Studies was established a year later, to provide a center for the development and supervision of all aspects of women's higher education. Women students now pursue their studies in a wide range of subjects including Arabic language, English language, geography, history, sociology and social work.

*Islamic University*

The Islamic University (PO Box 170, Madinah) was founded in 1961. Its main objectives are the following:

- Conveying the eternal message of Islam to the entire world by means of Dawa (Islamic Call).
- Inculcating the true Islamic spirit in the students, urging the individual and the community to practice the precepts of Islam in daily life and worship God alone, and to follow the example of the Prophet Muhammad, peace be upon him, with the utmost sincerity and devotion.
- Teaching religious knowledge to students from different parts of the world and enabling them to become highly qualified scholars, specializing in various Islamic Arabic disciplines.

- Collecting, verifying and publishing works relating to Islamic heritage.
- Maintaining and fostering scholarly and cultural ties with other universities and scientific institutions and organizations throughout the world to serve the cause of Islam and realize its objectives.

The University has 5,032 students, 3,452 of whom are non-Saudis. There are 15 professors, 42 associate professor, 138 assistant professors, 98 lecturers and 52 demonstrators, bringing the academic staff total to 345.

The University has the following faculties:

- Shariah (Islamic Law)
- Dawa & Usul-Ud-Din (Islamic Call & Theology)
- Holy Quran & Islamic Studies
- Arabic Language
- Hadith & Islamic Studies

The University also has the following centers:

Data Center: It is related to the Department of Administrative Development and its aims are the following:

- Preparing the developmental plan of the Center
- Introducing the computer system to the educational and administrative departments of the University
- Coordinating with other computer centers in universities and in governmental sectors
- Communicating with specialized companies in the fields of maintenance and computer information

Sunna and Sira Serving Center: The goals and objectives of the Center are the following:

- Preparing an encyclopedia in Hadith (Prophet's Traditions) and other encyclopedias in Sunna and Sira Serving
- Translation of Sunna and Sira books
- Refuting false matters in the field of Sunna and Sira
- Publishing the achievements of the Center
- Cooperating with other centers and organizations and scientific institutions in the field of Sunna and Sira
- Using the computer collecting Sunna and programming the relative information

The Scientific Research and Islamic Heritage Center: Its goals and objectives are the following:

- Preparing research and scientific studies in the field of Islamic and Arabic studies
- Publishing research and scientific studies
- Publishing a scientific magazine
- Preparing the periodicals and booklets on issues relating to Islamic society

- Explaining Islamic heritage
- Following up publications about Islam and Muslims in the world
- Cooperating with other organizations and institutions, which work in the field of scientific research inside and outside the Kingdom
- Communicating with famous Islamic characters
- Collecting manuscripts, documents and information
- Executing the policies of the scientific council in the field of scientific research and Islamic heritage

Document & Archiving Center: The Center classifies and stores all documents in the University, so that they may be easily found when needed.

### King Abdul Aziz University

The King Abdul Aziz University (PO Box 1450, Jeddah 21441), founded in 1967, has 2,071 teachers and more than 39,000 students.

Established initially as a private university, King Abdul Aziz University was converted to a State university in 1971. The Jeddah-based University is built on an area of 400 acres [162 hectares] and has the following colleges:

- Geology
- Marine Sciences
- Economics and Administration
- Arts and Human Sciences
- Science
- Engineering
- Medical Sciences
- Education
- Meteorology
- Earth Sciences
- Marine Sciences
- Dentistry

The University awards Master's degrees in Earth Sciences, Economics and Administration, Education, Humanities, Marine Sciences, Meteorology and the Environment, and Sciences. It awards Doctorates in Earth Sciences and Education.

The Research and Development Center (which forms part of the Faculty of Economics and Administration), the International Center for Research in Islamic Economics and the King Fahd Medical Research Center (all in Jeddah), are attached to the King Abdul Aziz University.

### Imam Muhammad Bin Saud Islamic University

The Imam Muhammad bin Saud Islamic University (PO Box 5701, Riyadh 11432), founded in 1953, was accorded university status in 1974. The

University and its supporting units are built on an area of 43 million square feet [4 million sq m]. It has more than 1,000 teachers and more than 30,000 students.

The Imam Muhammad bin Saud University is an international educational and cultural institution. Currently the University is composed of several faculties. The High Judiciary Institute was originally established in 1965 for the purpose of graduating qualified Shariah judges. The Faculty of Shariah (Theology) was established earlier in 1953 for the purpose of meeting the demand for qualified Ulama and preachers throughout the country. The Faculty of Arabic Language and Social Science was originally established as the Faculty of Social Science in 1970 and was expanded in 1974 by adding the Arabic Language major and a program in Library Science.

The University comprises the following colleges:
- Islamic Law (Shariah)
- Arabic Language
- Fundamental Studies in Islam
- The Higher Institute for Islamic Jurisdiction
- Social Studies
- Institute for Teaching Arabic Language (for non-native speakers)
- Propagation – at Madinah
- "Studies of Fundamental Principles in Islam" – Qassim area
- Social and Arabic Sciences – Qassim area
- "Shariah and Studies of Fundamental Principles of Islam" – in the southern region
- Arabic Language and Social Sciences – in the southern region
- Jurisdiction and Islamic Studies – in Al-Hasa area

*King Faisal University*

The King Faisal University in Dammam and Hofuf (PO Box 400, Al-Hasa 31982), founded in 1975, has some 500 teachers. The total student enrolment in 1999 was 8,126.

The idea of establishing a university in the eastern region was originated by King Faisal in 1974. The then Crown Prince Fahd's efforts brought into existence the King Faisal University, which was inaugurated during the academic year 1975–6 with two campuses. The first campus is in Hofuf in Al-Hasa and it comprises the faculties of Agriculture, Veterinary Medicine and Animal Resources. The second campus is located in Dammam and consists of the faculties of Medicine and Medical Sciences (established with the educational cooperation of Harvard University), and of Engineering. The campus at Al-Hasa now also caters for female students of home economics, medicine and dentistry.

One of the main objectives of the University is to modernize teaching methods. It is also committed to the development of study plans to serve the requirements of the local environment. In this context, the University offers consultancy, guidance and training programs for several bodies in the field of community service. The Community Service Center in the University encourages teaching staff to develop technical skills (in agriculture, commerce, education and engineering) to meet requirements at local community level.

The University has the following eight colleges:
- Agriculture and Nutrition Sciences
- Medicine and Medical Sciences
- Veterinary Medicine and Animal Resources
- Architecture and Planning
- Education
- Planning and Administrative Science
- Dentistry
- Applied Science of Medicine

*King Fahd University of Petroleum and Minerals*

The King Fahd University of Petroleum and Minerals (PO Box 5061, Dhahran 31261) was founded in 1963 under the name of the College of Petroleum and Minerals with fewer than 100 students. In 1964, the College decided to admit other Arab and Muslim students along with Saudi students. The College was officially inaugurated in 1965 by King Faisal who, on that occasion, declared that "it is a great pleasure for us to take part in inaugurating this great institution, of which the least that can be said is that it represents one of the pillars of our scientific, economic and industrial development". By 1974, student enrolment had increased to 1,500 and it was accorded university status in 1975. In December 1986, the University became the King Fahd University of Petroleum and Minerals. The University has some 800 teachers and, in 1995, there were 7,000 students.

The University is a semi-autonomous institution operating under an independent University Board, headed by the Minister of Higher Education. It has the following six teaching colleges:
- Applied Engineering
- Computer Science and Engineering
- Engineering Science
- Environmental Design
- Industrial Management
- Sciences

It also has a College of Educational Services, a Graduate School, a Center of Applied Geology and a Data Processing Center.

Studies in the University concentrate on the areas of petroleum and minerals and much encouragement is given to related scientific research. The University endeavors to promote awareness and understanding of petroleum and mineral issues in the Kingdom. Most important is that the University trains skilled manpower needed for the petroleum and mineral industries in the Kingdom. The University keeps abreast of the latest technological and scientific developments in the field. The University awards the Bachelor's degree in certain fields of engineering and science. There are also Master's and Doctoral programs in some fields of science, engineering sciences and industrial management.

The King Fahd University of Petroleum and Minerals can now claim to be a university with internationally acknowledged and respected standards of academic and technical excellence in the fields of petroleum and mineral technology.

Because of the importance of oil to the Kingdom's economy and the key role that the King Fahd University of Petroleum and Minerals plays in it, it is appropriate to give further details of the University's development since its foundation.

When the University (then a college) first started in 1963, student enrolment was 67; there was a faculty strength of 14. In 1978, student enrolment was 2,350, of whom 8% were non-Saudi students from 25 Arabian Islamic countries. The faculty strength had reached 388 from 25 different countries, including 37 Saudi professors with PhD degrees. Over 100 Saudi "faculty" members were in training in the United States, working for their PhDs. By 1983, 3,814 students had enrolled.

Saudi students enrolled at the University received generous financial aid from the Government (free tuition, monthly allowance, subsidized meals at the University's cafeteria, essential medical care, furnished and air-conditioned accommodation, free textbooks and round-trip air transportation to the student's place of residence once each academic year). The University offered similar scholarships to non-Saudi students from the Arab and Islamic world. It had students from Bahrain, Egypt, Ethiopia, Indonesia, Iraq, Jordan, Lebanon, Morocco, Pakistan, Qatar, Sudan, Syria, Tunisia and Yemen.

The University was governed by a Board consisting of prominent Saudi and non-Saudi scholars and governmental officials. The Saudi Minister of Petroleum and Mineral Resources was its chairman until 1976, when the Minister of Higher Education became Chairman of the Board.

The King Fahd University of Petroleum and Minerals' academic program to train the manpower for the petroleum and related industries was comple-mented by the decision to set up a major Applied Research Institute to help solve technical problems in this field. The Institute's program included six areas of focus – petroleum and gas; alternative sources of energy (such as solar power); minerals; water and the environment; standards metrology; and eco-nomic and industrial research.

A SR 900 million ($260 million) expansion of campus facilities began in 1977, including a 29,000 square-foot [24,000 sq m] building for the Research Institute; a building for the Graduate School, College of Industrial Manage-ment and the Data Processing Center; a Conference Center within the Department of Architecture; a 10,000-seat stadium; and a doubling of family and student housing.

By 1978, 1,000 engineers and industrial managers had graduated. By 1988, the University, now the King Fahd University of Petroleum and Minerals, had awarded more than 4,940 degrees, including 520 Master's and 4 PhD degrees.

The main instructional and research thrust of the University is supported by a number of services that are centralized and serve all departments. Among those of greatest importance to the academic program are the Library, the Information Technology Center, the Central Research Workshop, the English Language Center, the Physical Education Department, and the Cooperative Program (COOP).

## Umm Al-Qura University

The Umm Al-Qura University (PO Box 715, Makkah 21421), founded in 1979 and accorded university status in 1981, had on its register almost 14,000 undergraduate students in the year 1986, of whom more than 6,000 were female, and more than 400 postgraduate students. The number of students has now reached 20,600.

Originally, this institution included Colleges of Shariah and Education and an institute to teach Arabic language to non-Arabs, all of which functioned as branches of the King Abdul Aziz University. Later Colleges of Agricultural Sciences, Arabic Language, Applied Sciences and Engineering, Dawa and Usul-El-Din, Education (in Taif), and Social Sciences were opened.

A number of scientific centers are affiliated to the colleges of this University (for example, the Educational and Psychological Research Center, the Hajj Research Center, the International Center for Islamic Education, the Scientific and Engineering Research Center, and the Scientific Research and Islamic Heritage Rejuvenation Center). In addition, the Umm Al-Qura University cooperates with a number of foreign universities and other aca-demic institutions through scientific exchanges and scholarships.

*King Khalid bin Abdul Aziz University*

The King Khalid bin Abdul Aziz University began its life in the form of branches of King Saud University and Imam Muhammad bin Saud Islamic University in Abha, in the Asir region. In 1998 it was accorded university status.

Some 13,000 students study in the University's four faculties. These are the following:

- Faculty of Education
- Faculty of Medicine
- Faculty of Islamic Law and Fundamentals of Religion
- Faculty of Arabic and Administrative Studies

# KEY DOCUMENTS RELATING TO THE ARAB–ISRAELI CONFLICT

**Balfour Declaration**

2nd November 1917

*Balfour was the British Foreign Secretary, Rothschild the British Zionist leader.*

Dear Lord Rothschild,

I have much pleasure in conveying to you on behalf of His Majesty's Government the following declaration of sympathy with Jewish Zionist aspirations, which has been submitted to and approved by the Cabinet.

*His Majesty's Government view with favour the establishment in Palestine of a national home for the Jewish people, and will use their best endeavours to facilitate the achievement of this object, it being clearly understood that nothing shall be done which may prejudice the civil and religious rights of existing non-Jewish communities in Palestine, or the rights and political status enjoyed by Jews in any other country.*

I should be grateful if you would bring this declaration to the knowledge of the Zionist Federation.

Yours sincerely,

Arthur James Balfour.

\*\*\*\*\*

**Text of the UN Security Council Resolution 242**

22nd November 1967

*The Security Council,*

*Expressing* its continued concern with the grave situation in the Middle East,

*Emphasizing* the inadmissibility of the acquisition of territory by war and the need to work for a just and lasting peace in which every State in the area can live in security,

*Emphasizing further* that all Member States in their acceptance of the Charter of the United Nations have undertaken a commitment to act in accordance with Article 2 of the Charter

1. *Affirms* that the fulfillment of Charter principles requires the establishment of a just and lasting peace in the Middle East, which should include the application of both the following principles:

    (i)  Withdrawal of Israeli armed forces from territories occupied in the recent conflict;

    (ii) Termination of all claims or states of belligerency and respect for the acknowledgement of the sovereignty, territorial integrity and political independence of every State in the area and their right to live in peace within secure and recognized boundaries free from threats or acts of force.

2. *Affirms further* the necessity:

    (*a*) For guaranteeing freedom of navigation through international waterways in the area;

    (*b*) For achieving a just settlement of the refugee problem;

    (*c*) For guaranteeing the territorial inviolability and political independence of every State in the area, through measures including the establishment of demilitarized zones;

3. *Requests* the Secretary-General to designate a Special Representative to proceed to the Middle East to establish and maintain contacts with the States concerned in order to promote agreement and assist efforts to achieve a peaceful and accepted settlement in accordance with the provisions and principles in this resolution;

4. *Requests* the Secretary-General to report to the Security Council on the progress of the efforts of the Special Representative as soon as possible.

*Source:* UN Document S/RES/242 (1967).

\*\*\*\*\*

## UN Security Council Resolution on Jerusalem

25th September 1971

*The Resolution, No. 298 (1971), was passed* nem. con., *with the abstention of Syria.*

   *The Security Council,*

   *Recalling* its resolutions 252 (1968) of 21st May 1968, and 267 (1969) of 3rd July 1969, and the earlier General Assembly resolution 2253 (ES-V) and 2254 (ES-V) of 4th and 14th July 1967, concerning measures and actions by Israel designed to change the status of the Israeli-occupied section of Jerusalem,

*Having considered* the letter of the Permanent Representative of Jordan on this situation in Jerusalem and the reports of the Secretary-General, and having heard the statements of the parties concerned in the question,

*Recalling* the principle that acquisition of territory by military conquest is inadmissible,

*Noting* with concern the non-compliance by Israel with the above-mentioned resolutions,

*Noting with concern also* that since the adoption of the above-mentioned resolutions Israel has taken further measures designed to change the status and character of the occupied section of Jerusalem

1. *Reaffirms* its resolutions 252 (1968) and 267 (1969);

2. *Deplores* the failure of Israel to respect the previous resolutions adopted by the United Nations concerning measures and actions by Israel purporting to affect the status of the City of Jerusalem;

3. *Confirms* in the clearest possible terms that all legislative and administrative actions taken by Israel to change the status of the City of Jerusalem, including expropriation of land and properties, transfer of populations and legislation aimed at the incorporation of the occupied section, are totally invalid and cannot change that status;

4. *Urgently calls upon* Israel to rescind all previous measures and actions and to take no further steps in the occupied section of Jerusalem which may purport to change the status of the City, or which would prejudice the rights of the inhabitants and the interests of the international community, or a just and lasting peace;

5. *Requests* the Secretary-General, in consultation with the President of the Security Council and using such instrumentalities as he may choose, including a representative or a mission, to report to the Council as appropriate and in any event within 60 days on the implementation of the present resolution.

*Source:* UN Document S/RES/298 (1971).

\*\*\*\*\*

## UN Security Council Resolution 338

22nd October 1973

*UN resolutions between 1967 and October 1973 reaffirmed Security Council Resolution 242 (see above). In an attempt to end the fourth Middle East war, which had broken out between the Arabs and Israel on 6th October 1973, the UN Security Council passed the following Resolution:*

*The Security Council,*

1. *Calls upon* all parties to the present fighting to cease all firing and terminate

all military activity immediately, not later than 12 hours after the moment of the adoption of the decision, in the positions they now occupy;

2. *Calls upon* the parties concerned to start immediately after the ceasefire the implementation of Security Council Resolution 242 (1967) in all of its parts;

3. *Decides that,* immediately and concurrently with the ceasefire, negotiations start between the parties concerned under appropriate auspices aimed at establishing a just and durable peace in the Middle East.

*Source:* UN Document PR/73/29 (1973).

# WESTERN MEDIA ATTITUDES TO THE ARAB WORLD

WHY IS IT that the Western media retain their sympathy for Israel, even when Israel's conduct clearly offends against basic human rights? In 1989, as the Palestinian death toll in the *Intifada* rose inexorably, the Red Cross, after many months of fruitless remonstration with the Israeli authorities, condemned Israel in the strongest of terms for its brutal treatment of the Palestinians in the occupied territories. In 2000, when Ariel Sharon's ill-timed and intentionally provocative visit to Al Aqsa Mosque initiated another *Intifada*, the killing of Palestinians by the Israeli armed forces escalated, with deaths amongst the Palestinians facing an army of occupation far exceeding those amongst the Israelis. Yet the main tenor of press editorial comment in Britain and the United States still urged sympathy and understanding for Israel as it continued to obstruct attempts to find a peaceful means of according the Palestinians the right to self-determination in a land of their own.

The explanation for the Western media's biased treatment of events in the Arab–Israeli conflict, apart from a collective guilt over Nazi atrocities, seems obvious to Arabs. It was indeed a feature of the Nazi persecution of the Jews. The only "satisfactory" way to deny human rights to a people is to deny that people's humanity. If the Palestinians are viewed as decent human beings, to deny them basic human rights is clearly morally unacceptable. But if it can be shown that they and their supporters have forfeited their claim to belong to the world community of decent humanity – because they are, for example, deceitful, ignorant, uncivilized, undemocratic, unstable and violent – the moral dilemma is, at least, diminished.

In other words, to some (and probably to a large) extent, Western media hostility to the Arabs in the last few decades has ensued from a Western commitment to Israel's cause, and the consequent need to dehumanize those who oppose Israel, in order to justify Israel's inhumane behavior. The mechanism whereby this process is accomplished is a continuing emphasis on those aspects of Arab society which differ from Western culture – and, of course, an equally persistent emphasis on those aspects of Israeli society which Israel shares with the West.

Thus, Israel, which has effectively disenfranchized its Palestinian population, is nevertheless routinely described by the Western media as "democratic", in contrast with the "undemocratic" Arabs. Israel's judiciary, despite the random arrest and imprisonment of Palestinians, is characterized as based on Western principles of justice, in contrast with the "barbarity" of the Islamic penal system. Even Israel's ruthless suppression of the *Intifada* is often presented as the response of the forces of law and order to the violence of dissidents and terrorists, despite the fact that the *Intifada* is taking place in land which Israel has occupied as a foreign army.

So why do the Western media and Western politicians feel the need to placate Israel? It is generally recognized that in the United States (and, to a lesser extent, in Britain) politicians and the media alienate the Zionist lobby at their peril. It has even been said that no one becomes the President of United States without the support of the pro-Israeli pressure groups. Aware of the need to sustain support for Israel, the Zionists, through the American Israeli Public Affairs Committee (AIPAC) and its British counterpart (BIPAC) and through other pro-Israeli pressure groups, use their influence to maintain the image of Israel as part of the Western community and draw attention to any cultural difference which divides the West and the Arab world. They have their clearly defined objectives and they work effectively to fulfill them.

In the modern world of mass communications, we are all aware of how the media can be used to disseminate information or indeed distortions of the truth, literally at the speed of light. We have learned to discern the techniques that professional communicators use to put their "spin" on the facts they present. The language used (freedom-fighter or guerrilla or terrorist; the bombing of civilians or collateral damage; Government or regime), even the order in which facts are presented, can dramatically affect the information the reader or viewer "takes out" of any presentation.

Some of the distortions of the truth are conscious. More dangerous are those that are unconscious, those that are based on a fundamentally distorted view of an issue which automatically ensures that new information is filtered and realigned to confirm the distorted view before it is broadcast.

This is the world of today. The Arab world has an uphill task in shifting American and British opinion on the Palestine–Israel problem but, since the Arab view is rooted in history and reality, and the Palestinian cause is just, it may yet succeed.

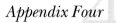

# CHRONOLOGY OF EVENTS
# MENTIONED IN THIS BOOK

## WITH A SELECTION OF OTHER EVENTS IN THE LIFE OF
## KING FAHD TOGETHER WITH A SELECTION OF HISTORICAL
## EVENTS IN THE REGION

APART FROM SETTING out a chronological sequence to the events described in the various chapters of this book, we hope this chronology will give a real flavor of the priorities that have infused the life of King Fahd bin Abdul Aziz bin Abdul Rahman Al Saud.

| YEAR | DAY/MONTH | SELECTED EVENTS IN KING FAHD'S LIFE | OTHER EVENTS IN THE KINGDOM | HISTORICAL MARKER |
|------|-----------|-------------------------------------|-----------------------------|-------------------|
| 1923 | | Prince Fahd is born, son of King Abdul Aziz bin Abdul Rahman Al Saud (Ibn Saud) founder of the modern Kingdom of Saudi Arabia | | |
| 1923 | | | Saudi Arabia grants first oil concession | |
| 1925 | | | Final consolidation of the Arabian Kingdom is accomplished | |
| 1926 | | | Abdul Aziz becomes King of Hijaz and Sultan of Najd and its Dependencies | |
| 1927 | | | | Major Iraqi oil field discovered in Kirkuk |
| 1930 | | | Charles R. Crane visits Saudi Arabia at King Abdul Aziz's invitation | |
| 1931 | May | | United States formally recognizes existence of Abdul Aziz's Kingdom | |
| 1931 | | | Karl Twitchell, the engineer, arrives in Jeddah to conduct a survey of the Kingdom | |
| 1932 | 23rd September | | Kingdom of Saudi Arabia officially founded | |
| 1933 | | | Oil discovered in Saudi Arabia | |
| 1935 | | | Oil found in a well drilled in Dhahran | |
| 1938 | | | Exploitation of Saudi oil fields begins | |

| YEAR | DAY/MONTH | SELECTED EVENTS IN KING FAHD'S LIFE | OTHER EVENTS IN THE KINGDOM | HISTORICAL MARKER |
|---|---|---|---|---|
| 1939 | 3rd September | | | Second World War starts |
| 1945 | 14th February | | King Abdul Aziz meets the US President Franklin D. Roosevelt on board the *USS Quincy* | |
| 1945 | 17th February | | King Abdul Aziz meets Winston Churchill | |
| 1945 | 22nd March | | | League of Arab States founded |
| 1945 | 8th May | | | End of Second World War against Germany |
| 1945 | 15th August | | | Japan surrenders to the Allies unconditionally |
| 1945 | 24th October | Prince Fahd member of Saudi delegation at signing of UN Charter | | United Nations formed |
| 1948 | April | | | First Arab–Israeli war |
| 1948 | 14th May | | | Israel founded |
| 1948 | | | King Abdul Aziz establishes a Shariah College in the Holy City of Makkah | |
| 1948 | | | Transmission from the first public radio broadcasting station in Jeddah | |
| 1952 | | | Saudi Arabian Monetary Agency founded | |
| 1953 | 18th June | | | Egypt becomes a republic |
| 1953 | 9th November | | King Abdul Aziz dies | |
| 1953 | 9th November | | Saud becomes King | |
| 1953 | | Prince Fahd appointed first Minister of Education and charged with establishing a nationwide educational system | | |
| 1956 | 26th July | | | Nasser nationalizes Suez Canal |
| 1956 | October–November | | | Suez/Sinai war: Israel, Britain and France send troops into Egypt |
| 1956 | 7th November | | | Ceasefire in Suez/Sinai war |
| 1957 | 7th March | | | Suez Canal reopens |
| 1957 | | | Riyadh University founded | |
| 1959 | | Prince Fahd heads Saudi delegation to 33rd session of League of Arab States in Casablanca, Morocco | | |
| 1960 | 14th September | | | Organization of Petroleum Exporting Countries (OPEC) founded |
| 1961 | | | Islamic University in the Holy City of Madinah founded | |
| 1962 | | Prince Fahd appointed Minister of the Interior | | |
| 1963 | | | Petroleum and Minerals College founded | |
| 1963 | | | Saudi Arabian Airlines established | |
| 1963 | | | Saudi Red Crescent founded | |
| 1964 | November | | Faisal becomes King and retains role of Prime Minister. Khalid is appointed Crown Prince and Deputy Prime Minister | |
| 1964 | | | Riyadh Broadcasting Station begins radio transmission | |

| YEAR | DAY/MONTH | SELECTED EVENTS IN KING FAHD'S LIFE | OTHER EVENTS IN THE KINGDOM | HISTORICAL MARKER |
|---|---|---|---|---|
| 1964 | | | Call of Islam Station in Holy City of Makkah begins radio transmission | |
| 1964 | | | Saudi Arabian Olympic Committee established | |
| 1965 | January | Prince Fahd represents Saudi Arabia at meeting of Arab Heads of State in Cairo, Egypt | | |
| 1965 | | | First test television transmission takes place from stations in Riyadh and Jeddah | |
| 1966 | | | Neutral zone between Saudi Arabia and Kuwait apportioned equally | |
| 1967 | 5th June | | | Six Day Arab–Israeli War: |
| 1967 | October | Prince Fahd appointed Second Deputy Prime Minister | | |
| 1967 | 22nd November | | | UN Resolution No. 242 sets out formula for Arab–Israeli peace settlement |
| 1967 | | | King Abdul Aziz University in Jeddah founded | |
| 1968 | 9th January | | | Organization of Arab Petroleum Exporting Countries (OAPAC) founded |
| 1969 | 3rd February | | | Yasser Arafat elected Chairman of PLO |
| 1969 | | | General Organization for Social Insurance (GOSI) established | |
| 1970 | | Prince Fahd leads Saudi delegation in talks with Britain on future of Arabian Gulf | | |
| 1970 | 28th September | | | President Nasser dies; Sadat becomes provisional President of the United Arab Republic (Egypt) |
| 1970 | December | Prince Fahd leads Saudi delegation on Buraimi border talks | | |
| 1970 | | Kingdom's first Five-Year Plan launched | | |
| 1970 | | | Dual-purpose water desalination plant built in Jeddah | |
| 1970 | | | Saudi Press Agency established | |
| 1971 | May | | | Organization of the Islamic Conference founded |
| 1971 | 2nd December | | | Six Trucial States merge to form United Arab Emirates (UAE) |
| 1971 | | | | PLO expelled from Jordan to Lebanon |
| 1972 | | | General Organization for Grains Silos and Flour Mills established | |
| 1972 | | | Saudi Arabian Arts Society established | |
| 1972 | | | | World Assembly of Muslim Youth founded |
| 1973 | March | | | Iraqi forces occupy a Kuwaiti outpost on the Kuwait–Iraq border and assert claim to two islands belonging to Kuwait |

| YEAR | DAY/MONTH | SELECTED EVENTS IN KING FAHD'S LIFE | OTHER EVENTS IN THE KINGDOM | HISTORICAL MARKER |
|---|---|---|---|---|
| 1973 | 6th October | | | Arab–Israeli October War |
| 1973 | 17th October | | | Arab oil producers cut supplies to exert pressure for Israeli withdrawal from occupied territory |
| 1973 | 22nd October | | | UN Resolution 338 calls for ceasefire in October War |
| 1974 | 22nd November | | | United Nations formally recognizes PLO |
| 1974 | | Prince Fahd makes first official visit to Washington. Saudi–US joint Commission on Economic Cooperation set up | | |
| 1974 | | | Saline Water Conversion Corporation established | |
| 1974 | | | Saudi Credit Bank established | |
| 1974 | | | General Presidency of Youth Welfare established | |
| 1974 | | | Saudi Industrial Development Fund established | |
| 1974 | | | Saudi Fund for Development established | |
| 1974 | | | Imam Muhammad bin Saud Islamic University, founded in 1953, given university status | |
| 1975 | 25th March | | Khalid becomes King on the assassination of King Faisal | |
| 1975 | 25th March | Prince Fahd becomes Crown Prince and Deputy Prime Minister | | |
| 1975 | 13th April | | | Lebanon Civil War starts |
| 1975 | 5th June | | | Suez Canal reopens |
| 1975 | 12th June | Crown Prince Fahd visits Iraq to discuss border issues | | |
| 1975 | 1st July | Crown Prince Fahd visits Tehran | | |
| 1975 | 2nd July | | Saudi Arabia and Iraq agree on partitioning of neutral zone | |
| 1975 | 21st July | Crown Prince Fahd visits France to discuss economic collaboration | | |
| 1975 | 9th September | | Royal Commission for Jubail and Yanbu established | |
| 1975 | October | | Saudi Cabinet increased by six ministerial posts | |
| 1975 | | Kingdom's second Five-Year Plan launched | | |
| 1975 | | | King Faisal University established | |
| 1975 | | | College of Petroleum and Minerals was accorded university status. (In 1986 the University became the King Fahd University of Petroleum and Minerals) | |
| 1975 | | | | Spain gives Western Sahara to Morocco and Mauritania |
| 1976 | 18th February | | Saudi Arabia and Iraq sign neutral zone agreement | |
| 1976 | | | Saudi Arabian Basic Industries Corporation (SABIC) established | |
| 1976 | | | Saudi Arabian Railway Corporation founded | |

| Year | Day/Month | Selected Events in King Fahd's Life | Other Events in the Kingdom | Historical Marker |
|---|---|---|---|---|
| 1976 | | | | Arab Satellite Communications Organization (ARABSAT) formed |
| 1977 | 19th May | Crown Prince Fahd hosts talks with President Assad of Syria and President Sadat of Egypt in Riyadh | | |
| 1977 | 23rd May | Crown Prince Fahd visits United States to discuss Middle East peace plans with President Jimmy Carter. Crown Prince Fahd puts forward a proposal that an independent Palestinian State should be set up, embracing the Israeli-occupied West Bank and the Gaza Strip, as part of a peace settlement. | | |
| 1977 | 26th June | | Saudi Arabia recognizes Republic of Djibouti | |
| 1977 | 19th November | | | Sadat visits Israel |
| 1977 | | | SCECO-East created | |
| 1978 | 3rd January | President Carter visits Riyadh for talks with King Khalid and Crown Prince Fahd | | |
| 1978 | 15th March | | | Israeli thrust into Lebanon |
| 1978 | June | | | Israel's withdrawal from Lebanon |
| 1978 | 17th September | | | Sadat and Begin sign peace agreement at Camp David |
| 1978 | | | Saudi Arabian Arts Society changes its name to Saudi Arabian Society for Culture and Arts | |
| 1979 | 15th January | | | Shah departs Iran for ever |
| 1979 | 1st February | | | Ayatollah Khomeini arrives in Tehran |
| 1979 | March | Crown Prince Fahd leads Saudi delegation to Arab Summit in Baghdad | | |
| 1979 | 26th March | | | Egypt makes a bilateral peace with Israel |
| 1979 | 16th July | | | Saddam Hussein becomes President of Iraq |
| 1979 | | | | Mauritania signs peace treaty with the Polisario |
| 1979 | 25th December | | | Soviet invasion of Afghanistan |
| 1979 | | | SCECO-South and SCECO-Central created | |
| 1979 | | | Saudi Public Transport Company established | |
| 1979 | | | Umm Al-Qura University in the Holy City of Makkah founded | |
| 1980 | 1st March | | | UN Resolution No. 465 deplores Israeli settlements on occupied territories |
| 1980 | 18th March | | Following Crown Prince Fahd's support for the plan, a committee to draft a "System of Rule", based on Islamic principles, appointed | |
| 1980 | 30th July | | | Israel annexes East Jerusalem |

| YEAR | DAY/MONTH | SELECTED EVENTS IN KING FAHD'S LIFE | OTHER EVENTS IN THE KINGDOM | HISTORICAL MARKER |
|---|---|---|---|---|
| 1980 | 22nd September | | | Open warfare between Iraq and Iran starts |
| 1980 | | | Aramco becomes 100% Saudi-owned | |
| 1980 | | Kingdom's third Five-Year Plan launched | | |
| 1981 | April | | "System of Rule" committee proposes plan for Consultative Committee, earlier endorsed by Crown Prince Fahd | |
| 1981 | 25th May | | | Gulf Cooperation Council (GCC) founded |
| 1981 | 7th August | Fahd Plan for resolution of Arab–Israeli conflict published | | |
| 1981 | 6th October | | | President Sadat of Egypt assassinated. Mubarak becomes President |
| 1981 | November | Fahd Plan is formally presented at the Arab Summit in Fez. | | |
| 1981 | 14th December | | | Israel annexes Golan Heights |
| 1981 | | Crown Prince Fahd leads Saudi delegation to North/South Conference in Cancun, Mexico | | |
| 1981 | | | King Abdul Aziz International Airport opens in Jeddah | |
| 1982 | May | | | Iran launches first counter-offensive against Iraq and retakes Khorramshahr |
| 1982 | 6th June | | | Israel invades Lebanon |
| 1982 | 13th June | | King Khalid dies | |
| 1982 | 13th June | Crown Prince Fahd becomes King. Prince Abdullah, Commander of the National Guard since 1962, becomes Crown Prince | | |
| 1982 | 5th August | King Fahd urges President Reagan to curb Israeli excesses in Lebanon | | |
| 1982 | 22nd August | | | Palestinian fighters evacuate Lebanon under US supervision |
| 1982 | 5th September | | | Arab Summit discusses Middle East peace plan |
| 1982 | 16th September | | | Phalangist militiamen, with Israel's blessing, enter Palestinian refugee camps of Sabra and Chatila and massacre 2,000 |
| 1982 | 11th November | King Fahd and Sheikh Isa bin Salman Al-Khalifa lay the cornerstone of King Fahd Causeway | | |
| 1982 | 14th November | President Amin Gemayel of Lebanon visits King Fahd | | |
| 1982 | | King Fahd donates $500,000 to Project Orbis, the flying eye hospital | | |
| 1982 | | | SCECO-West  established | |
| 1982 | | | Riyadh University renamed King Saud University | |

| YEAR | DAY/MONTH | SELECTED EVENTS IN KING FAHD'S LIFE | OTHER EVENTS IN THE KINGDOM | HISTORICAL MARKER |
|---|---|---|---|---|
| 1983 | February | | | Ariel Sharon held responsible for massacres at Sabra and Chatila, resigns post of Defense Minister but remains in Israeli cabinet |
| 1983 | 9th October | King Fahd attends fourth annual Summit Meeting of GCC at which peace initiative for Iraq–Iran war is discussed | | |
| 1983 | November | West German Chancellor Helmut Kohl visits King Fahd | | |
| 1984 | 29th July | | Saudi Arabia competes in Olympic Games for first time | |
| 1984 | 29th October | King Fahd lays foundation stone for the extension of the Holy Mosque in Makkah | | |
| 1984 | | | King Khalid International Airport opens in Riyadh | |
| 1984 | | King Fahd opens the King Fahd Complex for Printing the Holy Quran | | |
| 1984 | | King Fahd opens King Fahd Ship Repair Complex at the King Abdul Aziz Port in Dammam | | |
| 1985 | 8th February | | | First pan-Arab communications satellite launched |
| 1985 | 10th February | King Fahd visits Washington to pursue Middle East "peace process" | | |
| 1985 | 31st March | | UN Secretary General Perez de Cuellar meets Saudi leaders to discuss Iraq–Iran war | |
| 1985 | 14th April | King Fahd has talks with British Prime Minister Margaret Thatcher in Riyadh | | |
| 1985 | 10th June | | | Israel withdraws its own troops from Lebanon |
| 1985 | 17th June | | US space shuttle, with Prince Sultan bin Salman aboard, launches ARABSAT 1B | |
| 1985 | 1st October | | | Israeli aircraft attack PLO head-quarters in Tunis |
| 1985 | 2nd October | King Fahd condemns Israel's attack on PLO headquarters in Tunis as a threat to world peace and calls on the international community to condemn Israel | | |
| 1985 | 8th December | King Fahd has talks with Iranian Foreign Minister Ali Akbar Velayati in Riyadh | | |
| 1985 | | King Fahd launches the project of expanding the Prophet's Mosque in Madinah | | |
| 1985 | | Kingdom's fourth Five-Year Plan launched | | |
| 1986 | 20th February | | World's largest Islamic library opens in Holy City of Makkah | |

| YEAR | DAY/MONTH | SELECTED EVENTS IN KING FAHD'S LIFE | OTHER EVENTS IN THE KINGDOM | HISTORICAL MARKER |
|---|---|---|---|---|
| 1986 | March | King Fahd gives almost 3 million barrels of oil to Sudan, hit by drought and famine. The total cost is estimated to be $62 million | | |
| 1986 | 23rd May | | President of Somalia, injured in a car crash, is flown to Riyadh in Saudi air force "flying hospital" for intensive care on King Fahd's instructions | |
| 1986 | 5th October | King Fahd has talks with President Saleh of Yemen in Riyadh | | |
| 1986 | 26th October | King Fahd adopts the title Custodian of the Two Holy Mosques | | |
| 1986 | 26th November | Bahrain Causeway opened by King Fahd | | |
| 1987 | 25th March | King Fahd makes State visit to Britain | | |
| 1987 | 30th April | Sudanese conjoined twins successfully separated in London hospital at King Fahd's expense | | |
| 1987 | April | | Saudi Arabia attempts to negotiate ceasefire in Iraq–Iran war | |
| 1987 | April | | | Morocco completes a defensive wall in the Western Sahara along its border with Mauritania |
| 1987 | 20th July | | | UN Security Council passes Resolution 598 which calls for Iran and Iraq to implement an immediate ceasefire |
| 1987 | 27th December | King Fahd hosts eighth GCC Summit in Riyadh | | |
| 1988 | 9th January | King Fahd has talks with President Mubarak of Egypt in Riyadh | | |
| 1988 | 7th April | King Fahd has talks with US Secretary of State George Shultz | | |
| 1988 | 26th April | | Saudi Arabia signs Nuclear Non-Proliferation Treaty | |
| 1988 | May | | | Full diplomatic relations reestablished between Morocco and Algeria |
| 1988 | 5th June | King Fahd has talks with Austrian President Kurt Waldheim | | |
| 1988 | 7th June | King Fahd attends extraordinary meeting of Arab League Summit in Algeria which promises financial support for the Palestinian *Intifada* | | |
| 1988 | 31st July | | | King Hussein of Jordan relinquishes rights to West Bank in accordance with PLO wishes |
| 1988 | 13th August | King Fahd orders Saudi contribution to round-the-clock airlift of aid to flood-stricken Sudan | | |
| 1988 | 20th August | | | Ceasefire between Iraq and Iran comes into force |
| 1988 | | King Fahd initiates further efforts to end Iraq–Iran war | | |

| Year | Day/month | Selected Events in King Fahd's Life | Other Events in the Kingdom | Historical Marker |
|------|-----------|-------------------------------------|------------------------------|-------------------|
| 1988 | | King Fahd lays the foundation stone for the third Saudi expansion of the Holy Mosque in Makkah | | |
| 1989 | February | | | Soviet forces withdraw from Afghanistan |
| 1989 | 13th March | King Fahd hosts Organization of the Islamic Conference meeting in Riyadh at which Afghanistan and Palestine were at the top of the agenda | | |
| 1989 | 17th March | King Fahd receives Prince Charles on a private visit to the Kingdom at the invitation of Crown Prince Abdullah | | |
| 1989 | 28th March | King Fahd makes State visit to Cairo | | |
| 1989 | 17th May | King Fahd signs Universal Child Immunization Declaration | | |
| 1989 | 23rd May | At the Arab League Summit in Casablanca, King Fahd instigates the formation of Tripartite Arab Committee to bring an end to Lebanon's civil war | | Egypt readmitted to the Arab League |
| 1989 | May | King Fahd orders $12 million to support the Palestinian *Intifada* | | |
| 1989 | 4th June | | | Ayatollah Khomeini dies |
| 1989 | 22nd October | Taif Agreement, ending Lebanon's civil war, signed | | Signing of Charter of Reconciliation ends Lebanon's Civil War |
| 1989 | 23rd December | King Fahd and Sultan Qaboos sign agreement in Muscat settling the border demarcation between Saudi Arabia and Oman | | |
| 1990 | 17th April | King Fahd orders 30 flights to carry one million copies of the Holy Quran as gifts to Soviet Muslims | | |
| 1990 | May | | | At the Arab League Summit in Baghdad, Saddam Hussein criticizes unnamed States for exceeding their OPEC oil production quota |
| 1990 | 22nd May | | | North and South Yemen unite as Republic of Yemen |
| 1990 | July | | | Saddam Hussein tells Kuwait to cancel all war debts and "refund" the $2.4 billion of "stolen oil" and compensate Iraq for the loss of oil revenues resulting from the low oil price caused by Kuwait's over-production |
| 1990 | 31st July | | | Kuwaiti and Iraqi delegations meet in Jeddah, Saudi Arabia |
| 1990 | 2nd August | | | Iraq invades Kuwait |
| 1990 | 2nd August | | | UN Security Council passes Resolution 660, condemning Iraq's invasion of Kuwait and calling on Iraqi forces to withdraw from Kuwait |

| YEAR | DAY/MONTH | SELECTED EVENTS IN KING FAHD'S LIFE | OTHER EVENTS IN THE KINGDOM | HISTORICAL MARKER |
|---|---|---|---|---|
| 1990 | August | King Fahd condemns Iraq's invasion of Kuwait | | |
| 1990 | 7th August | | | The United States orders the deployment of American troops and aircraft to Saudi Arabia |
| 1990 | 10th August | | | Arab League meets in Cairo. Twelve of the twenty member countries present vote to contribute to the multinational force, assembling to protect Saudi Arabia; eight demurred. |
| 1990 | 12th August | | | Saddam Hussein announces he would withdraw from Kuwait if Israel withdraws from the occupied territories |
| 1990 | 4th October | King Fahd has talks with President Mitterand of France in Riyadh | | |
| 1990 | 10th November | King Fahd announces moves to form the new Consultative Council | | |
| 1990 | 21st November | King Fahd discusses the Gulf crisis with President Bush in Riyadh | | |
| 1990 | 29th November | | | UN drafts Resolution No 678, declaring that if Iraq does not fully comply with the UN resolutions demanding its withdrawal from Kuwait by 15th January 1991, then the alliance would use "all necessary means" to compel compliance |
| 1990 | | Kingdom's fifth Five-Year Plan launched | | |
| 1991 | 7th January | King Fahd visits units of the multinational force in the desert south of Kuwait | | |
| 1991 | 16th January | | | "Operation Desert Storm" begins |
| 1991 | 17th January | | Scud missile, launched by Iraq, hits Dhahran, killing 28 American soldiers | |
| 1991 | 24th January | | | Iraq spills oil from Kuwaiti storage tanks into the Gulf |
| 1991 | 28th January | | Iraqi forces occupy the deserted northern town of Ras al-Khafji in Saudi Arabia | |
| 1991 | 29th January | | Iraqi invaders of Ras al-Khafji repelled by alliance and Saudi forces | |
| 1991 | 28th February | | | Gulf War ends |
| 1991 | 15th April | King Fahd announces that a final report on the formation of the Consultative Council will be presented to the Council of Ministers shortly | | |
| 1991 | 3rd May | King Fahd announces $100 million in aid for victims of Bangladesh cyclone | | |
| 1991 | 21st May | | Saudi Arabia and Oman ratify border agreement | |
| 1991 | 29th May | King Fahd gives £1,750,000 to help a British charity to set up a center for research into schizophrenia at a British university | | |

| YEAR | DAY/MONTH | SELECTED EVENTS IN KING FAHD'S LIFE | OTHER EVENTS IN THE KINGDOM | HISTORICAL MARKER |
|---|---|---|---|---|
| 1991 | 4th June | King Fahd has meetings in the eastern region with the rulers of Bahrain and Qatar | | |
| 1991 | 9th June | King Fahd visits liberated Kuwait | | |
| 1991 | 17th September | | Saudi Ambassador to UN elected President of UN General Assembly | |
| 1991 | 18th September | | Middle East Broadcasting Center launched | |
| 1991 | November | | Saudi Arabia sets aside $450 million for Gulf oil clean-up operations | |
| 1992 | 1st March | King Fahd announces new regulations for the Basic System of Government, Regional Government and the Consultative Council | | |
| 1992 | 20th April | King Fahd has talks with Syrian President Assad in Riyadh | | |
| 1992 | 15th May | In response to an appeal by UNESCO, King Fahd offers $70 million to restore the Muslim Holy Sites in Jerusalem | | |
| 1992 | 18th May | King Fahd has talks with British Foreign Secretary Douglas Hurd | | |
| 1992 | 21st May | King Fahd pays for £150,000 liver and bowel transplant for 4-year-old English girl Laura Davies | | |
| 1992 | 4th June | King Fahd condemns Serbian aggression in Bosnia-Herzegovina and initiates political and aid efforts to alleviate situation | | |
| 1992 | 19th July | King Fahd orders the start of massive emergency aid program for Muslims in Bosnia | | |
| 1992 | 17th September | King Fahd names the first Speaker of the Consultative Council | | |
| 1992 | 12th October | King Fahd pledges $50 million to aid victims of Cairo earthquake | | |
| 1992 | December | King Fahd hosts OIC meeting on Bosnia at which the United Nations is urged to use force against the Serbs to protect the Bosnian Muslims | | |
| 1992 | 7th December | King Fahd agrees to send Saudi troops to assist with US relief operations in Somalia | | |
| 1992 | 30th December | On his last overseas trip as President, George Bush meets with King Fahd in Jeddah | | |
| 1993 | 8th January | King Fahd donates £75,000 towards bowel and liver transplant for 3-year-old English boy Stuart Masters | | |
| 1993 | 24th January | King Fahd calls for an end to the fighting amongst Afghan factions | | |
| 1993 | 4th March | King Fahd provides for 300 Bosnian Muslim families at an estimated cost of £400,000 | | |
| 1993 | March | King Fahd hosts meeting of Afghan leaders in Holy City of Makkah for signing of national reconciliation accord | | |

| YEAR | DAY/MONTH | SELECTED EVENTS IN KING FAHD'S LIFE | OTHER EVENTS IN THE KINGDOM | HISTORICAL MARKER |
|------|-----------|-------------------------------------|-----------------------------|-------------------|
| 1993 | 7th April | King Fahd receives Lebanese President Elias al-Harawi | | |
| 1993 | 14th April | | George Bush and the ruler of Kuwait praise King Fahd's firm resolution and unstinting efforts to bring about the liberation of Kuwait | |
| 1993 | 10th June | King Fahd donates $5 million for an Islamic law studies center at Harvard University | | |
| 1993 | 6th July | King Fahd calls for the lifting of the arms embargo on Bosnian Muslims | | |
| 1993 | 13th July | King Fahd awards US General Colin Powell the King Abdul Aziz Medal for his distinguished role in the Gulf War | | |
| 1993 | 15th July | King Fahd orders the construction of residential camps in Albania for Bosnian Muslims who are victims of Serb "ethnic cleansing" | | |
| 1993 | 15th July | King Fahd reorganizes the Kingdom's religious institutions | | |
| 1993 | 25th July | | | Israel launches attacks in southern Lebanon |
| 1993 | 29th July | King Fahd calls for a halt to Israeli aggression in southern Lebanon | | |
| 1993 | 2nd August | King Fahd orders ten flights to airlift aid to the victims of Israeli aggression in southern Lebanon | | |
| 1993 | 11th August | King Fahd contributes £100,000 to "Operation Irma" which moves sick Bosnians to hospitals in the UK | | |
| 1993 | 20th August | King Fahd orders Saudi aircraft to airlift 50 sick Bosnians to hospitals in the Kingdom | | |
| 1993 | 20th August | Consultative Council inaugurated, with 60 members | | |
| 1993 | 26th August | British newspaper gives King Fahd its Gold Award for "his kindness and generosity to sick children" | | |
| 1993 | 6th October | King Fahd pays £250,000 for further operation in US on Laura Davies | | |
| 1993 | 15th October | King Fahd has talks with President Mitterand of France | | |
| 1993 | 29th November | King Fahd donates £100,000 to British epilepsy charity | | |
| 1993 | 29th December | King Fahd addresses the first session of the Consultative Council | | |
| 1993 | | King Fahd pledges $100 million for social services and utilities in Gaza Strip and West Bank | | |
| 1993 | | King Fahd approves new Higher Education Council and Universities System | | |
| 1993 | | King Fahd introduces new regulations for the Council of Ministers | | |

| Year | Day/month | Selected Events in King Fahd's Life | Other Events in the Kingdom | Historical Marker |
|------|-----------|-------------------------------------|------------------------------|-------------------|
| 1993 | | Saudi forces sent to serve in UN peace-keeping contingent in Somalia | | |
| 1994 | 24th January | King Fahd receives PLO leader Yasser Arafat and reaffirms his total support for the Palestinian cause | | |
| 1994 | 28th January | King Fahd donates £2.5 million to the Prince Charles Institute of Architecture | | |
| 1994 | 2nd March | King Fahd orders the immediate dispatch of aid to relieve victims of the Indonesian earthquake | | |
| 1994 | 22nd March | On the instructions of King Fahd, $20 million (an instalment of the $100 million pledged) is provided through UNWRA for development projects in education, health and social welfare for the Palestinians living on the West Bank | | |
| 1994 | 25th March | King Fahd orders the provision of medical aid for Bosnia, including inoculation serums, to be given top priority | | |
| 1994 | 16th April | Expansion of Holy Mosques in Makkah and Madinah completed | | |
| 1994 | 10th July | King Fahd has talks with Yasser Arafat in Jeddah | | |
| 1994 | | King Fahd hosts 14th GCC Summit in Riyadh | | |
| 1994 | | King Fahd calls for resolution of Yemen crisis through dialogue | | |
| 1994 | | King Fahd provides funds for restoration of Islam's third holiest shrine and two other Mosques in Jerusalem | | |
| 1995 | July | | Saudi Arabia and Oman agree on demarcation of their joint borders | |
| 1995 | August | King Fahd makes Cabinet changes | | |
| 1995 | November | King Fahd admitted to hospital | | |
| 1995 | | Kingdom's sixth Five-Year Plan launched | | |
| 1996 | January | | Global System for Mobiles (GSM) launched in Saudi Arabia | |
| 1996 | 21st February | King Fahd resumes official duties | | |
| 1996 | 11th April | | | Israel launches "Operation Grapes of Wrath" |
| 1997 | March | | The Saudi Arabian Mining Company (MAADIN) created | |
| 1997 | September | | | Iran Air resumes flights to the Kingdom for the first time since the 1979 revolution |
| 1997 | 17th November | King Fahd receives US Secretary of State Madeleine Albright in Riyadh | | |
| 1997 | 3rd December | King Fahd mediates normalization of relations between Egypt and Qatar | | |

| YEAR | DAY/MONTH | SELECTED EVENTS IN KING FAHD'S LIFE | OTHER EVENTS IN THE KINGDOM | HISTORICAL MARKER |
|------|-----------|-------------------------------------|------------------------------|--------------------|
| 1998 | February | Saudi Arabia makes it clear US cannot use Saudi Arabia to launch airstrikes on Iraq | | |
| 1998 | 2nd March | King Fahd receives former Iranian President Rafsanjani | | |
| 1998 | 19th March | King Fahd Chair for Islamic Studies inaugurated in London | | |
| 1998 | April | King Fahd has talks with British Prime Minister Tony Blair in Jeddah | | |
| 1998 | 15th May | | King Fahd Dam in Bisha Valley inaugurated | |
| 1998 | 18th May | King Fahd expresses profound concern over India's nuclear test program | | |
| 1998 | May | | Saudi Arabia's telecommunications services privatized and the Saudi Telecommunications Company established | |
| 1998 | May | | King Khalid bin Abdul Aziz University founded | |
| 1998 | 1st June | King Fahd calls on India and Pakistan to show restraint | | |
| 1998 | 8th June | King Fahd urges Ethiopia and Eritrea to settle their dispute peacefully | | |
| 1998 | 13th July | King Fahd welcomes UN decision to accept Palestinian representation | | |
| 1999 | | | King Fahd Cultural Center opened | |
| 1999 | 7th February | | | King Hussein of Jordan dies |
| 1999 | | | Internet service launched in Saudi Arabia | |
| 2000 | | Kingdom's seventh Five-Year Plan launched | | |
| 2000 | | | Saudi Electric Company established | |
| 2000 | 23rd November | | Saudi Arabia donates $250 million to al-Quds *Intifada* and Al Aqsa Mosque funds | |

# BIBLIOGRAPHY AND OTHER SOURCES

*A Brief Account of the Life of King Abdul Aziz*, Knight Communications, 1998

*Achievements of the Development Plans, 1970–2000*, Ministry of Planning, Kingdom of Saudi Arabia

*A Country and a Citizen for a Happy Decent Life*, Ministry of Information, Kingdom of Saudi Arabia, 1999

*American Petroleum Institute website (www.api.org)*

*Bitter Harvest*, Sami Hadawi, Scorpion Publishing Ltd, 1983

*Custodian of the Two Holy Mosques King Fahd ibn Abdul Aziz*, Saudi Desert House Agency, 2000

*Desert Warrior*, HRH General Khaled bin Sultan, HarperCollins Publishers, 1995

*The Gulf Crisis, An Attempt to Understand*, Ghazi A. Algosaibi, Kegan Paul International, first published in English 1993

*The Holy Ka'bah and the Two Holy Mosques, Construction and History*, Obaid Allah Muhammad Amin Kurdi, Saudi Bin Ladin Group

*King Fahd and Saudi Arabia's Great Evolution*, Dr. Nasser Ibrahim Rashid and Dr. Esber Ibrahim Shaheen, International Institute of Technology Inc., USA, 1987

*Kingdom of Saudi Arabia, 100 Years in the Service of Islam and Muslims*, The Islamic Center for Information and Development, Beirut, Lebanon, 2000

*Kingdom of Saudi Arabia, One Hundred Years in the Service of Arabs and Arab Affairs*, Highlights of Development in Saudi Arabia, Dar Al-Ufuq for Publishing and Distributing

*Kingdom of Saudi Arabia, The March of Progress*, Ministry of Information, Foreign Information Department, Kingdom of Saudi Arabia, 1999

*Middle East and North Africa 2000,* Europa Publications

*Ministry of Higher Education website (www.mohe.gov.sa)*

*Ministry of Information website (www.saudinf.com)*

*Modernity and Tradition: The Saudi Equation*, Dr. Fouad Al Farsy, Knight
    Communications Ltd, 1999

*Opec Fund for International Development Annual Report 1999*

*Saudi Press Agency news releases*

*Story of the Great Expansion*, Hamid Abbas, Saudi Bin Ladin Group, 1996

*This is Our Country*, Ministry of Information, Kingdom of Saudi Arabia, 2000

The statistical information in this book has been drawn primarily from Saudi Arabian Government sources.

Extensive use has been made of *Achievements of the Development Plans, 1970–2000*, published by the Ministry of Planning.

The charts in this book have been created by the author, using the data in *Achievements of the Development Plans, 1970–2000*.

The photographs were supplied by the Saudi Press Agency, Kingdom of Saudi Arabia.

# INDEX